Black Women Writing Autobiography

A Tradition Within a Tradition

Temple
University
Press
Philadelphia

Black Women Writing Autobiography

A Tradition Within a Tradition

Joanne M. Braxton

"Lineage" from Margaret Walker's *For My People* in Chapter 5 is quoted by permission of the author. Copyright © 1942 by Yale University Press.

The passage from "Woman Me" in Chapter 6 is from *Oh Pray My Wings Are Gonna Fit Me Well* by Maya Angelou. Copyright © 1975 by Maya Angelou. Reprinted by permission of Random House, Inc.

Temple University Press, Philadelphia 19122
Copyright © 1989 by Temple University. All rights reserved
Published 1989
Printed in the United States of America

The paper used in this publication meets the minimum requirements of American National Standard for Information Sciences—Permanence of Paper for Printed Library Materials, ANZI Z39.48-1984

Library of Congress Cataloging-in-Publication Data

Braxton, Joanne M.
    Black women writing autobiography : a tradition within a tradition
    Joanne M. Braxton
        p.   cm.
    Bibliography: p. 227
    Includes index.
    ISBN 0-87722-639-3 (alk. paper)
  1. American prose literature—Afro-American authors—History and criticism.
  2. American prose literature—Women authors—History and criticism.
  3. Afro-American women authors—Biography—History and criticism.
  4. Slaves—United States—Biography—History and criticism.
  5. Afro-American women—Biography—History and criticism.
  6. Women—United States—Biography—History and criticism.
  7. Slaves' writings, American—History and criticism.
  8. Autobiography.   I. Title.
PS366.A35B73   1989
818'.08—dc19   89-30066
                                                                    CIP

For the spirit of the child quickening within me

Contents

Acknowledgments

First, I give thanks to God, Belinda's "great Orisha who made all things," in all of the forms that I know the Deity. I have strived to follow my grandmother's dictum to "put God in front of everything"; that faith has been the strength of my life.

I am grateful to my parents, Mary Ellen Weems Braxton and the late Harry McHenry Braxton, Sr., not only for creating the love that gave me life but also for the many sacrifices they made in order that I might have the sort of education I deserved and for bolstering me up when I was uncertain of my ability to go forward.

The teachers who honed my unformed intellectual faculties also deserve my thanks, especially Bernadette Mitchell Reid, the fifth- and sixth-grade teacher who opened my mind to the joys of reading, Bell Gayle Chevigny, who first introduced me to the slave narratives, and Gerda Lerner, who supervised an undergraduate oral history project that centered on my grandmothers.

The idea for this book originated in my Yale University American Studies doctoral dissertation. I owe much to the late Charles T. Davis and to John Blassingame, Margaret Homans, R. W. B. Lewis, Hazel Carby, Henry Louis Gates, and Robert Stepto, who read the manuscript or substantial portions of it in its dissertation format and offered generous commentary. I am also grateful to Shari Benstock, Mae Henderson, Irma McClaurin-Allen, and William Andrews, who commented on the manuscript in its subsequent phases.

Further, I am indebted to the American Council of Learned Societies, the College of William and Mary, the National Endowment for the Humanities, and the Andrew W. Mellon Foundation for support both direct and indirect. During the spring of 1984, I participated, as a Mellon National Scholar, in a semester-long Mellon-funded faculty development seminar at the Wellesley College Center for Research on Women. This seminar, directed by Peggy McIntosh, focused on including women and racial and ethnic minorities in the traditional liberal arts curriculum. *Black Women Writing Autobiography* reflects many of the theoretical and methodological issues discussed during that seminar. The following summer, I participated in a National Endowment for the Humanities summer seminar at Rutgers University on "Women's Writing and Women's Culture," directed by Elaine Showalter. She focused me on claiming my critical voice: Finally the poet and the scholar within could collaborate instead of working against one another.

The College of William and Mary supported *Black Women Writing Autobiography* during 1986 with a semester's faculty research assignment. A second semester of full-time work was made possible by a generous grant from the American Council of Learned Societies. The National Endowment for the Humanities supported *Black Women Writing Autobiography* with a Travel to Collections Grant that enabled me to spend additional time at the Moorland-Spingarn Research Center at Howard University, where archivists Esme Bahn and Sterling Hughes were especially helpful.

Materials from the Black Women's Oral History Project at the Schlesinger Library of Radcliffe College are quoted with the permission of the late Alfreda M. Duster, daughter of Ida B. Wells-Barnett, and the Schlesinger Library. I wish to thank Ruth Hill of the Black Women's Oral History Project for her help with the Duster interviews.

Maricia Battle of the Moorland-Spingarn Research Center and Betty Odabashian of the Schomburg Research Center of the New York Public Library assisted me in finding photographs of some of the autobiographers. I am also grateful to Jean Fagan Yellin for helping me to secure permission to reprint the striking photograph of Harriet A. Jacobs, which appears on the cover of her edition of *Incidents in the Life of a Slave Girl.*

Among my colleagues at the College of William and Mary, I wish to thank Tom Heacox and Elsa Nettels, who read and commented on portions of the manuscript, and Ann Reed, who helped rescue my mistakes from the word processor. Other individuals to whom my thanks are due include Bonnie Chandler and William Smyth, who assisted with the preparation of the final manuscript.

Every author prays for an editor like Janet Francendese, of Temple University Press, for her first scholarly work. In many ways, this book became possible only because of Janet's expert editorial advice and her friendship. Production editor Mary Capouya has been another force in shaping this book. I thank her for the sensitivity and care she has shown in producing *Black Women Writing Autobiography: A Tradition Within a Tradition.*

Finally, I wish to thank Julia Brazelton for helping this work to go forward and for being my first and sometimes my toughest critic. Thank you for being there for me, Julia.

Black Women Writing Autobiography

A Tradition Within a Tradition

A Tradition
Within a Tradition

I believe, with the critic James Olney, that students of autobiography are themselves vicarious autobiographers, and I know that I read every text through my own experience, as well as the experiences of my mother and my grandmothers. As black American women, we are born into a mystic sisterhood, and we live our lives within a magic circle, a realm of shared language, reference, and allusion within the veil of our blackness and our femaleness. We have been as invisible to the dominant culture as rain; we have been knowers, but we have not been known. This paradox is central to what I suggest we call the Afra-American experience.[1]

It was in the world of Afra-American autobiography that I first met the outraged mother on the conscious plane, but then I realized that I had known her all my life. With her hands on her hips and her head covered with a bandanna, she is the sassiest woman on the face of the earth, and with good reason. She is the mother of Frederick Douglass traveling twelve miles through the darkness to share a morsel of food with her mulatto son and to reassure him that he is somebody's child. She travels twelve miles back again before the dawn. She sacrifices and improvises for the survival of flesh and spirit, and as mother of the race, she is muse to black

1

poets, male and female alike. She is known by many names, the most exalted being "Momma." Implied in all her actions and fueling her heroic ones is outrage at the abuse of her people and her person.

She must be the core of our black and female experience, this American Amazon of African descent, dwelling in the moral and psychic wilderness of North America. Yet when I surveyed the literature of the critical wilderness proliferated from that moral and psychic one, I found her absent. I imagined our ancestor mothers lost forever in that fearsome place in search of a tradition to claim them.

The black woman's participation in the American autobiographical genre begins with "Belinda, or the Cruelty of Men Whose Faces Were Like the Moon" (1787), a short narrative petitioning the New York legislature for reparations. This "as told to" account reflects an African woman's shock at being taken while at prayer and sold into slavery: "Even when she, in a sacred grove, with each hand in that of a tender parent, was paying her devotion to the great Orisha who made all things, an armed band of white men, driving many of her countrymen in chains, rushed into the hallowed shades!"[2] "Belinda" records, therefore, not just the physical aspects of the capture in West Africa, and the dreaded "middle passage," but the complete disruption of the narrator's emotional and spiritual life and the corresponding loss of her sense of place, both physical and metaphysical. For the black woman in American autobiography, the literary act has been, more often than not, an attempt to regain that sense of place in the New World.

In America, the African woman met the problem of appropriating a new language as her own; she became an American. In the words of Belinda's narrative, "She learned to catch the ideas, marked by sounds of language, only to know her doom was slavery, from which death alone was to emancipate her."[3] "Belinda" reveals one black woman's early attempts to own her words, her freedom, and most assuredly, her own image. In order to restore God's power in her life after she was abducted to America, the African woman had to refashion the language she was forced to learn. In the movement from the spoken word to a written petition for reparations, "Belinda" crosses from the private sphere into a public arena to take a political position as spokesperson for millions of transported Africans.

Alice Walker raises a pertinent question, "What did it mean for a Black woman to be an artist in our grandmothers' time? And in our great-grandmothers' day? It is a question with an answer cruel enough to stop the blood."[4] Black women have been carriers of tradition, and values of care, concern, nurturance, protection, and, most important, the survival of the race. W. E. B. Du Bois spoke of the black man as a seventh son of a seventh son, gifted with a veil he could see out of but which others could not see into. For the black woman, there is a veil within a veil, a realm of shared knowledge communicated from generation to generation, both through literature and the oral tradition. Education in black womanhood begins in infancy with lullabies, nursery rhymes, and children's games. This education intensifies during adolescence when older black women initiate younger ones in their secret recipes, sayings, and the ways and wisdom of holding a man (for example, "If you got a good man, hold on, and watch out for your friends, cause they're the ones"). Motherhood can be a rite of passage, a vehicle for a new identity, as it was in 1861 for Harriet A. Jacobs in *Incidents in the Life of a Slave Girl,* or in 1966 for Maya Angelou in *I Know Why the Caged Bird Sings.* Others, like Zora Neale Hurston and Era Bell Thompson, suffered what the critic Margaret Homans has called "matraphobia," the fear of becoming what their mothers had been. Some women, like Charlotte Forten Grimké, who did not become mothers, were active Others, as Grimké was toward her motherless niece, the poet Angelina Weld Grimké.

From my own female elders I learned our family history and genealogy and folk medical formulas; I heard prayers both poetic and newsworthy, also ghost stories and preacher tales, as well as lullabies and nursery rhymes. My grand-mothers also related the struggles of black women to survive and raise their children, as can be seen in the words my father's mother, Emma Margaret Harrison, recorded for a student research project of mine in 1970:

> My Mama had 16 children. Didn't but seven of us grow up. William Taylor Harrison, James Taylor Harrison, Edith Virginia, Iris—they was all much older than me—and Sarah, Joe, and Agnes they were younger. One set of twins. They died at birth. Oh, yeh, I do remember Bertina. Bertina died when she was 19 months old right in my arms. She was younger than I was and Joe and Agnes—she was the baby. We got diphtheria. I was sick in bed with it, she was sick with it, too, and she come upstairs and got in my arms. I took care of her and she loved me. I don't have no trouble with children. And she laid in my arms and I thought she was asleep and Mama come up there and said, "Lay her down." And I didn't lay her right down, I said "I can hold her." Mama took her out of my arms and laid her down and then Mama said to me "Bertina's dead."
>
> … after I was born and Cleveland was the President and everything got so hard and tight around Muirkirk, and they put up a soup house for to feed the people. And Papa got a job up in Anne Arundel—a foreman on a farm, Joe Benson's farm, up near Lansdowne, near Baltimore. And Mama was the row boss, and Mama was out there in that snow and dew and stuff in the morning. Mama learn how to work like a dog.
>
> And she wasn't well. She had gall stones all through. A lot of her babies were still born, and a lot of her babies died—right at birth. Them days infants died anyhow. They don't die no more, but they did. And I thank God that they don't die no more like they did. But people didn't raise they children in them days much.[5]

There began my fascination with autobiography, at my grandmother's knee, where I sat completely enthralled by her stories, which described a way of life I would never know. And yet I sensed my connection with this knowledge, which I had not yet found in books. My consciousness was ready shaped for the study of the slave narrative. I had learned to *listen*. This early intellectual curiosity and affinity would intensify through the years, and lead, in 1984, to the completion of my Yale doctoral dissertation, "Autobiography by Black American Women: A Tradition Within a Tradition," an early version of this book.

I come to these texts as a listener, with the understanding that I have everything to learn about this tradition within a tradition, and that it has everything to teach. As Henry Louis Gates has observed, perhaps somewhat shortsightedly, "Literary works configure into a tradition not because of some mystical collective unconscious determined by the biology of race or gender, but because writers read other writers and *ground* their representations of experience in models of language provided largely by other writers *to whom they feel akin* [emphasis mine]. It is through this mode of literary revision, amply evident in the *texts* themselves—in formal echoes, recast metaphors, even in parody—that a 'tradition' emerges and identifies itself."[6] Gates's point about literary forms is well taken, but not all the texts in the literary tradition of black American women were written down. In the words of Temma Kaplan, "Often in the most oppressive situations, it is the memories of mothers handed down through the daughters that keeps a community together. The mother tongue is not just the words or even the array of cultural symbols available to a people to resist its tormentors. The mother tongue *is* the oral tradition."[7] Indeed, this "unwritten literature" and the juxtaposition of literary and oral forms create a linguistic vitality that informs written literature on many levels. Black women autobiographers are grounded in a chosen kinship with their literary antecedents from blueswomen and evangelists to the works of the founding fathers, both black and white. Like the blues, most autobiographies by black Americans, male and female, tend to have a dominant internal strategy of action rather than contemplation. And, like the blues singer, the autobiographer incorporates communal values into the performance of the autobiographical act, sometimes rising to function as the "point of consciousness" of her people. Thus black women writers are joined together by forces both tangible and real, no more mystical than Du Bois's veiled seventh son of the seventh son, and insist on their own terms. For while "mysticism" cannot define a tradition, there *are* unwritten texts and subtexts that black women bring to the reading or creation of written literature. This is not to assert that those born outside the "magic circle" of the black and female "world of love and ritual" are forever locked outside the text. For the text is accessible to whoever would first establish its proper cultural context, thus gaining access to a sphere of privileged (and valuable) knowledge—which was often what Toni Morrison has called "discredited knowledge."[8] The critic who is *not* a black woman must simply work harder to see the black woman at the center of her own (written) experience. From this understanding, and a close reading of important literary antecedents, the tradition unfolds and defines itself.

Until very recently, women's autobiography has not been treated with much sophisticated literary analysis. The pace of development of critical literature for autobiography as a genre did not begin to quicken until the 1960s, and there was little adequate treatment of black literature as a tradition until the 1970s. Two books published in the 1970s helped define black autobiographical tradition and provide some notice of works by women. In 1974, Stephen Butterfield's *Black Autobiography in America* demonstrated the parallel development of the slave narrative with colonial and early federal autobiographies, journals, and diaries, and noted the probable influence of the founding fathers on the slave narrators' use of Christian rhetoric. Butterfield also mentioned black women's autobiography as a "high course of literary interest different from one pursued by males," but ultimately he failed to define the "high course of literary interest" in any way.[9] Also in 1974, Sidonie Smith's *Where I'm Bound* traced the thematic and structural patterns established in slave narratives, which recur in subsequent autobiographies. Smith recognized the need for a volume of criticism on the autobiography of black women and treated Maya Angelou's *I Know Why the Caged Bird Sings* as an example of autobiography used as a vehicle for growth into "self-conscious black womanhood," yet her focus is on the "black version" of Benjamin Franklin's well-known formula, a formula that has appealed primarily to men.[10]

By the 1980s, the autobiography of black American women had begun to win the critical attention it merits. The critic James Olney saw this "sign of the critical/cultural times" as paradigmatic of increased interest in the genre as well as the "literary enfranchisement of the black woman." Writing in 1980, Olney observed:

> If black autobiography is a paradigm, the history of Maya Angelou's *I Know Why the Caged Bird Sings* is a paradigm of a paradigm. Until fairly recently, black writing in general was barely mentioned as literature—if mentioned at all it was usually in some other context—and until very recently, autobiography received the same treatment. Moreover, women writers have not always been given due consideration as makers of literature. But here we have an autobiography by a black woman, published in the last decade (1970), that already has its own critical literature. Is this to be attributed solely to the undoubted quality of Maya Angelou's book? Surely not. And here is the most striking sign of the critical/cultural times: *her autobiography was Maya Angelou's first book....* We can only conclude that something like full literary enfranchisement has been won by black writers, women writers, and autobiography itself.[11]

This enfranchisement has been demonstrated by the literary flowering of black women writing autobiography, fiction, and poetry as well as literature and cultural history. Alice Walker, Toni Morrison, Gloria Naylor, Paula Giddings, Nikki Giovanni, and Angela Davis have become familiar to both white and black Americans. Therefore the black woman autobiographer (and in this case, the critic) arrives in not only a literary renaissance of the study of autobiography, but a renaissance of black women writing.

Contemporary feminist literary criticism offers many approaches to reading the work of women. Lillian S. Robinson insists that "where the subject matter of art has explicit race, sex or class content, this content must be understood and experienced to the full extent that it participates in meaning."[12] Annette Kolodny finds a feminist literary perspective useful because it demands that "we give women writers the same kind of critical attention we have always accorded our male writers." Kolodny believes that the informed feminist critical perspective must "embrace the inherited tools of literary analysis" and undertake the responsibility of developing a critical vocabulary that is difficult to misread—to examine how and if the experience of women writers, as mediated by culture, is "qualitatively different" and if their writings are therefore "structured into a different kind of literary language."[13] Despite this increased literary awareness, feminist critics (especially white feminist critics) have been almost as guilty of overlooking black women's autobiographical writings as have critics of the so-called mainstream of Afro-American literature. For example, Estelle Jelinek, the editor of *Women's Autobiography*, has helped establish a tradition of women's autobiography and "women's autobiographical criticism" as "substantial literary discipline," yet only one essay in her 1980 book pays even passing treatment to the autobiography of black American women.[14] Fortunately, such oversights have been remedied somewhat by the contemporary critical commentary of William Andrews, Hazel Carby, Nellie McKay, Valerie Smith, and others. The 1988 *Schomburg Library of Black Women Writers of the Nineteenth Century* includes about twenty nineteenth-century narratives, along with informative introductions that supply both the critical and cultural contexts for the reading of these works within a larger tradition of black women writing. William Andrews's gender-balanced writing on black American autobiography is among the most inclusive in its treatment of the works of women; this is especially true of *To Tell a Free Story*, easily the most comprehensive work on black American autobiography.[15]

The study of black women's participation in the literary genre of autobiography reveals much about the ways in which the experience of racial and sexual difference influences the development of identity and the selection of language within a given narrative. *Black Women Writing Autobiography: A Tradition Within a Tradition* views the autobiography of black American women as an attempt to define a life work retrospectively and as a form of symbolic memory that evokes the black woman's deepest consciousness. Black women's autobiography is also an occasion for viewing the individual in relation to those others with whom she shares emotional, philosophical, and spiritual affinities, as well as political realities. The methodology of the present study acknowledges the problem of treating the texts both as literature and history, following the model provided by Albert E. Stone in his *Autobiographical Occasions and Original Acts*. Stone insists on "the need to adjust critical focus from *individual text* to *social context* to *appropriate conceptual framework—and back to the single text again.*"[16] Additionally, the present study requires each individual text to be read in relation to others within the tradition of black women writing autobiography.

The following chapters treat the participation of black American women in the written autobiographical genre and examine representative occasions that have called forth their written autobiography. *Black Women Writing Autobiography* treats different subgenres: slave narrative, travelogue, reminiscence, historical memoir, and modern autobiography. Even without considering the volumes of autobiography published since Angelou's *I Know Why the Caged Bird Sings* in 1969, about a hundred texts could have been examined. The problem of selection has been a prickly one, especially considering the early narratives, many of which have not been studied previously as part of a literary tradition. Therefore, I have chosen representative situations or occasions for autobiography and analyzed them as such. I argue for a redefinition of the genre of black American autobiography to include the images of women as well as their memoirs, reminiscences, diaries, and journals—this as a corrective to both black and feminist literary criticism. This book places the black woman at the center of critical discourse and her own literary experience, instead of at the margins, where she has been too often found. The text itself, consisting of six interrelated chapters, has been divided into three parts, "Making a Way Out of No Way," "Emerging from Obscurity," and "Claiming the Afra-American Self." Each part has its own brief introduction, designed to help the reader establish a cultural context appropriate to the understanding of the autobiographies discussed therein.

In the words of Albert Stone, this book also "inevitably questions definitions of authorship which literate people have assumed for themselves and imposed upon others."[17] Chapter 1 takes a look at some of the criteria that have been used to define the slave narrative genre so that it has generally excluded women. It suggests a reconsideration of those criteria through a discussion of the controversy surrounding the authorship of Harriet ("Linda Brent") Jacobs's pseudonymously published *Incidents in the Life of a Slave Girl, Written by Herself* (1861). The main body of Chapter 1 speculates on ways in which the experience of racial and sexual oppression influences the appropriation of language in this narrative written by a heroic female fugitive. "Sass" is examined as a mode of verbal discourse and as a weapon of self-defense, and the outraged mother is introduced as a variation of the articulate hero archetype defined by the critic Robert Stepto in his early work on black narrative.

Chapter 2 studies representative narratives by freeborn black women of the nineteenth century and the postemancipation accounts of former slaves. As a group, these autobiographies reflect a shift from the preoccupation with survival found in the slave narratives to a need for self-expression and self-identification. But black women created vital and sometimes hybrid forms, such as the spiritual autobiography/travelogue, travelogue/adventure story, and slave narrative/memoir, as they grappled with the challenges of freedom and the problem of attaining a public voice. These early works are represented by two examples of confessional spiritual autobiographies, *The Religious Experience and Journal of Mrs. Jarena Lee* (1849) and *Gifts of Power: The Journals of Rebecca Cox Jackson* (written between 1830 and 1864 and published in 1981); by Elizabeth Keckley's *Behind the Scenes: or Thirty Years a Slave and Four Years in the White House* (1868); and by Susie King Taylor's *Reminiscences of My Life in Camp with the U.S. 33rd Colored Troops* (1902). Additionally, this chapter examines *Harriet, Moses of Her People* (1869) and *Narrative of Sojourner Truth* (1878) as the works of women William Andrews has called "inheritors of a black and female autobiographical tradition of activism founded on a commitment to religious faith, human rights and women's struggles."[18] I discuss the ways in which Tubman and Truth "radicalize" and secularize the form of the spiritual autobiography to create a tool of personal and political liberation.

These first two chapters embrace the pressures of acculturation as they relate to the foundation of a distinctively black and female autobiographical tradition, as well as the problem of attaining freedom and literacy and the problem of "telling a free story."

In Chapter 3, "A Poet's Retreat: The Diaries of Charlotte Forten Grimké," I examine some of the problems faced by a well-educated and extremely literate nineteenth-century black woman as she attempts to find a public voice. This chapter looks at Forten's use of a private autobiographical form, the diary, for recording the growth of her mind and as a tool for restoration and self-healing. I present the diaries as a series of interrelated texts, including the final diary, which has received very little critical attention. This chapter also treats the relationship of the diaries to Forten's attempts at writing romantic poetry and speculates on the prospects of an autobiographical form less restrictive than the slave narrative, as heralded by Forten's work. While at first glimpse Forten might be viewed as outside a tradition of black women writing because of her choice of such European literary models as Wordsworth, Keats, and Elizabeth Barrett Browning, a closer look reveals her modal improvisation on the

forms and themes of the black experience, including spirituals and slave narratives. Forten, daughter of an influential,
progressive, and well-to-do black family from Philadelphia,
emerges as a truly bicultural voice, yet she was ever aware of
her difference.

Chapter 4 examines *Crusade for Justice: The Autobiography
of Ida B. Wells*, the posthumously published historical and
personal memoir of a well-known journalist and antilynching
activist. The analysis of *Crusade for Justice* does much to
establish continuity in black female autobiographical tradition, for this autobiography has distinct characteristics that
are common to both nineteenth-century narratives and modern autobiographies by black American women. Wells's autobiographical consciousness moderates between the form of
the confessional narrative and the historical memoir, permit-
ting her to discuss not only her public but her private duty.
Wells requires this dual form in order to demonstrate her
development as a political activist and as an outraged
mother. In discussing the development of Wells's autobiographical consciousness and her shifting autobiographical
stance, this chapter makes use of the theories of Patricia
Spacks and Albert Stone on autobiography and the psycho-
historical theories of Erik Erikson on identity formation.

Chapter 5, "Motherless Daughters and the Quest for a
Place: Zora Neale Hurston and Era Bell Thompson," analyzes
Hurston's *Dust Tracks on a Road* and Thompson's *American
Daughter*, and attempts to place them in a tradition of black
women writing autobiography. Hurston and Thompson represent the first generation of black and female autobiographers who did not continually come into contact with former
slaves; their works turn away from the restrictions and
limitations of the slave narrative and extend the quest for a
dignified and self-defining identity to include a search for
personal fulfillment. As formally literary enterprises, these
two autobiographies vary in coherence, wholeness, orderliness, and artistic achievement, as individual works in
any genre will do. More significant for my purpose of looking
at them at this particular stage in the development of black

women's autobiography is their shared bonding and conformity to a "female" narrative mode—Thompson's narrative of isolation and transcendence and Hurston's narrative of vision and power.

I have chosen Maya Angelou's *I Know Why the Caged Bird Sings* as representative of the autobiography of modern black women. As the focus of Chapter 6, it illustrates how the archetypal patterns and narrative concerns established in early autobiographies renew themselves in contemporary works by black American women. Like Thompson and Hurston, Angelou speaks with the triple consciousness of the *American Daughter*. She knows who she is, where she has come from, and what the source of her strength has been. In *I Know Why the Caged Bird Sings*, she finds the place to re-create the self in her own image—the place Hurston and Thompson and all those who had gone before had been searching for.

Part I
Making a Way
Out of No Way

Emerging from a culture in which teaching
slaves to read and write met with disapproval or, in some places, was a criminal
act, the early autobiographical writings of
black Americans linked the quest for freedom with the quest for literacy. To be able
to write, to develop a public voice, and to
assert a literary self represented significant
aspects of freedom. The critic William
Andrews suggests that the American writer
of African descent was burdened with the
task of winning the attention of an audience
overwhelmed with racial difference; the
Afro-American's autobiographical impulse
and imperative have been "to tell a free
story"—to be politically free and to achieve
narrative freedom within a given text. Freed
slaves and fugitives who could not write
shared a disadvantage: Their words had to
be taken down by others, and they could not
exert full control over their life stories.[1]

The autobiographical writings of black
women in nineteenth-century America bear
witness to the continuity and vitality of
black women asserting images of self in
many and varied forms.

Like the narratives of questing male
fugitives, narratives of female fugitives and
former slaves echo the values and language
of the founding fathers as they traverse the
path from slavery to freedom, literacy, and
self-empowerment. Yet, within this
"pregeneric quest" for freedom and literacy
lies another myth—that of the female slave
(or former slave) trying to protect her family
and create a hearth and home for them. Her
tools of liberation include sass and invective
as well as biblical invocation; language is
her first line of defense. Like her fugitive
brothers, she knows that God is on the side
of the oppressed. Her relationship with God
is direct and self-authorizing; her Creator
speaks to her through dreams and visions
and through her own inner voice. Her
strength and protection come from both
within and without. Her spirituality is
expressed in myriad and diverse forms.[2]

The chapters in this part consider both
kinds of autobiography—that written by
women who were slaves and that written for
them. These chapters demonstrate that slave
women were no less challenged by the
pressures of acculturation and the barriers
to literacy than were men, and they show
that women were subject to the additional
burdens of sexual exploitation; the shape
and texture of their stories differ as a result
of the differences between men's and

women's experiences. Women writing slave
narratives and spiritual autobiographies developed common themes and archetypal
figures, establishing an enduring tradition
within the genre of black autobiography.

1

Outraged Mother and Articulate Heroine: Linda Brent and the Slave Narrative Genre

Until recently, and with few notable exceptions, the critical treatment of the slave narrative has almost always dealt with the narratives of heroic male slaves, not their wives or sisters. By focusing almost exclusively on the narratives of male slaves, critics have left out half the picture. Resistance to a gynocritical or gynocentric approach to the slave narrative genre has been dominated by linear logic and by either/or thinking. We have been paralyzed by issues of primacy, authenticity, and authorship, and by criteria of unity, coherence, completion, and length. Academic systems that do not value scholarship on black women, or reward it, have told us that we are not first, not central, not major, not authentic, suggesting that neither the lives of black women nor the study of our narratives and autobiographies have been legitimate.[1]

Transforming our understanding of the slave narrative means reconsidering the criteria used to define the genre in such a way that the works of women have been excluded.[2] This chapter seeks to expand the genre's definition by re-evaluating the either/or thinking that has limited both the consideration of evidence surrounding the narratives of women and the inclusion of works by women in the slave narrative genre. Instead of asking, "Is it first? Is it major? Does it conform to established criteria?" this study asks, "How did slave women shape their experience into a different kind of literary language?" A balanced understanding of the slave narrative relies, first, on a close reading of narratives written by women and, second, on an expanded range of terms used in writing about those narratives. This chapter seeks to accomplish this transformation through a brief discussion of the participation of black women in the slave narrative genre and through Harriet "Linda Brent" Jacobs's 1861 account, *Incidents in the Life of a Slave Girl: Written by Herself*, a narrative that can be considered exemplary of the autobiographical writing of slave women even as it might be seen as atypical of the narratives of male slaves.[3]

Traditionally, the 1845 *Narrative of the Life of Frederick Douglass, An American Slave, Written by Himself* is viewed as the central text in the slave narrative genre. Based on this narrative, the critic Robert Stepto has defined the primary Afro-American archetype as that of the articulate hero who discovers the links among freedom, literacy, and struggle. Stepto's definition disregards the narrative experience of the articulate and rationally enlightened female slave,[4] probably because few slave women wrote narratives. Women's experiences are seldom related firsthand, but slave women are often represented in accounts of slave men as mothers and nurturers (generally of their own) or, often, as degraded and dehumanized individuals who have lost their self-respect and self-esteem. I propose that such women should be brought forth from this obscurity, that we consider as a counterpart to the articulate hero the archetype of the outraged mother. She is a mother because motherhood was virtually unavoidable under slavery; she is outraged because of the intimacy of her oppression.[5]

One important difference between *Incidents in the Life of a Slave Girl* and narratives of heroic male slaves is that the heroine celebrates the cooperation of all the people, slave and free, who make her freedom possible. She celebrates her liberation and her children's as the fruit of a collective effort, not an individual one. In her introduction to the Schomburg Library edition of *Incidents,* Valerie Smith argues that "the narrators of the male-authored accounts were able to represent themselves as solitary figures because the circumstances of their captivity granted them a greater degree of relative autonomy than that allowed to female slaves." Smith asserts that "women slaves were more likely than men to be tied to the plantation by the demands of child care; moreover, men were more likely than women to be sold separately from their offspring." These factors, she suggests, help to explain "why male slave narrators would figure themselves as self-sustaining individuals" and "isolated heroic subjects" who "defined their humanity in terms of prevailing conceptions of American male identity."[6]

As laborers and producers of children for the market, slave women were objects of sexual desire as well as profitable commodities. In the words of "Linda Brent," "Women are considered of no value, unless they continually increase their owner's stock."[7] Frederick Douglass, in his *Narrative,* cites the master's "base ingratitude" to his "poor old grandmother," informing the reader that "she had been the source of all his wealth; she had peopled his plantation with slaves; she had become a grandmother in his service." Douglass also writes of Caroline, a woman bought by a cruel slavebreaker, Covey, "as he said, for a *breeder*." Too poor to afford more than one slave, Covey hired a married man from a neighboring plantation and "him he used to fasten up with her every night. The result was that at the end of the year the miserable woman gave birth to twins," reared as "quite an addition" to Covey's wealth.[8] In addition to women exploited as "breeders," others were treated as objects of sexual pleasure. William Wells Brown writes that his sister was sold into a life of enforced prostitution with a sensual master, who bought, at the same time, three other women "for his own use."[9] And Solomon Northup relates the story of Patsey, a field hand forced to function as her master's concubine. These women are the mothers, grandmothers, wives, and sisters of the heroic male slave who moves North in his quest for freedom and literacy.

Not entirely indifferent to the bonds of maternal affection between slave women and their children, slaveholders worked, Frederick Douglass contended, to "blunt and destroy the natural affection of the mother for the child." Speaking from his own experience, Douglass wrote: "My mother and I were separated when I was but an infant—before I knew her as my mother. It is a common custom, in the part of Maryland from which I ran away, to part mothers from their children at an early age" (*Narrative*, 2–3). Frederick Douglass's mother once walked twelve miles through the darkness to share a morsel of food with her mulatto son and to reassure him that he was "somebody's child"; before dawn, she walked twelve miles back to the plantation where she lived and worked. Even so, Douglass remembered seeing his mother fewer than half a dozen times.

The outraged mother appears repeatedly in Afro-American history and literary tradition, and she is fully represented in *Incidents in the Life of a Slave Girl*. In the words of "Linda Brent," the outraged mother "may be an ignorant creature, degraded by a system that has brutalized her from childhood; but she has a mother's instincts, and is capable of feeling a mother's agonies" (*Incidents*, 16). The archetypal outraged mother travels alone through the darkness to impart a sense of identity and "belongingness" to her child. She sacrifices and improvises to create the vehicles necessary for the survival of flesh and spirit. Implied in all her actions and fueling her heroic ones is abuse of her people and her person.

Prefiguring *Incidents*, an 1831 account, *The History of Mary Prince*, treats the perils of slave girlhood in a West Indian setting.[10] This "as told to" account depicts the separation of families as well as the physical exploitation and sexual abuse of black women from a first-person point of view. Like Linda Brent, Mary Prince enjoys a happy childhood that ends abruptly with the death of a "kind mistress." Mary is initiated into the suffering of slave womanhood when the family is separated. (This theme of feminine suffering is highlighted when we later learn that Mary's mother loses her mind after being separated from her children.) Not only does *Mary Prince* prefigure the later *Incidents* in its criticism of sexual liaisons forced on slave women but also in specific uses of language. *Incidents* and *Mary Prince* employ similar modes of verbal discourse. There are clear uses of "sass" and invective as verbal weapons. One occurs when Mary defends the young mistress from the blows of her drunken father, another when Mary rebukes the same man for submitting her to a sexual indecency. Elsewhere, a "mulatto woman" is described as being "saucy, very saucy." Also, within the narrative strategy of *Mary Prince*, there seems to be a tendency, found later in *Incidents*, to alternate between confrontations with the reader and concealment of certain details considered "too horrible" to report. The authenticating documents appended to the text support the idea that *Mary Prince* was considered "shocking" in its day.

Other early women's slave narratives survive. Included among them are *Memoir of Jane Blake* (1834), *Narrative of Joanna, an Emancipated Slave of Surinam* (1838), *Aunt Sally; or the Cross the Way to Freedom* (1858), *Narrative of the Life of Jane Brown* (1860), *Louisa Picquet, The Octoroon: A Tale of Southern Slave Life* (1861), and *Memoir of Old Elizabeth, A Colored Woman* (1863). All are antebellum works that have more in common with traditional slave narratives than postemancipation accounts of slaves. I consider *Incidents* to be the most representative of this genre.

Harriet Brent Jacobs published *Incidents* in 1861. As I have argued elsewhere, the kinds of questions scholars asked about this text prohibited them from seeing it as part of the slave narrative genre and prevented them from looking for historical evidence to establish Jacobs's authorship. Although Marion Starling, a black woman, argued for Jacobs's authorship of *Incidents* as early as 1946, critics like Sterling Brown and Arna Bontemps contested that claim.[11] The issue was complicated by the fact that Lydia Maria Child had edited the

Jacobs narrative, which was published under the pseudonym "Linda Brent." Not until 1981 did Jean Yellin publish evidence that establishes the author's identity and the authenticity of her narrative. Yellin found evidence readily available in the form of letters from Jacobs to Lydia Maria Child, from Jacobs to her confidante, the Rochester Quaker Amy Post, and from Jacobs to William Lloyd Garrison, as well as in the apprentice pieces Jacobs published in the *New York Tribune*.[12] Another piece of evidence overlooked by many scholars was a May 1, 1861, review that appeared in the London *Anti-Slavery Advocate* and was written by someone who had knowledge of the manuscript in both the original and published versions and who had talked with the author. This *Anti-Slavery Advocate* review contains a wonderful description of Jacobs and her text and reads in part: "Her manners were marked by refinement and sensibility, and her utter absence of pretense or affectation, and we were deeply touched by the circumstances of her early life which she then communicated and which exactly coincide with those of the volume now before us."[13] Questions of authenticity, then, camouflaged the narrative's importance, though they were relatively easy to answer.

The only known full-length work by an Afra-American writing about her experiences as a slave woman, *Incidents* is at the same time a representative document, speaking for many lives. An analysis of *Incidents* moves us closer to a characterization of the behavior of the outraged mother and to a more balanced understanding of the slave narrative genre. *Incidents* evolves from the autobiographical tradition of heroic male slaves and a line of American women's writings that attacks racial oppression and sexual exploitation. It amalgamates the patterns of movement of the slave narrative with conventional literary forms and stylistic devices in an attempt to transform the so-called cult of true womanhood and to persuade women in the North to take a public stand against slavery, the most political issue of the day. Jacobs's text interweaves the twin themes of abolition and feminism. According to Hazel Carby, *Incidents* "is the most sophisticated sustained narrative dissection of the conventions of true womanhood by a black author before emancipation."[14] Like Harriet Beecher Stowe's *Uncle Tom's Cabin*, *Incidents* focuses on the power relationships of masters and slaves and the ways in which slave women learn to manage the aggressive sexuality of white masters. Unlike Stowe, who demonstrated her anxiety about the authorship of *Uncle Tom's Cabin* by saying that "God wrote it," the author of *Incidents* claims responsibility for every word, yet she publishes under the pseudonym "Linda Brent." It is Linda Brent who obscures the names of persons and places mentioned in the text, and although she denies any need for secrecy on her part, she writes that she deems it "kind and considerate towards others to pursue this course" (*Incidents*, 1). Thus she speaks as a disguised woman, a woman whose identity remains partly obscured. As Yellin astutely points out, Linda Brent speaks at once as a hero and as a fallen woman (*Incidents*, xiv). Her quest includes liberation from the realities of slavery and sexual exploitation as well as the search for a home for herself and her children.

The double nature of the narrator's experience is reflected not only in the use of a pseudonym but also in the form of the text, which alternates between the confessional mode and the form of genteel fiction. Her ordeal is that of a beautiful and desirable woman forced to live under slavery. *Incidents* links the details of this experience by a series of "turning points" that culminate in an escape from slavery that is viewed as a divine act. The pattern of movement, as in the narratives of questing male slaves, is one of geography as well as consciousness, being in "hate, the atmosphere of hell," and moving toward "the Northern Star, at all hazards" (*Incidents*, 40, 150). In this confessional narrative of a slave woman, the growth of intellectual maturity parallels certain female "peak experiences." These include Linda's first love affair (with a free black man whom she despairingly sends away for his own good), a planned pregnancy that might well be viewed as an act of rebellion in itself, and the birth of her two children, Benjamin and Ellen.

Much of the narrative action, especially after the birth of Benjamin and Ellen, is motivated by Linda's concern for their freedom and well-being. Sacrificing opportunities to run away without her children, she endures a long and voluntary confinement in the hopes of an eventual "redemption from slavery." She leaves her place of concealment only twice, once to plead with the children's father for their emancipation, and again to speak with her daughter, apparently to nullify the father's assertion that the children are "motherless" and Linda herself dead. Finally, she arrives at a symbolic action, escape, which is the first step on the road to freedom and her redemption from "sin and disgrace." Through her confessional narrative, she begins to expiate her guilt and to find a physical and spiritual community where her humanity and sensitivity will be valued and where she can rise above her painful past.

The preface of *Incidents* constitutes the first of many appeals to her intended audience:

> Reader, be assured this narrative is no fiction. I am aware that some of my adventures may seem incredible; but they are, nevertheless, strictly true. I have not exaggerated the wrongs inflicted by slavery; on the contrary, my description falls far short of the facts. I have concealed the names of places, and given persons fictitious names. I had no motive for secrecy on my own account, but I deemed it kind and considerate towards others to pursue this course.
>
> I wish I were more competent to the task I have undertaken. But I trust my readers will excuse deficiencies in consideration of circumstances.

Essentially, the preface explains why and how Jacobs came to write the narrative; not for herself but for those still in bondage:

> I have not written my experiences in order to attract attention to myself; on the contrary, it would have been far more pleasant to me to have been silent about my own history. Neither do I care to excite sympathy for my own sufferings.

> But I do earnestly desire to arouse the women of the North to a
> realizing sense of the condition of two millions of women at the
> South, still in bondage, suffering what I suffered, and most of
> them far worse. (*Incidents*, 6)

Jacobs hopes to move northern women to rise up against the
cruel abuses suffered by black women in the South. She
addresses the preface to the reader to establish both intimacy
and trust; she asserts the truth of the narrative despite her
deliberate attempts to obscure identities and place names. In
order to lead the reader to moral action, she must establish
this confidence. She also establishes her literacy by apologiz-
ing for her inability to write well and by asking the reader to
consider her "circumstances." This underscores her assertion
of authorship, that *Incidents* is indeed not fiction, and that it
was truly "written by herself."[15]

The virtual "madwoman in the attic," Linda leads a veiled
and unconventional life. Although *Incidents* serves as a kind
of open letter to the women of the North, Jacobs's narrative
strategy alternates between confrontation and concealment,
seeking to establish what Patricia Spacks describes as "a
conciliatory relationship" with her reader, "attempting to
justify ... untraditional ways of living and writing so as to
gain public acceptance."[16] A marked quality of reticence is
observed in the narrator's voice; she affects a conciliatory
tone, asking the reader to pardon her for the indelicacy of her
topic and to pity her for the sake of her sisters still enslaved:
"I know I did wrong. No one can feel it more sensibly than I
do. The painful and humiliating memory will haunt me to my
dying day. Still, in looking back, calmly, on the events of my
life, I feel that a slave woman ought not to be judged by the
same standards as others" (*Incidents*, 55–56). The "cult of true
womanhood" provides a backdrop for the genteel northern
readers of this narrative. *Incidents* demonstrates that it is
impossible for "true womanhood" to flourish under slavery
because slave women are not allowed to practice the virtues
of modesty, chastity, and domesticity. "The slave woman is
not allowed to have any pride of character. It is deemed a

crime in her to wish to be virtuous" (*Incidents*, 31). Jacobs emphasizes that double jeopardy of the slave woman: "If God has bestowed beauty upon her, it will prove to be her greatest curse. That which commands admiration in the white woman only hastens the degradation of the female slave" (*Incidents*, 28).

A portion of the narrator's experience and identity must remain concealed, and yet, paradoxically, this autobiographical act is Jacobs's route to self-validation. Initially insecure with her audience, she seeks not to present factual information for verification but to obscure it. Through the persona of Linda Brent, she achieves a coherent first-person narrative, radical because of its treatment of the topic of sexual abuse and the oppression of slave women. The "cult of true womanhood" decreed that sexuality was not to be discussed, and few women dared raise it in public, let alone in print; therefore, this "autobiographical act" may be viewed as a radical one. Yellin argues: "By creating a narrator who presents her sexual history as a subject of public political concern, Jacobs moves her book out of the world of conventional nineteenth-century polite discourse. In and through her creation of Linda Brent, who yokes her success as a heroic slave mother to her confession as a woman that she is not a storybook heroine, Jacobs articulates her struggle to assert her womanhood and projects a new kind of female hero" (*Incidents*, xiv).[17] Linda Brent, an outraged mother, adheres to a system of black and female cultural values that motivates her actions and informs the structure of her text. Above all, her stated purpose is to "arouse the women of the North to a realizing sense of the condition of two millions of women at the South." If white women in the North know the true conditions of slave women in the South, then they cannot fail to answer this call to moral action.

In the introductory chapter, Linda details her background and narrates her childhood in a scant five pages. Her "parents were a light shade of brownish yellow, and were termed mulattoes" (*Incidents*, 5). "They lived together in a comfortable home," and Linda was "so fondly shielded" that she knew nothing of her slave status until she was six years old. "When I was six years old, my mother died; and then, for the first time, I learned, by the talk around me, that I was a slave" (*Incidents*, 6). According to the narrative, Linda's first mistress values her unusually close relationship with the slave family and teaches young Linda to read and spell. "My mistress was so kind to me that I was always glad to do her bidding, and proud to labor for her as much as my young years would permit. I would sit by her side for hours, sewing diligently, with a heart as free from care as that of any free-born white child" (*Incidents*, 7). When Linda is twelve years old this "kind mistress" sickens and dies.

Recalling that the mistress had promised Linda's dying mother that her children should never want for anything, Linda hopes that she might be set free, but she is not. Linda points out the religious hypocrisy implicit in her mistress's lack of consideration:

> My mistress had taught me the precepts of God's Word: "Thou shalt love thy neighbor as thyself." "Whatsoever ye would that men should do unto you, do ye evenso unto them." But I was her slave, and I suppose she did not recognize me as her neighbor. I would give much to blot out from my memory that one great wrong....
>
> She possessed but few slaves; and at her death those were all distributed among her relatives. Five of them were my grandmother's children, and had shared the same milk that nourished her mother's children. (*Incidents*, 8)

Stunned by the inconsistency of her mistress's biblical teachings and her actions, Linda is forced to accept the fact that as a slave girl entering womanhood, she has become an increasingly valuable commodity. No one, not even her "kind mistress," could overlook that value—especially her potential as a future mother and producer of slaves. "Five of them... had shared the same milk that nourished her mother's children," she observed. The "kind mistress" is a traitor, then, not only to her religion but to her womanhood, even the veritable "mother's milk."[18]

Although Linda becomes the legal property of the young niece of her former mistress, she is, in fact, under the domination of the girl's father, Dr. Flint, a neighborhood physician who had married the sister of Linda's late mistress. Linda describes Dr. Flint as a person of a "restless, craving, vicious nature" who "roved about by day and night, seeking whom to devour" (*Incidents*, 18). Not long after her arrival at the Flints, the doctor presses his determination to break Linda's spirit. Ironically, Flint's attacks serve to fortify rather than shatter the slave girl's psyche; in fact, they bolster her spirit of rebellion: "When he told me that I was made for his use, made to obey his command in *every*thing; that I was nothing but a slave, whose will must and should surrender to his, never before had my puny arm felt half so strong" (*Incidents*, 18). As Carby has pointed out, Linda is portrayed as having inherited the spirit of her grandmother, Aunt Marthy, who did not possess the submissiveness of "conventional womanhood."[19]

Five chapters of the autobiography deal explicitly with the sexual oppression encountered by slave women: "The Trials of Girlhood," "The Jealous Mistress," "The Lover," "A Perilous Passage in a Slave Girl's Life," and "A New Tie to Life." As Linda enters adolescence, described as "A Perilous Passage in a Slave Girl's Life," she sees several slave women sold with Dr. Flint's children suckling at their breasts: "I knew that as soon as a new fancy took him, his victims were sold far off to get rid of them; especially if they had children. I had seen several women sold, with his babies at the breast. He never allowed his offspring by slaves to remain long in sight of himself and his wife" (*Incidents*, 55). Flint thus compounds his guilt by the immorality of selling his own children. A slave woman who becomes pregnant by him can expect to be sold, while Flint himself realizes a measurable financial profit through his sexual misconduct.[20]

Linda shares the male fugitive's quest for freedom and literacy, but she learns to reconcile her heroic aspirations with her sexual vulnerability. Before she can achieve her final escape from slavery and complete her quest for literacy, she must achieve a temporary escape from the sexual advances of the master. When Flint finds the beautiful slave girl teaching herself to write, he attempts to pervert her quest for literacy into a seduction: "One day he caught me teaching myself to write. He frowned, as if he was not well pleased; but I suppose he came to the conclusion that such an accomplishment might help to advance his favorite scheme. Before long, notes were often slipped into my hand. I would return them saying, 'I can't read them, sir.' 'Can't you?' he replied" (*Incidents*, 31).

Underclothed and underfed, Linda comforts herself with secret trips to her grandmother's house. "Aunt Marthy," a free woman, becomes Linda's sustaining force and primary role model. Intelligent, self-sufficient, quick-witted, pious, protective, nurturing, and morally strict, Aunt Marthy is also wise, noble, and courageous. Aunt Marthy herself is an outraged mother. Skilled in the use of invective and insult, as well as silence, Aunt Marthy successfully confronts Dr. Flint at crucial points in the narrative; she sasses him, she outwits him, and she provides food and shelter for both Linda and Linda's children. Aunt Marthy is, in short, the bearer of a system of values as well as the carrier of the female version of the black heroic archetype. Aunt Marthy teaches and demonstrates the values and practical principles of sacrifice and survival; without her example and her brilliant organization of Linda's support system, escape for Linda would have been impossible.

Throughout the text, Linda and her grandmother use language as a weapon, dueling with Dr. Flint, gaining psychological space and strength. The many references to "sass" and "impertinence" underscore the importance of its use in regaining self-esteem; they also suggest a feminine reflection of the trickster figure. The use of disguise and concealment, and of trickery and wit, to overwhelm a larger and more powerful foe, long important to the slave narrative genre, takes on new meaning in relation to the slave woman, her abject status, and the atmosphere of moral ambiguity that surrounds her. Women resort to wit, cunning, and verbal warfare as forms of rebellion; in *Incidents in the Life of a Slave Girl,* Linda employs verbal warfare and defensive verbal postures as tools of liberation. Quick thinking and invective play vital roles, and Linda becomes a veritable trickster.

Sass is a word of West African derivation that is associated with the female aspect of the trickster. The *Oxford English Dictionary* attributes the word's origin to the poisonous "sassy tree." A decoction of the bark of this tree was used in West Africa as an ordeal poison in the trial of accused witches, women spoken of as being wives of Exu, the trickster god. In her 1893 *Autobiography*, Amanda Smith, an independent black missionary, wrote: "I don't know as any one has ever found what the composition of this sassy wood really is; but I am told it is a mixture of certain barks. They say that it is one of their medicines that they used for punishing witches so you cannot find out what it is. The accused had *two gallons* to drink. If she throws it up, she has gained her case."[21] So, obviously, "sass" can kill.

Webster's Dictionary defines *sass* as talking impudently or disrespectfully to an elder or a superior, or as talking back. Whenever Linda is under sexual attack, she uses sass as a weapon of self-defense; she returns a portion of the poison the master has offered her. The first time that Flint hits Linda, she hits back, not with her fists, but with sass: "You have struck me for answering you honestly. How I despise you." When he threatens to send her to jail, she responds, "As for the jail, there would be more peace for me there than there is here" (*Incidents*, 39, 40). In one instance, Flint demands: "Do you know that I have a right to do as I like with you,—that I can kill you, if I please?" Negotiating for respect, Linda replies: "You have tried to kill me, and I wish you had; but you have no right to do as you like with me" (*Incidents*, 39). Sass preserves the slave girl's self-esteem and increases the psychological distance between herself and the master. Ironically, Linda's sass becomes a shield against Flint's physical sexual aggression: "Sometimes I so openly expressed my contempt for him that he would become violently enraged, and I wondered why he did not strike me" (*Incidents*, 32). In short, Linda uses sass the way that Frederick Douglass used his fists and his feet, as a means of resistance.

In time, however, Flint begins to build a cottage for Linda in the isolated countryside, forcing the young woman to make a desperate choice: "I would do anything, every thing, for the sake of defeating him. What *could* I do? I thought and thought, till I became desperate, and made a plunge into the abyss" (*Incidents*, 53). When Flint threatens to kill Linda if she tells her grandmother, he completes her psychological isolation. Desperate, Linda resorts to the use of her own body, not for happiness or fulfillment, but as a weapon against the master: "Revenge, and calculations of interest, were added to flattered vanity and sincere gratitude for kindness. I knew nothing would enrage Dr. Flint so much as to know that I favored another; and it was something to triumph over my tyrant, even in that small way" (*Incidents*, 55). Thomas Doherty argues that it is Linda's identity and not her "honor" that is at stake in this duel of wills.[22]

Mr. Sands, a white single gentleman, has learned of Linda's predicament through neighborhood gossip. Linda chooses him to play a part in her scheme. She "allows" herself to be "seduced" by this younger, "purer" man: "It seems less degrading to give one's self, than to submit to compulsion. There is something akin to freedom in having a lover who has no control over you, except that which he gains by kindness and attachment" (*Incidents*, 55).[23] While Sands enjoys Linda's charms, he does what he can to purchase her, and though he will later betray her trust, he is for a time an invaluable friend, a man who keeps her secret, when to reveal it would mean her destruction and the ruin of her family.

Learning of her pregnancy, Linda rejoices over the prospect of telling the master. When Flint orders Linda to the completed cottage, she assails him with sass. Confident of his goal, he decrees: "You shall go, if you are carried by force; and you shall remain there." Again she returns his poison. "I will never go there. In a few months I shall be a mother"

(*Incidents*, 56). She increases the master's rage by refusing to reveal the identity of her child's father to him, another act of defiance. But at this moment of triumph, Linda mourns over revealing her secret to her grandmother, who has worked hard to protect her granddaughter's virtue. "I thought I should be happy in my triumph over him. But now that the truth was out, and my relatives would hear of it, I felt wretched. Humble as were their circumstances, they had pride in my good character. Now, how could I look them in the face? My self-respect was gone!" (*Incidents*, 56). Linda experiences a loss of self-esteem with her sexual fall and disgrace; much of the remainder of the autobiography, and indeed the act of writing, seems a kind of expiation, an attempt to regain what she has lost.

In *Incidents in the Life of a Slave Girl* the narrative and geographical movement parallel the development of intellectual capacity and emotional maturity, as well as the narrator's concern for the well-being of her two children. Motherhood opens the pathway to greater self-awareness and, like sass, becomes a vehicle for the retrieval of lost self-respect. With the birth of her son, Benjamin, the young mother experiences the beginnings of an illumination: "When I was most sorely oppressed I found a solace in his smiles" (*Incidents*, 62). It is a distinctive feature of the outraged mother that she sacrifices opportunities to escape without her children; Linda is motivated by an overwhelming concern for the freedom and literacy of her children, a concern that is not apparent in the narratives of questing male slaves. This concern is reflected in such chapter titles as "The Children Sold," "New Destination for the Children," and "The Meeting of Mother and Daughter." After the births of Benjamin and Ellen, each major "turning point" building toward freedom is linked with the mother's concern for their freedom and well-being. The birth of her children toughened the slave mother and steeled her to the sacrifices she would make for their sake. In Linda's words: "I had a woman's pride, and a mother's love for my children; and I resolved that out of the darkness of this hour a brighter dawn should rise for them. My master had power and law on his side; I had a determined will. There is might in each" (*Incidents*, 85).

The prospect of her daughter Ellen's future finally enables Linda to find the nerve to run away. "When they told me my new-born babe was a girl, my heart was heavier than it had ever been before. Slavery is terrible for men; but it is far more terrible for women. Superadded to the burden common to all, *they* have wrongs, and sufferings, and mortifications peculiarly their own" (*Incidents*, 77). Following Ellen's birth, events leading to "The Flight" begin to mount rapidly, showing the narrative growth toward the "conviction" and escape stage. Linda's desires for her own freedom are rekindled through her hopes for her children: "I could have made my escape alone; but it was more for my helpless children than for myself that I longed for freedom. Though the boon would have been precious to me, above all price, I would not have taken it at the expense of leaving them in slavery" (*Incidents*, 89).

For refusing to become Flint's concubine, Linda is sent to his son's secluded plantation. Leaving behind her son, Benjamin, who is ill, Linda sets off for the plantation, there to have her suspicions confirmed. She has been sent to the isolated location to break her spirit of resistance. Observing other slave mothers on the plantation, her chief fears are for her daughter: "How much easier it would be to see her die than to see the master beat her about, as I daily saw him beat other little ones. The spirit of the mothers was so crushed by the lash, that they stood by, without courage to remonstrate. How much more must I suffer, before I should be 'broke in' to that degree?" (*Incidents*, 133). The outraged mother's determination to save herself and her children spurs her to plan a secret escape. "My mind was made up; I was resolved that I would foil my master and save my children, or I would perish in the attempt. I kept my plans to myself; I knew that friends would try to dissuade me from them, and I would not wound their feelings by rejecting their advice" (*Incidents*, 86–87). Thus the master's persecution only increases the slave mother's determination to achieve her freedom.

Masking her true feelings, Linda tries to appear content. This becomes more difficult when Ellen breaks down under the "trials of her new life": "One day, she sat under the window where I was at work, crying that weary cry which makes a mother's heart bleed. I was obliged to steel myself to bear it" (*Incidents*, 87). Moved by her concern for her children, Linda begins to finalize plans for her escape:

> My plan was to conceal myself at the house of a friend, and remain there a few weeks till the search was over. My hope was that the doctor would get discouraged, and, for fear of losing my value, and also of subsequently finding my children among the missing, he would consent to sell us; and I knew somebody would buy us. I had done all in my power to make my children comfortable during the time I expected to be separated from them. (*Incidents*, 91)

Again, it is the projection of her daughter's life under slavery that motivates her to action: "I knew the doom that awaited my fair baby in slavery, and I determined to save her from it, or perish in the attempt. I went to make this vow at the grave of my poor parents, in the burying-ground of the slaves" (*Incidents*, 90). Praying at her parents' graves, Linda links the dead, the living, and the unborn; she is part of an Afro-American continuum as well as a part of a continuum of women's oppression.

Linda realizes her plans for escape through disguise and concealment, as well as the direct assistance of family and friends. On a morning when a cart is loaded with shingles to be sent to town, she puts Ellen into it and sends her back to the relative safety of the town and Aunt Marthy. Although the master is annoyed, he takes no punitive action. This act reflects the protective values of the outraged mother, who resists her situation not so much on her own behalf as on her children's. Aided by a female slave friend, Linda conceals herself in the home of a neighboring slaveholder who is sensitive to her plight. During this time, she experiences a vision: "I rose from my sitting posture, and knelt. A streak of moonlight was on the floor before me, and in the midst of it appeared the forms of my two children.... Some will call it a dream, others a vision. I know not how to account for it, but it made a strong impression on my mind, and I felt certain something had happened to my little ones" (*Incidents*, 107–108). As it turns out, Mr. Sands, the children's father, has tricked Flint into selling them, along with Linda's brother William, to a slave trader acting on his behalf. With the help of Betty, her slave friend, and Peter, a carpenter who had been her father's apprentice, Linda is disguised as a sailor and taken to the Snaky Swamp, a location she finds more hospitable than landed slave culture: "Even those large, venomous snakes were less dreadful to my imagination than the white men in that community called civilized" (*Incidents*, 113).

Later, Linda is concealed in a carefully constructed crawl space in her grandmother's home: "My uncle Phillip, who was a carpenter, had very skillfully made a concealed trap-door, which communicated with the storeroom. He had been doing this while I was waiting in the swamp. The storeroom opened upon a piazza. To this hole I was conveyed as soon as I entered the house. The air was stifling; the darkness total" (*Incidents*, 114). Here she remains seven years. Constantly sitting or lying in a cramped position, she speaks of being tormented by insects and heat in the summer and of being frostbitten in the winter. "But I was not comfortless," she writes; "I heard the voices of my children" (*Incidents*, 114). Ironically, no one suspects that she may be hiding anywhere in the immediate area. Through a series of ingenious and heroic performances, Linda thus outwits Flint to attain freedom for her and her children. While hidden in her grandmother's house, she deceives Flint by writing letters that a friend mails from New York. Three times he sets out for New York to look for her; each time, she is practically in his own back yard.

The remainder of the text describes the outraged mother's long struggle to bring about the reunion of her family in the free states. When her friend Peter alerts Linda to an opportunity to leave for the free states, she at first hesitates because of her grandmother's disapproval and offers another slave woman her place. But at the last minute she changes her mind, with the result that both women board a freedom-bound ship, under the cover of being taken to a reunion with fictitious husbands in the North. In time, Linda, William, Benjamin, and Ellen are reunited in the North, but they are not yet safe. Only when a friendly employer pays Flint's son-in-law $300 to relinquish all claims to Linda and the children are they "free at last." Linda writes that she "had objected to having [her] freedom bought." "Yet I must confess that when it was done I felt as if a heavy load had been lifted from my weary shoulders. When I rode home in the cars I was no longer afraid to unveil my face and look at people as they passed" (*Incidents*, 200). The lifting of this veil symbolizes both a physical and a spiritual liberation. Yet the outraged mother's goal of a home for herself and her children remains unfulfilled at the end of the narrative.

Because of her moral compromise, there can be no totally "happy ending," and when Linda's story ends, the outraged mother's dream is "not yet realized." She wishes "for a hearthstone of [her] own, however humble," adding that she wants it "for [her] children's sake far more than for [her] own." The narrative concludes with a final play on the "cult of true womanhood": "Reader, my story ends with freedom; not in the usual way, with marriage. I and my children are now free! We are as free from the power of slaveholders as are the white people of the north; and though that, according to my ideas, is not saying a great deal, it is a vast improvement in *my* condition. The dream of my life is not yet realized. I do not sit with my children in a home of my own. I still long for a hearthstone of my own, however humble. I wish it for my children's sake far more than for my own" (*Incidents*, 201). The final image is that of the narrator's reflection on the memory of her grandmother: "fleecy clouds floating over a dark and troubled sea." The heroine never sees her "good old grandmother" again.

Speaking to a predominantly white and female northern audience, the outraged mother espouses conventional nineteenth-century notions of ideal womanhood, but she acts on black cultural values. Linda inverts the traditional "happy ending" of the nineteenth-century domestic novel and amalgamates the elements of that fiction with the traditional slave narrative to create an original form. The only work in the slave narrative genre in which the articulate hero is a woman, a mother, and the author of a coherent first-person narrative, *Incidents* is also the only full account of a maturing slave girl's initiation into the sorrows of slave motherhood. In this respect, *Incidents* emerges as a text central to the slave narrative genre and to the autobiographical writing of black Americans.

Incidents in the Life of a Slave Girl reveals the outraged mother as another version of the black heroic archetype and emphasizes the importance of female bonding, especially between the narrator, her grandmother, and her daughter. An articulate and rationally enlightened heroine engaged in a quest for freedom and literacy, as well as for a hearth and a home for herself and her children, Linda displays many of the nurturing and protective values and characteristics observed in the "good old grandmother." Through her descent into "sin," she discovers motherhood as an avenue to identity. Paradoxically, her fall is a fortunate and necessary step toward a "brighter dawn." *Incidents in the Life of a Slave Girl*, in its departure from the conventional slave narrative, reflects ways in which women structure their experiences into a different kind of literary language. Further study of all such texts and testimonies by women can help us correct and expand analyses based exclusively on male models of experience and writing. Thus the study of black women's writing helps us to transform definitions of genre, of archetype, of narrative traditions, and of the African–American experience itself.

2
Fugitive Slaves
and Sanctified Ladies:
Narratives of Vision
and Power

In addition to the slave narratives, the autobiographical writing of nineteenth-century black American women took many and varied forms. They include the journals, memoirs, and reminiscences of freeborn teachers and missionaries; the "as told to" accounts of such historical figures as Harriet Tubman and Sojourner Truth; the postemancipation accounts of women who were slaves; and the confessional spiritual autobiographies of black women preachers, notably Jarena Lee and Rebecca Cox Jackson, whose proto-feminist religious perspectives were formed in response to African Methodism. This chapter examines representative situations and occasions that called forth the literary assertion of self among black women in nineteenth-century America. Like Frances E. W. Harper, perhaps the most popular black poet before Paul Laurence Dunbar, these women saw themselves and their race "as a living force, animated and strengthened by self-reliance and self-respect."[1] The force of this self-assertion, this "making a way out of no way," is revealed in their work and their progress from degradation and voicelessness to literacy and freedom. Narratives of free women and former slave women tend to differ from those of fugitives in that the writing of autobiography stands as a literary experience wherein slavery has less importance as a theme. The author is involved in creating a public persona, but the impulse to write is less overtly political because the need to raise public opinion against slavery has diminished. While these works lack the emotional confessional quality of such fugitive narratives as *The Narrative of Frederick Douglass* and *Incidents in the Life of a Slave Girl*, they sustain the themes of family and survival, and they reflect a movement toward self-sufficiency and self-expression, and toward an intelligent and self-conscious sensibility that seeks to satisfy its own needs. In the postemancipation accounts of slaves, the central concerns for family and self-sufficiency do not cease but extend the ideal of service to one's community, state, and nation. Susie King Taylor's *Reminiscences of My Life in Camp with the U.S. 33rd Colored Troops* (1902) and Elizabeth Keckley's *Behind the Scenes: or Thirty Years a Slave and Four Years in the White House* (1868) serve as representative examples.

Behind the Scenes reveals much about the transition from slavery to freedom. Elizabeth Keckley, the child of a slave woman whose husband lived on a neighboring plantation, suspected her mother's master of being her true biological father. When she reached the age of eighteen, this master placed Elizabeth with another white man, by whom she bore a son.[2] Later, the master took her to live with him in St. Louis, along with her son and her mother. When his business failed, he proposed that Elizabeth's mother be hired out as a servant. *Behind the Scenes*, like *A Narrative of the Life and Travels of Mrs. Nancy Prince*, *Incidents in the Life of a Slave Girl*, and Susie King Taylor's *Reminiscences*, displays strong evidence of female bonding. Keckley is outraged by the impending separation of her family and directs her resources toward helping her family achieve liberation from slavery. "The idea was shocking to me. Every gray hair on her old head was dear to me," she writes, "and I could not bear the thought of her going to work for strangers" (*Scenes*, 44). Thus, Keckley serves the master's interests to protect her mother and prevent the separation of her family. Her desperate need for self-sufficiency begins the rise to freedom, just as surely as Linda Brent's rebellion did in the earlier text: "In a short time I had acquired something of a reputation as a seamstress and a dressmaker. The best ladies in St. Louis were my patrons, and when my reputation was once established I never lacked for orders. With my needle I kept bread in the mouths of seventeen persons for two years and five months" (*Scenes*, 45).

Yet Elizabeth Keckley realizes that, ultimately, she cannot secure freedom for others until she has achieved her own freedom. Later, when she proposes to buy herself and her son, "the proposition was bluntly declined, and I was commanded never to broach the subject again. I would not be put off thus, for hope pointed to a freer, brighter life in the future" (*Scenes*, 46–47). Keckley, another outraged mother, asks a question similar to that raised by the heroine of *Incidents in the Life of a Slave Girl:* "Why should my son be held in slavery?" Despite this outlook, however, Keckley's reaction appears to be much more accommodating than that of the rebellious heroine of *Incidents*.

Like Harriet "Linda Brent" Jacobs and the slave narrator Ellen Craft, Elizabeth Keckley puts a value on the importance of producing only freeborn children; she delays marriage until she can be assured that she has a prospect of freedom. As these narratives demonstrate, a slave woman might resist a "legitimate" marriage to a free man, even one who was her own choice for a husband, out of a desire to protect both him and their future progeny. The logic of such resistance is revealed by probing into a complex and contradictory situation composed of conflicting loyalties, affinities, and values.

Family attachments inspired black women to seemingly impossible feats in their determination to protect their children, preserve family unity, and secure the freedom of loved ones. Choosing not to become a fugitive, Keckley instead determines to purchase her freedom and that of her son. The master at first resists and then reluctantly enters into a contract, the conditions of which he knows will be difficult for her to meet. "[He] told me that he had reconsidered the question, that I had served his family faithfully; that I deserved my freedom, and that he would take $1200 for myself and boy." Only after "taking a prospective glance at liberty" does she decide to marry (*Scenes*, 49). In this and other ways, Keckley's slave experience sharply contrasts with that of Linda Brent. Elizabeth Keckley's master permits her to marry the man of her choice and gives her a lavish wedding party, whereas Linda Brent had to send her love away. Although both women grow up in genteel environments, only Linda Brent revolts and escapes. Elizabeth Keckley cannot leave her mother behind; for her, the break between slavery and freedom is not a clear one. Because of the demands on her labor by the master's family, she struggles to accumulate the funds necessary to execute the contract to purchase herself and her son. When the master dies, the executor of his estate, in an uncommon act of generosity, agrees to do what he can to help her raise the money.

Like *Incidents*, *Behind the Scenes* also praises the cooperation of white women of the South, who assist Elizabeth in gaining her freedom, such as the white woman patron of her seamstress trade who raises the needed $1200: "At last my son and myself were free. Free! the bitter heart-struggle was over. Free! the soul could go out to heaven and to God with no chains to clog its flight or pull it down. Free! the earth wore a brighter look, and the very stars seemed to sing with joy. Yes, free! free by the laws of man and the smile of God—and Heaven bless them who made me so" (*Scenes*, 55). Significantly, Elizabeth places her son before herself in announcing her freedom.

Although Elizabeth Keckley's ascent from slavery is comparatively easy—her circumstances were not so extreme as those of Linda Brent—she is no less an outraged mother. Had Keckley's master not been her father, had she encountered more oppression in her daily life or more overt resistance to her determination to be free, had she the projection of a daughter's life under slavery instead of that of a son, or had she been denied the privilege of marrying her chosen lover, she might have reacted more closely to the Linda Brent model.

In Washington, Keckley serves a distinguished clientele, including the First Ladies of both the Confederacy and the Union. Apparently, Mrs. Lincoln became quite attached to "Madame Elizabeth," seeking her assistance in the days and months after the assassination of President Lincoln and regarding her as a confidante. Their friendship is later destroyed, partly as a result of conflict surrounding the publication of Keckley's ghost-written autobiography. In her efforts to authenticate her work and her professed intimacy with the former First Lady, Keckley depicts Mrs. Lincoln as an emotionally unstable and financially destitute woman, who sold her wardrobe in order to meet her expenses.

Like many other autobiographies by black women in the nineteenth century, *Behind the Scenes* is marked by unpredictable shifts in the narrative action. Similar to Nancy Prince's *Narrative,* Keckley's work is really two texts: a slave narrative and a confidential memoir. The second part of the text, concerning Keckley's life in Washington in the days leading up to and including the Civil War, lacks the vitality of the earlier portions. Additionally, we should note that *Behind the Scenes,* which was published in 1868, is a postemancipation account written in the form of a memoir, not a political slave narrative like *Incidents in the Life of a Slave Girl.* Hence, by definition, the goals of the two narratives are different.

Another narrative that shows the transition from slavery to freedom is Susie King Taylor's *Reminiscences of My Life in Camp with the U.S. 33rd Colored Troops,* published in 1902. As James McPherson has suggested, *Reminiscences* makes a valuable companion piece to Thomas Wentworth Higginson's *Life in a Black Army Regiment.*[3] The Taylor text is as interesting as the Higginson one from a historian's point of view; indeed, Taylor's achievement prompts the reader to wonder what she might have accomplished as an autobiographer if she had spent ten years studying at Harvard, as Higginson did. *Reminiscences* clearly demonstrates that Taylor had both intellectual ability and literary talent. She expands the idea of service that emerged in Keckley's *Behind the Scenes,* and growth of consciousness in this autobiography may be correlated with an apparent growth of self-reliance. Taylor's concept of her Christian duty extends not only to her family and her immediate community but to her race and nation. Again, there are parallels with the slave narrative tradition in the nurturing and self-sacrificing qualities of the heroine. With the attainment of freedom, former slaves like Susie King Taylor were able to turn their talents to new areas of interest and concern; nursing and teaching were two acceptable roles.

Susie King Taylor was "born under slave law" in 1849 on an island off the coast of Savannah, Georgia. Because her mother, like Elizabeth Keckley and Linda Brent, was a favored house servant in an established family, at the age of seven Susie was allowed to live in Savannah with her free maternal grandmother. Thus, Susie King in Savannah, like Frederick Douglass in Baltimore, knew the myriad advantages of an urban environment. One detail of particular interest concerns the manner in which Susie King Taylor "stole" her education. In her quest for freedom and literacy, young Susie learned to hide her books and her intentions, in silent defiance of laws forbidding slaves to read and write: "We went everyday about nine o'clock, with our books wrapped in paper to prevent the police or white persons from seeing them. The neighbors would see us going in sometimes, but they supposed we were learning trades."[4] Susie remained in this secret school for more than two years, until she had learned all that her teacher could teach. Then, like Frederick Douglass, she received advanced lessons from white playmates, including the landlord's son. This "theft" of knowledge indicates that Susie learned to use weapons of indirection and deception as forms of self-defense in creating psychological space for herself and in maximizing her opportunities to attain literacy. In using her special talents to acquire letters and language, Taylor places herself even closer to the tradition of the fugitive slaves; she discovers the bond between freedom and literacy—a theme noticeably absent from Keckley's *Behind the Scenes*. Perhaps because of the early age at which she was freed, Susie King Taylor does not provide an extensive description of her slave experience, as do Jacobs and Keckley. Although the focus of this narrative is Taylor's life as a free woman, *Reminiscences* reveals parallels with the slave narrative tradition, especially in the recurrence of the archetypal nurturing and self-sacrificing qualities of the individual women. In general, the Taylor narrative bears an even closer relation to the slave narrative model, both in form and content, than does the Keckley memoir. Although Taylor makes no direct reference to any given slave narrative, it is difficult to imagine any literate slave who would not have had reading knowledge of some of them.

Like many other female narratives, Susie King Taylor's work emphasizes the importance of bonding with a close female relative, in this case, her grandmother, a free woman. At this time in Georgia history, "all colored persons, free or slave, were compelled to have a pass." Consistent with the spirit of the archetypal trickster figure who relies on wit, speed, and intelligence to deceive, beguile, overwhelm, and defeat a more powerful foe, Taylor characteristically uses her newly found literary talents to gain some "here and now" transcendence by counterfeiting passes for her grandmother, thus expanding the elder woman's freedom (*Reminiscences*, 21). This studied deceit echoes the theme of disguise and concealment found in the narratives of Frederick Douglass, Harriet Brent Jacobs, William and Ellen Craft, and Henry "Box" Brown. Like countless other slave narrators, Susie King Taylor also learns to use the weapon of deception as a form of self-defense. More significantly, she uses her special talents to acquire the use of letters and language, the first tools of the autobiographer, and to liberate further her grandmother—a woman who is at once her ancestor, her link with tradition, her protector, and her sister in the face of common oppression.

In contrast to Linda Brent and Elizabeth Keckley, Susie King Taylor realized her freedom as the result of a historical moment. Early in the Civil War (1861), the U.S. Navy steamed into South Carolina's strategically important Port Royal Sound, began bombardment of the shore, and landed troops within twenty-four hours. The whites in rebellion evacuated quickly, leaving behind some ten thousand former slaves as "contrabands" of war, many of whom crossed Confederate lines to join Union forces. Thus, during the same year that Elizabeth Keckley set about establishing herself as a Washington *modiste* and dressmaker to the First Ladies of the two rival governments, Susie King, with her uncle and his family, escaped from Confederate-held territory in a small boat, landing under the protection of the Union blockade. Later in the same year, 1861, at the age of fourteen, she married Edward Taylor and went to live with him off Port Royal Island, where he joined the First South Carolina Volunteers, the first black regiment in the Union Army. Two "great questions" were of concern in what some saw as the social problem of their time: "One is, will the people of African descent work for a living? and the other is, will they fight for their freedom?"[5] The fate of the "contrabands" had not yet been decided. A full two years away from the Emancipation Proclamation, black hands who had grown cotton for white slaveholders now grew corn for the Union.

"On the first of January, 1863," Taylor attended "services for the purpose of listening to the reading of President Lincoln's proclamation." At the same time, the U.S. 33rd Colored Troops received "two beautiful strands of colors ... as the crowning event we had a grand barbecue. A number of oxen were roasted whole, and we had a grand feast." As the wife of a black enlisted man, Taylor supported him and his unit in what they saw as the struggle for freedom; she worked as a nurse, a laundress, and teacher within the camp. Passing on her love of learning, she taught soldiers in her husband's company: "I taught a great many of the comrades in Company E to read and write, when they were off duty. Nearly all were anxious to learn. My husband taught some also when it was convenient for him. I was very happy to know my efforts were successful in camp, and also grateful for the appreciation of my services" (*Reminiscences*, 21). As a nurturer and healer, she also nursed the sick and wounded; in her narrative, she describes a herbal preparation that she asserts prevented her from contracting smallpox while treating diseased men: "I drank sassafrass tea constantly, which kept my blood purged and prevented me from contracting the dread scourge, and no one need fear getting it if they will only keep their blood in good condition with this sassafrass tea, and take it before going where the patient is" (*Reminiscences*, 17). Thus the Taylor narrative further exemplifies the ideal of service to others.

After the war, Taylor's work was of necessity directed at survival rather than larger social goals. Widowed in 1866, Taylor supported herself briefly by running a school, then moved to Boston, where she, like Nancy Prince, entered domestic service. Her life as a servant was all too similar to her previous life as a slave.

Although her circumstances are less dramatic, Susie King Taylor, like Harriet Brent Jacobs and Elizabeth Keckley, is an outraged mother, risking herself for her child. In 1898, when her only son grows ill while traveling in Louisiana, she goes by train to see him. Forced into a confrontation with a group of white men, she uses language and silence as a means of self-defense. Playing the naive narrator, Taylor writes that she asked the conductor if the railroad "allowed persons to enter the car and insult passengers" (*Reminiscences*, 70). Like Aunt Marthy and Linda Brent, Susie King Taylor is skilled at using sass and invective as life-preserving measures that put distance between her and potential sources of danger. Taylor is first aware of this danger when a black porter asks her why she is traveling in Louisiana; she responds that only the illness of her son could have taken her there. In Shreveport, she finds her son hemorrhaging and in need of a specialist's care. Anxious to take him North, where such care might be more easily obtained, she attempts to secure him a berth on a sleeper, "as he was not strong enough to travel otherwise" (*Reminiscences*, 72). Predictably, the railroad refuses them on account of Jim Crow racial restrictions. The text does not explain exactly why she then leaves her son behind, and this seems a curious omission. Having made the dangerous trip to Shreveport, it seems unlikely that she would have quit her task easily. Concluding her narrative, Taylor notes this painful irony: "It seemed very hard, when his father fought to protect the Union and our flag, and yet this boy was denied, under the same flag, a berth to carry him home to die, because he was a Negro."

On the return trip to Boston, in Clarksdale, Mississippi, she sees a man hanged, describing it as "a terrible sight." She fears for her own safety until she crosses the Ohio, the boundary between slavery and freedom. It is a disillusioned but not broken woman who writes these words of outrage: "For two hundred years we have toiled for them; the war of 1861 came and ended, and we thought the race was forever freed from bondage, and the two races could live in unity with each other, but when we read almost every day of what is being done to my race by some whites in the South, I sometimes ask, 'Was the war fought in vain?' " And then she adds, appropriately: "There are many people who do not know what some of the colored women did during the war. These are things that should be kept in history before the people" (*Reminiscences*, 61).

Bearing witness, in the tradition of the confessional slave narrative, Taylor, outraged by the needless death of her son, attempts to move public sentiment against the practices of white supremacy that replaced slavery in the South following Reconstruction. Assuredly she is not the only one who wonders if the war had been fought in vain. Like Harriet Brent Jacobs and Nancy Prince, who commented on the racism they encountered in the North, the alleged land of freedom, Taylor criticizes the failure of the "War of 1861" to make a significant change in the lives of former slaves and their children.

In Keckley's *Behind the Scenes*, the theme of family and family unity found in the female slave narrative is transformed and expanded into an ideal of service to others. *Reminiscences* expands this concept even further to include the ideal of service to one's community and nation. Both Elizabeth Keckley and Susie King Taylor conform to the outraged mother archetype and demonstrate the importance of ties with close female relatives. Moreover, the formal tone of conciliation, the shifts in the pattern of narrative movement, and the "curious omissions" all serve to tie these works into a larger tradition of women writing. This link is significant. For women writers generally, a lack of educational opportunity, limited literacy models, and the many demands on their labor thwarted literary ambitions; for black women, the barriers were higher. The mere fact that women who were formerly slaves produced autobiography in nineteenth-century America at all shows the strength of their impulse to assert the self in the form of personal narrative.

Power with God

Nineteenth-century spiritual autobiographies by black American women also include the narratives, memoirs, and reminiscences of missionaries, exhorters, preachers, and visionaries. This chapter next explores their quest for personal power and their assertion of the literary self; included in this discussion are the problem of attaining freedom and literacy and the problem of "telling a free story." Personal power, in this context, should be understood to mean "power with God"; it is expressed in dreams, premonitions, and visions, which may be, as likely as not, profoundly disturbing to the narrator/pilgrim/seeker. William Andrews has made a valuable contribution to the study of black American autobiography in *Sisters of the Spirit*, the collected nineteenth-century spiritual autobiographies of Jarena Lee, Zilpha Elaw, and Julia A. J. Foote. As he argues in his introduction to these three works, these narratives, like other American spiritual autobiographies, are records of a pilgrimage toward spiritual salvation. "Whether written by blacks or whites," Andrews asserts, "American spiritual autobiography chronicles the soul's journey not only from damnation but also to a realization of one's true place and destiny in the divine scheme of things."[6]

Like *Pilgrim's Progress* or John Woolman's *Journal*, spiritual autobiographies by black Americans, both men and women, center on the quest for spiritual perfection in an imperfect world. For these Americans, the autobiographical act was a form of spiritual witnessing; their narratives record a journey characterized by trials, temptations, and, finally, triumph. These narratives of vision and power, an important "type" among early spiritual autobiographies, include *The Life and Religious Experience of Mrs. Jarena Lee* (1936); *Memoirs of the Life, Religious Experience and Travels of Mrs. Zilpha Elaw* (1846); *A Brand Plucked from the Fire: An Autobiographical Sketch by Mrs. Julia A. J. Foote* (1879); *Elizabeth: A Colored Minister of the Gospel Born in Slavery* (1889); and *Gifts of Power: The Writings of Rebecca Cox Jackson, Black Visionary, Shaker Eldress* (1981), a nineteenth-century journal edited by the contemporary feminist scholar Jean Humez. This study focuses primarily on *The Life and Religious Experience of Mrs. Jarena Lee* and *The Writings of Rebecca Cox Jackson*, two closely related visionary texts.

In addition to documenting the trials, temptations, and triumphs of black American women, spiritual autobiography illuminates sex-specific aspects of the black woman's early intellectual history and her quest for self-definition and self-determination, especially in the case of free black missionary women. Many free women found relative acceptance as missionaries and teachers; their evangelical travel narratives are underscored by the same reliance on divine deliverance and the same "orality" that they share with the "pure" spiritual autobiographies and the confessional slave narratives. *A Narrative of the Life and Travels of Mrs. Nancy Prince* (1850) is such a hybrid.

Prince's *Narrative* really consists of two narratives: a travelogue/adventure story of her nine-year sojourn in Russia, and a record of her experiences as a missionary in Jamaica, where she encountered extreme gender bias. Although Prince did not claim great literary talent, her object was more than "a vain desire to appear in public."[7] Her *Narrative* represents an attempt to rise above perceived cultural isolation to lay claim to a dignified, self-defining identity in the creation of autobiography and the assertion of a literary self. In writing her *Narrative,* she discovers and rediscovers the power of personal narrative and writing, as well as the use of language as a means of self-defense and self-expression.

Like many other female narratives, Prince's autobiography is marked by shifts in the patterns of movement that contribute to the overall impression that the story lacks order. But these changes in narration reflect Prince's discontinuous experience. One such sudden shift centers on Prince's decision to leave America for Russia. Deeply affected by her personal experience of racial, sexual, and economic oppression while working as a "free" servant in Massachusetts, Prince, "after seven years of anxiety and toil," chooses to leave America, having married a black man (referred to only as "Mr. Prince") in the service of the czar. Prince never says much about her marriage or her relationship with her husband, but the marriage does initiate a change in the movement of her *Narrative*. On one level, it might even be argued that part of the resulting discontinuity of the *Narrative* is caused by the marriage. Yet this notion is not confirmed by the narrator's voice, which seeks to overcome the confines and limitations of physical abuse and overwork, as well as psychological anxiety about her racial and sexual difference and her perceived cultural isolation.

Prince sails for Russia on April 24, 1824, and arrives in St. Petersburg on June 21. She documents her observations of the manners and customs of the Russians, as well as her life as a seamstress at the Imperial Court. She spends nine and a half years in St. Petersburg; then, overwhelmed by the cold Russian climate, she leaves Russia and returns to America. Her husband remains behind in an attempt to acquire some property, but he dies before he can do so. Concluding this section of the narrative with her return, Prince becomes involved in efforts to establish an orphanage for black children who had been shut out of other asylums. This assertion affirms Prince's quest for a dignified, self-defining identity, her drive for self-sufficiency and public respect, and her desire to make a contribution to her race.

Prince's departure for Jamaica initiates the second radical shift in the narrative. Like many other free black women of this era, Prince found relative acceptance as a teacher and a missionary. In 1840, she leaves for Jamaica to "aid, in some small degree, to raise up the emancipated inhabitants, and teach the young children to read and fear God, and put their trust in the Savior" (*Narrative*, 45). She survives pirates and tropical storms to arrive in St. Ann Harbor, Jamaica. Progressing from the role of passive observer to that of active participant, Prince describes a population living in "sin of every kind" and exploited by hypocritical missionaries who charge excessive rates for Bibles. Not surprisingly, considering the experiences of her sister Silvia, who became a prostitute in Boston, the problems of destitute young women rank high on her list of priorities. Like many other women involved in preaching and missionary work, Prince, a Baptist, disagrees with church officials regarding the appropriateness of her role as a female missionary. Her difficulties result from her assertive behavior and from giving away Bibles, an act that subverts the profit-making motives of others, who find more favor with the church.

Born of an attempt to provide for her necessities, Prince's *Narrative* also sprang from the impulse to render experience more bearable through the confessional retelling of her story. Prince devotes a large portion of the narrative to detailing the things she saw, felt, and experienced. As in the narratives of slave women, the family plays a role of central importance, yet the search for a self-defining identity is more strongly developed here than in the reminiscences of former slaves. Nancy Prince achieved a greater degree of self-definition than either Susie King Taylor or Elizabeth Keckley. Born free, she set larger horizons for herself and tested the limitations of her freedom.

Some missionary accounts, such as *An Autobiography: The Story of the Lord's Dealings with Mrs. Amanda Smith* (1893), incorporate the journey motif within an adventure story to seek an identity that would merit the respect of a largely white and northern audience. While Smith asserts that her purpose in writing this narrative is religious, the

Autobiography also carries a subtext of "gospel temperance." Smith hopes that other young women will follow her example "so that when I have fallen in the battle, and can do no more, they may take the standard and bear it on."[8]

The two main themes of this text are the quest for education and the achievement of religious purification. As a child, Amanda was urged by her parents to secure an education. In Africa, she teaches "little Bob" to read and write in order to demonstrate his potential for literacy and intellectual improvement. All the while, she is longing for the sanctification of her soul through good deeds and constant prayer, acquiring an international reputation as a preacher and prayer leader. The "escape" of this text is an escape from sin, achieved by her early religious conversion; ironically, when Smith is converted, she runs to the mirror to see if her color has changed:

> There seemed to be a halo of light all over me; the change was so real and so thorough that I have often said that if I had been as black as ink or as green as grass or as white as snow, I would not have been frightened. I went into the dining room; we had a large mirror that went from the floor to the ceiling, and I went and looked in it to see if anything had transpired in my color, because there was something wonderful had taken place inside of me, and it really seemed to me it was outside, too and as I looked in the glass I cried out, "Hallelujah, I have got religion; glory to God, I have got religion!" (*Autobiography*, 47)

Because of her preaching ability, her power to sway large groups of people emotionally, and her mobility, Smith succeeds in escaping the limitations of her culture to some extent. She travels to England, Ireland, Scotland, Wales, Africa, and India as an independent missionary, acquiring an international reputation as a preacher and prayer leader. In Africa, after she teaches "little Bob" to read, she fulfills both the spiritual journey and what the critic Robert Stepto has defined as "the quest for freedom and literacy."[9]

A member of the African Methodist Episcopal (A.M.E.) Church until she left to become, in the words of Jean Humez, "a great holiness preacher," Smith was but one of many women whose religious philosophies developed almost in direct response to (and sometimes as a revolt against) African Methodism. Another example of this drive for spiritual power by women within the A.M.E. Church can be found in *The Life and Religious Experience of Mrs. Jarena Lee.* Both Lee's *Life* and the writings of Rebecca Cox Jackson employ traditional biblical imagery and languages that set them apart from traditional black women's writings. Punctuated as they are with visions and visitations, these narratives also share the quest for literacy and/or religious instruction; the trial, temptation, and triumph motif; and the importance of a spiritual journey or pilgrimage.

The central thematic concern of Lee's *Life and Religious Experience* is the quest for spiritual sanctification, augmented by Lee's struggle, as a woman, to answer God's call to preach the gospel in a male-dominated temporal religious world.[10] In its language, visionary content, and quest for sanctification, the narrative resembles the Puritan model of confessional spiritual autobiography. For Lee, as for Puritan and Quaker women of the eighteenth century, the writing of autobiography represents "the fulfillment of a sacred duty to family, both immediate and extended."[11]

There the similarity ends, however; the quest for sanctification is primarily a product of Methodism and the Holiness movement. The Puritans would have been horrified by anyone who claimed to have sought or achieved sanctification. Lee's *Life and Religious Experience* exemplifies a concern both for spiritual liberation and for the development of self-sufficiency and community; in the quest for sanctification, Lee offers her life as an exemplary model. Her spiritual energy expresses itself through the traditional biblical imagery of her visions: "a form of fire," "a man robed in white," and the "savior, nailed to the cross," all symbols of transformation and regeneration (*Life*, 12–14). Structurally, Lee's *Life* can be divided into an untitled introductory section and three chapters: "My Call to Preach the Gospel," "My Marriage," and "The Subject of My Call to Preach the Gospel Renewed."

This Is the People to Which My Heart Unites

The introductory section of *The Life and Religious Experience* describes Lee's family background and documents her early conversion to Christianity under the teaching of the Reverend Richard Allen, founding bishop of the African Methodist Episcopal Church:

> During the labors of this man that afternoon, I had come to the conclusion, that this is the people to which my heart unites, and it so happened, that as soon as the service closed he invited such as felt a desire to flee the wrath to come, to unite on trial with them—I embraced the opportunity. Three weeks from that day, my soul was gloriously converted to God, under preaching, at the very onset of the sermon....
>
> For a few moments I had the power to exhort sinners, and tell of the wonders and of the goodness of him who had clothed me with his salvation. During this, the minister was silent, until my soul felt its duty had been performed, when he declared another witness to the power of Christ to forgive sins on earth, was manifest in my conversion. (*Life,* 5)

This first section narrates Lee's subsequent progress in the quest for salvation, a quest that had three distinct "degrees": conviction (or conversion), justification, and finally, sanctification.

Unlike the narratives of missionaries, which incorporate the journey motif within an adventure story to seek a dignified and self-defining public identity, narratives of vision and power by black women preachers focus almost wholly on spiritual matters and show less concern with temporal issues, except as they relate directly to spiritual development.

The preoccupation with religious perfection and the relationship between these women and the Methodist Church are fascinating. John Wesley was one of the first to preach the possibility of achieving perfection, or "sanctification," the ultimate goal of these women preachers who formed their self-authorizing and proto-feminist concepts on their direct experience of the Holy Spirit, which divine source they viewed as no respecter of either gender or the hierarchies of temporal-based religious. For these women, access to the Holy Spirit through visions and the inner voice became a vehicle for defining themselves in opposition to the unjust world around them, the logical outcome of their quest for spiritual perfection in an imperfect world. They were not consciously antinomian, but the force of life and the vitality of their own being asserted itself from within. They "rose up"; they were "resurrected souls" oblivious to the laws, barriers, and restrictions in their way. Owning "power with God" derived directly from the Holy Spirit in its various forms, they went against the external limitations imposed on them by their respective denominations and in their personal secular lives. Jean Humez refers to this sanctification as "a second experience of divine grace in the soul following conversion."[12] According to Humez, the experience of "sanctification" was rooted in "the Holiness current in Methodist thought and practice," a current of which Lee was most decidedly a part: "The individual experienced 'justification' at conversion—the conviction that her sins were forgiven and she was 'made just' through Christ's love. The state of blessedness beyond justification, sanctification, was one in which the individual experienced full freedom from 'intentional sin'—the liability, to which all fallen humanity was heir, to commit sins in full knowledge that they were sins."[13] The quest for sanctification, like the journey motif in the spiritual autobiography, is characterized by trials, temptations, and, finally, spiritual triumph.

Lee's *Life and Religious Experience* follows this movement, detailing the trials and temptations that beset her soul on the path to spiritual salvation and sanctification. The trials encountered during the conviction stage twice include the temptation to commit suicide by drowning, and on another occasion to hang herself. Paradoxically, these temptations lead her to deliverance; in fact, spiritual salvation seems to be the very reason for these temptations. Because she fell, she could rise again in the Holy Spirit. A vision of Hell puts her on the path to salvation:

But notwithstanding the terror which seized upon me, when about to end my life, I had no view of the precipice on the edge of which I was tottering, until it was over, and my eyes were opened. Then the awful gulf of hell seemed to be open beneath me, covered only, as it were, by a spider's web, on which I stood. I seemed to hear the howling of the damned, to see the smoke of the bottomless pit, and to hear the rattling of those chains, which hold the impenitent under clouds of the judgment of the great day.

I trembled like Belshazzar, and cried out in the horror of my spirit, "God be merciful to me a sinner." That night I formed a resolution to pray; which, when resolved upon, there appeared, sitting in one corner of the room, Satan, in the form of a monstrous dog, and in a rage, as if in pursuit, his tongue protruding from his mouth to a great length, and his eyes looked like two balls of fire; it soon, however, vanished out of my sight. From this state of terror and dismay, I was happily delivered under the preaching of the Gospel as before related. (*Life*, 6)

For Lee, this vision served as corroboration of "the Bible account of a hell of fire, which burneth with brimstone, called in Scripture the bottomless pit." It cemented her conversion and brought about an end to her temptations: "Day and night my joy was full, no temptation was permitted to molest me. I could say with the psalmist, that 'God had separated my sins from me, as far as the east is from the west.' "

Soon Lee began to pray for "sanctification," the last stage in the journey toward "salvation." When at last she realized her goal, she felt as if she had been struck by lightning: "A new rush of the same ecstasy came upon me, and caused me to feel as if I were in an ocean of light and bliss" (*Life*, 10). Despite the conventional format of this introductory section, however, Lee's *Life* also treats public and political aspects of her spiritual experience: specifically, her call to preach, her travels, and her trials as a female preacher. Like many other women in the Holiness movement, Lee, a clairvoyant, had premonitions and perceived events happening at a distance. Lee heard an inner voice and followed its dictates. She received her call to go and preach from just such a voice: "Again I listened, and again the same voice seemed to say— 'Preach the Gospel. I will put words in your mouth and turn your enemies to become your friends' " (*Life*, 10). Lee's inner voice is important, especially in the context of a sexist, slaveholding antebellum culture, in that it is essentially self-authorizing, defying secular laws, and, ultimately, the settled ways of white (and black) patriarchy; for Jarena Lee, black, female, and thus denied a public voice, the promise of a divine gift of words and friends had a powerful effect. Ultimately, Lee's inner voice sets up a tension between her inner self and external religious authority, a tension she will use to carve out an identity and a voice for herself.

In keeping with the doctrinal restrictions of traditional pre–A.M.E. Methodism, Bishop Richard Allen denies Lee's request for a license to preach; nevertheless, he gives her permission to exhort and to lead prayer meetings, a more "acceptable" practice. Lee writes: "But as to women preaching, he said our Discipline knew nothing at all about it—that it did not call for women preachers. This I was glad to hear because it removed the fear of the cross." Despite Lee's surface acquiescence, however, her narrative becomes openly polemical on the question of women preaching:

> O how careful aught we to be, lest through our by-laws of church government and discipline, we bring into disrepute even the word of life. For as unseemly as it may appear now-a-days for a woman to preach, it should be remembered that nothing is impossible with God. And why should it be thought impossible, heterodox, or improper, for a woman to preach? Seeing the Savior died for the woman as well as the man.
>
> If a man may preach, because the Savior died for him, why not the woman? seeing he died for her also. Is he not a whole Savior, instead of a half one? as for those who hold it wrong for a woman to preach, would seem to make it appear. (*Life*, 11)

Not long after being denied a license to preach, Jarena, at age twenty-eight, married the Reverend Joseph Lee. Overcoming her initial uneasiness about her new role in life, she became the model minister's wife, bearing two children. The oldest was two years and the youngest six months of age when their father died. At the sudden end of her six-year marriage, Lee again felt the "call" to preach: "The subject now was renewed afresh in my mind; it was a fire shut in my bones" (*Life*, 15). She continued to exhort publicly until Bishop Allen gave her his verbal permission to preach. In one of her exhortations, Lee raised the issue of her calling:

> I told them that I was like Jonah; for it had been then nearly eight years since the Lord had called me to preach his gospel to the fallen sons and daughters of Adam's race, but that I had lingered like him, and delayed to go at the bidding of the Lord....
>
> During the exhortation, God made manifest his power in a manner sufficient to show the world that I was called to labour according to my ability, and the grace given unto me, in the vineyard of the good husbandman. (*Life*, 17)

For this "indecorum," she feared she might be expelled from the church. Instead: "The Bishop rose up in the assembly, and related that [Lee] had called upon him eight years before, asking to be permitted to preach, and that he had put me off; but that he now as much believed that I was called to that, as any of the preachers present." Lee notes: "These remarks greatly strengthened me, so that my fears of having given an offence, and made myself liable as an offender subsided, giving place to a sweet serenity, a holy job of a peculiar kind, untasted in my bosom until then" (*Life*, 17). Finally having received the bishop's permission to preach, Lee traveled through the Middle Atlantic and New England states, winning souls for African Methodism.

Buried in the Tradition of My Forefathers

Drawing on both Eurocentric and Afrocentric systems of belief, some black women sought and claimed direct contact with a "divine Spirit" and sought spiritual purification in predominantly female "praying and singing bands." Before and during the 1820s, the testimonial, the praying band, and the class meeting were vital sources of spiritual power for black women in America. Attracted by the popular "spiritual extempore preaching" of African Methodism, many of these women grew up in the A.M.E. Church or joined the church only to find that church leaders considered their weeping and fasting "extravagant" and many of the old-fashioned spirituals "heathenish." Threatened by this rising female power, the church adopted rules about who could raise a song and when. In the 1840s, Bishop Daniel Payne also headed a drive to increase the educational requirements for the ministry, a drive that had the effect of excluding most women. This period of A.M.E. Church history is also associated with the rise of the Holiness movement, another manifestation of female "power with God."

Like Jarena Lee, the Shaker eldress Rebecca Cox Jackson was raised in the African Methodist Episcopal Church and was rooted in the Holiness movement. Both women were itinerant ministers engaged in the quest for sanctification (and, later, holiness), and both struggled with issues of church discipline regarding their appropriate roles as women, and, in the case of Jackson, her radical self-empowering theology. William Andrews suggests that *The Life and Religious Experience of Jarena Lee* may have served as a model for the autobiographical writings of Rebecca Jackson. *Gifts of Power* also records a spiritual life heavily influenced by dreams and visions, frequently expressed in symbolic imagery and language. In *Gifts of Power*, however, the importance of dreams and visions as vital sources of information is more pronounced, fulfilling essentially the same role as the inner voice in Lee's narrative; they authorize antinomian and sometimes defiant behavior, setting up a tension between the inner self and external religious authority. Rebecca Cox Jackson used her dreams and visions as a way of distancing herself from the life around her and ultimately in the creation of a private space wherein she could create her own unique identity and voice. Jackson's narrative, with its attendant questioning of authority, is more radical than Lee's or any of the other spiritual autobiographies by black American women that preceded hers. Jackson's autobiography also differs from Lee's in that Jackson's writings were essentially private documents that were not intended for publication. Lee also had more control over the structure of her printed narrative than did Jackson, whose work appeared post-humously.

Jean Humez located Jackson's work "in various Shaker archives" and arranged the manuscript of *Gifts of Power* chronologically in six sections: "Awakening and Early Gifts (1830–1832)," "Breaking Away from Family and Churches (1833–1836)," "Finding God's True People on Earth (1840–1843)," "Shaker Doctrine and the First Residence at Watervliet (1844–1851)," "Interim in Philadelphia: Experiments in Séance Spiritualism (1851–1857)," and "Second Residence at Watervliet: Establishment of the Philadelphia Shaker Community (1857–1864)." Rebecca Jackson underwent what Humez calls "a rich, lifelong education in religiosity": "Listening to the testimony in the praying bands and class meetings, she would have derived much of her sense of the fitness, the probability, the appropriateness, the meaning of certain kinds of visionary and spiritual events, the language in which the divine expressed itself."[14] Jackson herself describes her experience of this educational process as being buried: "I was so buried in the tradition of my forefathers that it did seem as if I never could be dug up."[15]

The dream language of Jackson's autobiography concerns itself almost wholly with spiritual matters; her dreams, her visions, and her "inner voice" provide the inspiration and direction for her physical actions and the authorization for her unique mission. Jackson followed these inner guides absolutely, even when to do so was to risk confrontation in her marriage, her family, and her church organization. "In the years following her conversion and sanctification," Humez notes, "Jackson derived much of her ability to stand alone, unsupported by husband, brother or church, from her visionary experience."[16] In her journal, Humez suggests, "Jackson wove together the peaks of her visionary experience, attempting to show how they related to her situation in the world outside herself."[17] The "peaks" of Rebecca Jackson's "visionary experience" correspond with some of the major turning points in her life and her spiritual journey: her conversion, her sanctification, and her discovery of self-control as a means of attaining personal power. Jackson's autobiographical writings also reflect her struggle to reconcile her visions and her inner voice with externally imposed religious authority—first the A.M.E. Church and then the Shakers. This crucial tension defines the narratives of both Rebecca Cox Jackson and Jarena Lee.

As in Lee's *Life*, Jackson's inner voice is sometimes the voice of temptation, such as the voice she heard in the midst of a thunderstorm just prior to her conversion: "It was suggested to me, 'the first clap will break your neck down the stairs.' " And then she knelt and prayed with the thought, "I might as well go to Hell off my knees a crying for mercy as anywhere else." "The more I prayed the worse I felt," she wrote. "My sins like a mountain reached to the skies, black as sack cloth of hair and the heavens was as brass against my prayers and everything above my head was one solid blackness." And then she vowed "never to rise from [her] knees" until she was either converted or sent to hell for her sins (*Gifts*, 71–72).

Jackson's apparently unreflective use of conventional biblical language and imagery, especially "blackness" to represent sin, is perplexing and confusing. It suggests her acceptance of the symbolic polarities of whiteness to represent purity and goodness and blackness to represent impurity and evil. Did Jackson see herself as inherently evil because of her blackness? Was part of the "purification" process in search of religious salvation the stripping away of her awareness of racial identity and gender difference? This "moment of despair" became a turning point for Jackson when she "found the Lord," whose divine presence she expresses in conventional images of light:

> The cloud bursted, the heavens was clear, and the mountain was gone. My spirit was light, my heart was filled with love for God and all mankind. And the lightning, which was a moment

ago the messenger of death, was now the messenger of peace, joy, and consolation. And I rose from my knees, ran down the stairs, opened the door to let the lightning in the house, for it was like sheets of glory to my soul. (*Gifts*, 72)

"Ever since," she wrote, "I have been made to praise God in time of storm, to rejoice and be exceeding glad." This ecstatic conversion from sin was the first step in Jackson's quest for sanctification or release from the burden of her sins; however, it might also be seen as a step away from a self-conscious race- and gender-specified identity.

Not long after her conversion, Jackson challenges the authority of her husband and brother to leave her sickbed and attend the prayer meeting where she is sanctified. "I knew my husband would be angry, and my brother also, and I had given them great cause to be," she admits. At the prayer meeting she asks the Lord to sanctify her: "So I asked, in prayer and crying to God with all my might, soul, body, and strength, until my body became faint and weak. I could no longer kneel on the chair, so I prostrated myself on the floor and there I labored from early in the morning until 12 o'clock" (*Gifts*, 76). With sanctification comes the knowledge of "the sin of the fall of man":

> At that hour the burden rolled off. I felt as light as air. I sprang upon my feet, shouting and leaping the high praises of God. So I praised God aloud with all my faculties from 12 until 1 o'clock. I never felt so happy in all my life. I then saw for the first time what the sin of the fall of man was, and I thought if I had all the earth, I would give it, to be a single woman. How to return to my husband I knowed not. These were my thoughts, for they had never entered into my mind that was the sin. (*Gifts*, 76–77)

"However," she writes, "I went home shouting through the streets."

With knowledge of "the sin of the fall of man" comes Jackson's discovery of sexual self-control as a means of attaining personal power. This self-control includes not only mastery of one's sexual appetite but also mastery over every aspect of one's physical body. Jackson demonstrates her spiritual strength to her husband by repeatedly placing her hands on a red-hot stove and pulling them away unharmed: "The coffee aboiling on the top while my hands was on the stove. He had not the power to touch me, and when I was permitted to open my eyes, I saw him with his two hands under his chin and ashaking like a person with a heavy fit of ague" (*Gifts*, 77).

The identification of sex as sin also serves to liberate Jackson from male domination. (Note that the stove and the bed, domestic symbols of women's limited sphere, are key sites in Jackson's rebellion, when she confronts her husband with superior and unchallengeable demonstrations of power.) Her inner voice and its subsequent revelation of sex as sin lead Jackson to further confrontation with her family and the A.M.E. Church. Unlike Jarena Lee, who was licensed by Bishop Allen, Jackson preaches and prays on her own authority, drawing considerable opposition. Yet she remains determined: "I had started to go to the promised land, and I wanted husband, brother, and all the world to go with me, but my mind was made up to stop for none." During this stage of her quest, she writes, "I had no friends at home or abroad." The topic of sexual abstinence is indeed an explosive one; at prayer meetings, she feels as if she "had opened a bottle of cayenne pepper among the people" (*Gifts*, 87).

Jackson receives much of her spiritual instruction through visions she has while fully awake. On one such occasion, she experiences a vision of her "holy leader," or spiritual teacher, significantly, a female figure. This vision corresponds with Jackson's search for spiritual guidance concerning her deportment toward the outer world, both in deed and appearance. In the midst "of fasting, praying, and crying to God to know his will," Jackson sees a woman:

> She was dressed in light drab. Her bonnet was close to her face. Her arms hung down at her side. She walked straight forward. She neither looked nor turned to the right nor left....

> And it was spoken in my heart, "This is the way I want you to walk and to dress and when you are as you ought to be, you will look like this woman and be like her." (*Gifts*, 93)

When first viewed, the woman is twelve feet in front of Jackson and is headed east. Jackson follows her, unable to see the face of her teacher or to catch up to her, though she "labored hard day and night so to do." Yet she knows that she will catch up with the woman "in God's own appointed time" (*Gifts*, 93). This proves to be one of the most prophetic and significant visions Jackson will record.

Jackson's dreams are another vital source of information; she finds "A Dream in the Garden" troubling. Jackson dreams that she is alone in the midst of a garden of blackberries, having entered through a path that is the only entrance and the only exit. The berries "was ripe, long, and beautiful," but just as she is about to begin picking, she realizes the bushes are full of snakes:

> And when I looked the bushes was full all around me and over my head. Every one had their mouth open, their strings out, and they were ready to spring upon me. I saw nothing but death for me if I stayed there and it was death to attempt to come out. They were hanging between me and the door. I saw no hand could save me but the hand of Almighty God, so in faith and humble prayer I cried out unhurt and made for the house. I had to pass through a shed and as I was coming through, they were killing a dog. As I passed the blood spun on my white apron. I shook my apron and all the blood was off and my apron was as clean as if it had not been on. (*Gifts*, 93–94)

The reader should probably resist the temptation to analyze the symbolism of Jackson's dreams or interpret them in psychological terms. Without an understanding of the context, especially a knowledge of Jackson's own established dream language, she is easily misread. Nevertheless, careful attention should be paid to her *own interpretation* of the dream, which again borrows much from the conventional (and/or white) religious imagery of the Bible. And in Jackson's dream language, the sexual symbolism of this dream is dramatically clear. Putting aside her troubled spirit, she "got understanding." "This garden," she writes, "was my fallen nature." "These berries was the fruit on which my carnal propensities subsisted. My person was my soul. My picking was my soul taking an active part in all its pleasures. So I found that the Lord was teaching me the way of life." For Rebecca Jackson, "the way of life" could no longer include sexual relations, and though she entered this new stage in her spiritual quest with a symbolically clean white apron, she knew the difficulty she would encounter: "I saw in my dream the great opposition I would have to go through in my pilgrimage, and how I was to believe it was by living in obedience to all that God required of me, and then I should have faith of God in the time of trouble." She writes: "Faith and prayer are my weapons of war" (*Gifts*, 94).

Jackson's autobiographical writings recall her personal struggle to reconcile her visions and her inner voice with externally imposed religious authority—first the A.M.E. Church and then the predominantly white Shakers. In "A Dream of Slaughter" Jackson dreams of being flayed by a man who subsequently disembowels her and then mangles her body with a "long knife." She wakes up in her husband's arms: "I was all in a tremble. And these words was spoken to me, 'Thy Life is hid in Christ. Thy Life is hid in Christ.' Three times these words was spoken to me. And I was strengthened and my soul filled with the love of God." Jackson identifies her tormentor as a Methodist minister who "about four years after I had this dream...persecuted me in as cruel a manner as he treated my body in the dream" (*Gifts*, 95). Jean Humez says this man was probably Jeremiah Miller, one of three Methodist ministers who persecuted Jackson; the other two she identifies as Henry and Isaac Lowers. So violently were these men opposed to her ministry, Jackson asserts, that they "appointed what death I ought to die. One said I ought to be stoned to death, one said tarred and feathered and burnt, one said I ought to be put in a hogshead, driven full of spikes, and rolled down a hill" (*Gifts*, 149). The specific verbal attack Jackson sustained from two A.M.E. ministers "probably occurred in 1835"; retrospectively, therefore, she may have interpreted her earlier dream, circa 1831, as something of a warning.

Among the gifts of power Jackson receives as a result of her quest for holiness are the gifts of literacy, healing, and the ability to control the weather. Of all these gifts, literacy is perhaps the greatest. Tired of her brother's censorship of the letters he writes for her ("I don't want thee to *word* my letter. I only want thee to *write* it"), Jackson longs to be able to read the Bible and conduct her own correspondence. In the midst of her trials, her inner voice speaks to her, "Be faithful, and the time shall come when you can write" (*Gifts*, 107). Heeding her inner voice, she puts down her sewing, picks up her Bible, reads a chapter without stopping, and finds that she can both read and understand. Her subsequent religious instruction comes from guides and teachers, such as the "holy leader" revealed in her earlier vision, as well as from angels, who speak to her spirit when it has left her body and ascended "through all substance" (*Gifts*, 111). These are her rewards for taking up a new "way of life" consistent with the dictates of her visions and her inner voice, and for putting aside the life of the flesh.

In the next phase of her experience, Jackson's visions lead her to go out and preach as well as to continue to pray for the sick and to conduct prayer meetings. During this time, she meets with increased opposition from her husband, Samuel, her minister brother, Joseph Cox, and the A.M.E. ministry. At the same time, she increases her following and develops a radical theology that precludes sexual relations, whether within or outside the marital relationship:

> And that man and that woman who thinks God will give them an inheritance with His dear Son in light, while they live in this world according to this generation, instead of living in the regeneration, as His dear Son did to show us the way of eternal life, so that we might with Him possess all things and that

God might be glorified in His Son.... For when we live in the
regeneration, which is to live without sin, herein we glorify
God and herein also God's power is made manifest through all
the obedient, to the Children of men.

This is the New Heaven and the New Earth, wherein
dwelleth righteousness, and it is the First Resurrection. For the
souls of men and women are hereby raised out of their fallen
nature into the spirit of Christ, and this is external life. (*Gifts*,
131–132)

At this point in her quest or struggle for holiness or a
"redeemed life," Jackson continues to experience conflict in
her church and family life because of her determination to
live a "Christ-like life" that does not include sexual intimacy.
She still has not found the Shakers, even though she feels led
by her spiritual teacher, the female figure she saw in a vision
three years earlier. Soon, however, Jackson testifies that her
"heavenly lead" enters her: "And as she entered me, the
heavenly influence of her divine spirit overcame my soul and
body and I can't tell the heavenly feeling I had" (*Gifts*, 133).
This near-erotic spiritual experience strengthens Jackson's
"gift of foresight," or prophecy, and her gift of healing.
Through Jackson, the gift of sight is restored to a blind
woman; later, she will predict both this woman's death and
the exact time and place of her funeral. Such extraordinary
gifts make Jackson even more controversial in her social
sphere.

In 1831, at a time when she suffered the greatest "sorrow
and suffering about living a holy virgin life" in a world where
"everything seemed to stand in opposition to that life,"
Jackson experiences a vision of "God's true people on earth."
"I then entreated the Lord to tell me why it was that I was
called to live a life that nobody lived on earth." In answer to
her request, she is told, "I have a people on earth that lives the
life that I have called you to live" (*Gifts*, 137). These people
are, of course, the Shakers, and this vision becomes an
important turning point in Jackson's life. Now she feels she
has divine sanction for her decision to join the Shakers and
live a "holy virgin life":

> Then my spiritual eyes was opened and I saw in the distance
> flocks of kids, white as snow, on beautiful green grass. They
> laid close to the ground. Their forefeet were crossed and their
> chin rested on their forefeet. They were many miles apart.
> They all looked like one kid, yet I seen them distinct. And when
> I saw them, it was said to me, "These are my people. These
> lived the life that I have called you to live. And if you are
> faithful, I will bring you to see them." (*Gifts*, 137)

She sees these chosen people for the first time in 1836 when
she is in New York to preach in Albany. On visiting a public
Shaker meeting, her inner voice speaks to her: "These are my
people and if you are faithful, when you are done the work
which I have given you to do in the world, I will gather you to
my people" (*Gifts*, 139).

Two other events in 1836 presage her discovery of the
Shakers: what she calls her "release from bondage," and her
discovery in herself of "a Mother in the Deity." Shortly after
"A Dream of Three Books and a Holy One" in which she is
provided with a new spiritual teacher (this time a man),
Jackson's inner voice commands her to tell her husband she
will no longer have sexual relations with him. "And now from
this day and forever, I shall never strive again," she tells him.
"But I shall serve to the Lord and Him only. And when I have
done it, He will be pleased" (*Gifts*, 147). This conviction and
her increasing public testimony against "living in generation"
earn Jackson new adversaries among the Methodists, and her
persecution increases. Yet she writes, "This great persecution
opened doors before me." Throwing herself on the Lord, she
sees for herself, for the first time, a "Mother in the Deity":

> This was indeed a new scene, a new doctrine to me. But I
> knowed when I got it, and I was obedient to heavenly vision—
> as I *see* that I hold forth, that is, with my spirit eye. And was I
> not glad when I found that I had a Mother! And that night She
> gave me a tongue to tell it! The spirit of weeping was upon me,
> and it fell upon all the assembly. And though they never heard
> it before, I was made able by Her Holy Spirit of Wisdom to
> make it so plain that a child could understand it. (*Gifts*,
> 153–154)

Jackson's attraction to the Shakers is both understandable and paradoxical. She was pulled, first and foremost, by the Shaker doctrine of celibacy and by the inherently feminist theology of the four-in-one Shaker godhead, which included Mother and Daughter as well as Father and Son. Holy Mother Wisdom balanced the Almighty Father and played a vital role in Shaker life and religious writing. Jean Humez sees this "perfectly balanced male and female Godhead" as a "deliberate reflection of Shaker communal organization, in which a female-headed sisterhood and a male-headed brotherhood lived together" in a "parallel hierarchy" of "spiritual 'union.' "[18] They were, in Jackson's terminology, "living to live forever" (*Gifts*, 139). In addition, Jackson may have been attracted to the Shakers' pacifism, their antislavery sentiment, and their rejection of state authority; as a sect, they were equalizing, if not equalitarian. For a woman oppressed because of her race, her gender, and her spiritual beliefs, these tenets of Shaker belief must have provided a strong pull indeed. Paradoxically, leaving "the world" meant cultural isolation from other blacks. For although the Shakers welcomed everyone, without regard to race, they felt no special mission to blacks, most of whom were invested in an essentially patriarchal religious experience as well as the accumulation of wealth and status in a society where these things had been denied them.

In this regard, Jackson strongly differed from white Shaker leaders. Rebecca Cox Jackson *did* feel a responsibility, a mission, to blacks, which she dreamed about in 1843:

> Then I woke and found the burden of my people heavy upon me. I had borne a burden of my people for twelve years, but it now was double, and I cried unto the Lord and prayed this prayer, "Oh, Lord, God of Hosts, if Thou art going to make me useful to my people, either temporal or spiritual—for temporally they are held by their white brethren in bondage, not as bound man and bound woman, but as bought beasts, and spiritually held by their ministers, by the world, the flesh, and the devil. And if these are not a people in bondage where are there any on earth?" (*Gifts*, 181–182)

The doctrinal conflict that arose between Jackson and the Shaker leaders—that is, whether she would submit to their authority over her inner voice—is tied to her personal sense of having a mission to black people. Although Jackson's visionary experience was both direct and immediate, visions and messages from angels and holy spirits required approval from Shaker sect leaders before they could be regarded as authentic. When, after having lived separate from "the world" amid the Shakers at Watervliet since 1847, Jackson in 1854 decided to return to Philadelphia to convert blacks to Shakerism and to establish a permanent mission there, the presiding Shaker eldress Paulina Bates refused to sanction Jackson's plan. At this time, Shakers permitted only "unavoidable business contacts with the outside world ... and those were carefully monitored" (*Gifts*, 31). For Jackson, who believed that the exact day and year she should begin her mission to black people had been ordained by her inner voice, the eldress's objection to her plan caused serious inner conflict. Nevertheless, Jackson's inner self authorized her external reality and strengthened her resolve to take the Shaker religion to black people. With her constant companion, Rebecca Perot, Jackson spent six years spreading the Shaker religion in Philadelphia before returning to Watervliet in 1857, following her signal "Dream of Home."

Ultimately, however, the same inner authority that brought her into conflict with Shaker religious authority helped resolve that conflict. Jackson's "Dream of Home" showed how her unconscious sleeping self helped bring about a resolution to issues that confronted her waking self, for this dream summoned her to Watervliet to make amends with Eldress Paulina.

In "Dream of Home," Eldress Paulina welcomes Jackson with open arms and then chastises her for her willfulness. The dream ends with Jackson receiving the sanction she desires for her Philadelphia mission, to form a Shaker community among blacks. Not long after this vision, Jackson returns to Watervliet and submits to the authority of Eldress Paulina, promising to obey her. For her reward, she receives a divine commission from Holy Mother Wisdom via Eldress Paulina: "Now you are endowed with power and authority. Now the Lord hath sent you. You have waited for the Lord, and you go under a blessing. All that you bless, we bless—and whoever sets out to you, and honestly confesses their sins, we own and bless, and receive into our Society—and we will withhold no good thing for you or your people" (*Gifts*, 277). In 1859, Jackson returns to Philadelphia with Rebecca Perot and two other women and holds her first meeting as a Shaker eldress.

Jackson's last known writing is dated June 4, 1864, and she died in 1871, but her Philadelphia "family" survived her by forty years. Jackson's radical narrative records the growth of an essentially self-authoring and defiant inner self in conflict with external forms of authority, both religious and secular. The logical outcome of this strong spiritual orientation (and the form of the spiritual narrative itself in the hands of nineteenth-century black women) may be seen in the "secular" narratives of Harriet Tubman and Sojourner Truth, where black women question secular authority in order to establish both themselves and a space of difference.

"To Tell a Free Story"

Unlike Rebecca Jackson and Jarena Lee, neither Harriet Tubman nor Sojourner Truth would acquire the gift of literacy. Both women had to rely on others to transform their spoken narratives into written words and to structure this symbolic language into a version of the self if their desire were to be partly satisfied, as William Andrews calls it, "to tell a free story."[19] As neither autobiographer had been empowered to control the form of her written narrative, more than any of the self-authored narratives, *Harriet Tubman, The Moses of Her People,* and *Narrative of Sojourner Truth* exemplify the problem of "speaking freely." The first edition of Sarah H. Bradford's *Scenes in the Life of Harriet Tubman* appeared in 1869. An expanded second version was published under the current title in 1886. Both were printed privately by Bradford in order to raise funds for Tubman. Olive Gilbert prepared Sojourner Truth's 1850 *Narrative and Book of Life* as well as *Narrative of Sojourner Truth: A Bondswoman of Olden Time. Emancipated by the New York Legislature in the Early Part of the Present Century; With a History of Her Labors and Correspondence Drawn from her "Book of Life"* "for the author" in 1878. Authorial control of the speaker's words and images, and the final shape of the narrative, had to rest with others.

Harriet Tubman, The Moses of Her People, and *Narrative of Sojourner Truth* also demonstrate the parallel development of autobiography, biography, and what Andrews calls "religious social activism" among black women in America. Andrews views Tubman and Truth as "inheritors of a black and female autobiographical tradition of activism founded on a commitment to religious faith, human rights and women's struggles."[20] These remarkable accounts of two of the greatest social movers of their time possess the quality of orality, a vitality reminiscent of the act of speaking. They show the secularization and oralization of the written spiritual autobiography in the personal "as told to" narrative. This important development demonstrates the parallel currents of written and oral literature, especially the spiritual testament or testimony, a form that historically has appealed to black Americans of varied social, economic, and educational backgrounds—a popular outlet of spiritual self-expression. Drawing on both Eurocentric and Afrocentric systems of belief, Sojourner Truth and Harriet Tubman make radical uses of traditional forms of spirituality more explicitly than Jarena Lee or Rebecca Jackson ever did. This is evidenced by Tubman's willingness to risk her life repeatedly to save others via the Underground Railroad and in Truth's feminist/abolitionist and temperance activities. By questioning what they saw as illegitimate authority, they established a "wild zone," or space of difference, from which to wage rebellion against an intemperate, sexist, and slaveholding society; they believed that God was on their side and that they acted on divine authority. Taken altogether, these narrators might be said to "radicalize" the form of spiritual autobiography and re-create it as a tool for temporal liberation. With such "power with God," they wielded an almost superhuman influence over the world around them as they sought to restructure that world in their own image.

Both Harriet Tubman and Sojourner Truth experienced an immediate and personal relationship with Christ Jesus. They believed in the power of prayer and the presence and accessibility of God; nothing they asked for would be denied. Both experienced dreams and visions of a prophetic nature and were so guided in their daily experiences; both relied on inner voices, which they presumed to be of divine origin. God was their immediate protector. African-born Sojourner Truth was an outraged mother before she became a social activist, though all of her heroic actions were fueled by the same spirit. When her mistress sold Sojourner's five-year-old son to a wealthy planter in Alabama (illegally, as New York law prohibited the sale of any slave out of state, and all minors were to be freed at age twenty-one), Sojourner (then Isabella Bomefree) confronted the woman directly and demanded the return of her son:

> I tell you, I stretched up. I felt as tall as the world!
> "Missis," says I, "*I'll have my son back again!*"
> She laughed.
> "*You* will, you nigger? How you goin' to do it? You ha'nt got no money."
> "No Missis—but *God* has—an' you'll see he'll help me!"[21]

Looking back on this experience, Truth pronounced, "Oh, my god! I knowed I'd have him agin. I was sure God would help me to get him. Why I felt so *tall within*—I felt as if the *power of a nation* was with me!" (*Sojourner*, 45). Indeed, the "power of a nation" was with her, and in time she did retrieve her son, though he returned to her with his "back all covered with scars and lumps," the result of floggings he received in the South (*Sojourner*, 163). The spirit that Truth showed in challenging her mistress was the same she would later show in speaking out for abolition, temperance, and black and women's rights. Her values were not formed on the public stage, but in the crucible of slavery. Her public activism was the natural flowering of her private rage, which was also the rage of her mother, who had been taken from Africa and separated from her children in the New World.

Like Rebecca Jackson, Harriet Tubman (née Araminta Ross) felt herself chosen by God to lead her people out of bondage, but in Tubman's case it was the literal, physical bondage of slavery to be conquered, not the bondage of flesh. She, "Moses," was to lead her people's exodus out of the hell of southern Egypt into the Promised Land of Canaan. *Harriet Tubman, The Moses of Her People*, demonstrates her secularization of the spiritual "sorrow songs" of the slave as a vehicle of physical liberation:

> What dat ar old chariot comes,
>   I'm gwine to lebe you.
> I'm boun' for de promised land,
>   Fren's, I'm gwine to lebe you.
>
> I'm sorry, fren's, to lebe you,
>   Farewell! oh, farewell!
> But I'll meet you in de mornin',
>   Farewell! oh farewell!
>
> I'll meet you in de mornin',
>   When you reach de promised land!
> On de oder side of Jordon,
>   For I'm, boun' for de promised land.[22]

Both *Harriet Tubman, The Moses of Her People*, and *Narrative of Sojourner Truth* incorporate the journey and the trial motif. For Tubman, each physical journey out of the slaveholding territories into Canada was a spiritual journey; her own freedom would be meaningless until she secured that of her family:

> I was free; but dere was no one to welcome me to de land of freedom, I was a stranger in a strange land, and my home after all was down in de old cabin quarter, wid de ole folks and my brudders and sisters. But to dis solemn resolution I came; I was free and dey should be free also; I would make a home for dem in de North, and de Lord helping me, I would bring dem all dere. (*Harriet*, 31–32)

By some accounts, Tubman rescued as many as three hundred people from slavery, sometimes carrying babies drugged with paregoric or opium in a basket. She was successful in rescuing her parents and all but one of her sixteen siblings and in bringing them north. Tubman's God was ubiquitous and omnipresent, all-knowing and all-powerful, like the God of the precolonial African. Once, "Moses" ordered her party to lie down "in the tall wet grass" of a swamp where she prayed "and waited for deliverance" (*Harriet*, 55–56). In time, they were rescued by a Quaker "friend" who seemed to appear almost miraculously. The Lord told Tubman when danger lay ahead or behind and what to do to avert it. The Lord told her when to seek help for her people and whom to seek it from and in what form—even, at times, from perfect strangers.

Perhaps the most astonishing evidence of Tubman's faith in divine deliverance came in the form of her premonition of freedom, which, according to her text, she experienced three years before the Emancipation Proclamation. Visiting the Reverend Henry Highland Garnet in New York, Tubman awoke and came to breakfast singing "My people are free! My people are free!" When challenged by Reverend Garnet, Tubman exclaimed, "I tell you, sir, you'll see it, and you'll see it soon. My people are free! My people are free! My people are free!" When the friends of abolition rejoiced at the actual Proclamation, a sober Harriet explained, "I had *my* jubilee three years ago. I rejoiced all I could den; I can't rejoice no more" (*Harriet*, 92–93). If God said it, it was so, and her dreams and visions were messages from God; this was the modus of her faith, and she acted on the revelations she received, perfectly self-actualized.

Sojourner Truth chose her own name, a highly symbolic act. She called herself Sojourner Truth because her life mission was to journey and testify, showing "the truth" to the people. She too experienced a direct relationship with God, and she felt herself to be under His continual protection and guidance. For example, she felt His divine providence made possible her escape from bondage: " 'Now,' says I, 'I want to git away; but the trouble's jest here; if I try to git away in the night, I can't see; an' if I try to git away in the day-time, they'll see me an' be after me.' Then the Lord said to me, 'Git up two or three hours afore daylight, an' start off.' 'An',' says I, 'Thankee Lord! that's a good thought' " (*Sojourner*, 156). Having started out, she realizes she has no place to go: "Well Lord, you've started me out, an' now please to show me where to go" (*Sojourner*, 156). Then the Lord shows her a vision of a house and tells her to walk on until she sees it. She travels late into the night before she sees the house, goes inside, and tells the occupants, the Van Wageners, that the Lord has sent her.

Sojourner lives with this family two or three years, during which time she "forgot all about God." Soon afterward, slavery is abolished in New York, and her former master comes to take her to visit "the folks on the old place" she had escaped from. Then she "met God" and is fully converted:

> Well, jest as I was goin' out to get in the wagon, *I met God!* an' says I, "O God, I didn't know as you was so great!" An' I turned around an' come into the house, an' set down in my room; for 't was God all around me. I could feel it burnin', burnin', burnin' all around me, an' goin' through me; an' I saw I was so wicked, it seemed as ef it would burn me up. An' I said, "O somebody, somebody, stand between God an' me! For it burns me!" Then honey, when I said so, I felt as it were somethin' like an amberill [umbrella] that stood between me an' God; an' it felt cool, like a shade; an' says I, "Who's this stands between me an' God?" (*Sojourner*, 157–158)

After some time of questioning the identity of this presence, Sojourner realizes she had found not only God the Father but also His Son:

> An' finally somethin' spoke out in me an' said, *"This is Jesus!"* An' I spoke out with all my might, an' says I, *"This is Jesus! Glory be to God!"* And then the whole world grew bright, an' the trees they waved an' waved in glory, an' every little bit o' stone on the ground shone like glass; and I shouted an' said, "Praise, praise, praise to the Lord!" An' I begun to feel sech a love in my soul as I never felt before—love to all creatures. (*Sojourner*, 158–159)

Although she seemed to have "no preference for one sect more than another," Sojourner Truth, like many other black women of her day, joined the Methodist Church. She frequently attended religious gatherings and camp meetings in New York, Connecticut, and Massachusetts, and she visited the New York Shaker communities. She occasionally organized meetings to give herself the opportunity to speak, and she reserved as her singular text the story of her religious conversion, which she called "When I Found Jesus." In time, Sojourner Truth became known, not primarily as a religious figure, but as a social activist and public speaker. Her audiences were largely, but not exclusively, white. She felt authorized for her unique mission by the Holy Spirit: "The Lord had made me a sign unto this nation an' I go round a testifyin', an' showin' on 'em their sins agin my people." "The Spirit calls me there and I must go," she proclaimed. Thus, Sojourner Truth lived to travel and to bear witness. Like Jarena Lee, Rebecca Cox Jackson, and Harriet Tubman, she depended on God as her sole help, and she acted accordingly.

A Living Force

Each generation of black women autobiographers revises the one that went before; the works of Susie King Taylor and Elizabeth Keckley revise those of "Belinda" and "Linda Brent," all playing the role of the outraged mother. Rebecca Jackson revises Jarena Lee, whose spiritual narrative it seems likely Jackson knew. Lee traveled far and wide, saving souls for her larger family, and Rebecca Jackson, who was no one's biological mother and a member of a sect that abstained from sex, was "Mother Rebecca" to the members of her predominantly black Philadelphia Shaker community. Harriet Tubman and Sojourner Truth, although they never gained access to the tools of literacy and therefore could never "tell a free story" completely, radicalized the form of the spiritual narrative, improvising on earlier established forms in their well-informed outrage. They too were mothers of the race and a tradition of black women writing. In fact, black women writing autobiography constitute the strongest thread in the rich tapestry that is the black woman's literary tradition in nineteenth-century America. Although there were a few prominent poets, novelists, and essayists, autobiographical narratives constitute the bulk of black women's writing in that century; the literary connections are stronger in autobiography than in poetry, essay, or fiction. These black women autobiographers dared to step outside the racist and sexist stereotypes of the dominant culture and to re-create themselves, and God, in their own images. They made "a way out of no way" for those who would follow, even as they built on the foundation they inherited from books, the oral tradition, and, indeed, their own mothers.

Harriet Jacobs in 1894.
Courtesy of
Harvard University Press

Elizabeth Keckley,
probably in Washington, D.C.,
at the turn of the century.
Courtesy Moorland-Spingarn
Research Center,
Howard University

Susie King Taylor circa 1902.
Courtesy Schomburg Center
for Research in Black Culture,
New York Public Library

Amanda Smith circa 1893.
Author's collection

Charlotte L. Forten Grimké
in Washington, D.C.,
probably 1870s.
Courtesy Schomburg Center, NYPL

"General" Harriet Tubman circa 1865.
Courtesy Schomburg Center, NYPL

Harriet Tubman in old age.
Courtesy Schomburg Center, NYPL

Sojourner Truth in 1860s.
Courtesy Schomburg Center, NYPL

*Sojourner Truth with President Lincoln,
Washington, D.C., circa 1864.
Courtesy Schomburg Center, NYPL*

Ida B. Wells as a young journalist.
Courtesy Schomburg Center, NYPL

Ida B. Wells-Barnett circa 1917.
Courtesy Schomburg Center, NYPL

Era Bell Thompson, Chicago, circa 1946.
Courtesy Schomburg Center, NYPL

Zora Neale Hurston in 1946.
Courtesy Schomburg Center, NYPL

Zora Neale Hurston, probably in 1930s.
Courtesy Schomburg Center, NYPL

Maya Angelou at Howard University in 1986.
Courtesy Moorland-Spingarn Center

Part II
Emerging
from Obscurity

The chapters on Charlotte Forten Grimké and Ida B. Wells treat the autobiographical writings of two black women active in the struggle for freedom, literacy, and justice during Reconstruction and the post-Reconstruction era. An ardent abolitionist and feminist, the young Charlotte Forten sought refuge from the sting of white racism in the pages of her private diary; she also used the diary as a testing ground for the development of her public voice as a poet and essayist. Although this diary is in a form Estelle Jelinek would call "analogous to the private sphere to which women's lives have primarily belonged," it shows the impact of a black and female consciousness coming into contact with the moral, literary, and philosophical issues of the day.[1] More than Charlotte Forten Grimké's diary, *Crusade for Justice: The Autobiography of Ida B. Wells,* as the memoir of a well-known public figure who was also a woman, constitutes part of

the "lost ground" of Afro-American literary
tradition.[2] In *Crusade for Justice*, the outraged mother of the slave narrative re-
emerges as a journalist, public speaker, and
race leader decrying the brutality and injustice of lynching. A text with distinct
characteristics common to both nineteenth-
and twentieth-century autobiographies by
black American women, Wells's autobiography presents prime source material for
speculation on the role of racial and sexual
oppression in Wells's psychosocial identity
and autobiographical point of view. Although this text was not published until
1970, almost four decades after her death,
Ida B. Wells wrote *Crusade for Justice*
between 1928 and 1934, intending it not only
as the story of her life but also as the story
of "the storm and stress immediately after
the Civil War, of the Ku Klux Klan, of ballot
stuffing" and the "wholesale murders of
Negroes who tried to exercise their new-
found rights as free men and citizens."[3] Predictably, therefore, an analysis of *Crusade for
Justice* does much to establish continuity in
the black female autobiographical tradition.

3
A Poet's Retreat:
The Diaries of
Charlotte Forten Grimké

To be burned in case of my death immediately.
He who dares read what here is written,
Woe be unto him.

   —Unpublished pencil inscription,
     Diary 2 (January 1, 1857–January 27, 1858)

In the earnest path of duty
  With the high hopes and hearts sincere,
We, to useful lives aspiring
  Daily meet to labor here.

No vain dreams of earthly glory
  Urge us onward to explore
Far-extending realms of knowledge
  With their rich and varied store;

But with hope of aiding others,
  Gladly we perform our part;
Nor forget, the mind, while storing,
  We must educate the heart,—

              —"Poem" (1856)

Charlotte Forten Grimké, turn-of-the-century black woman poet, scholar, teacher, and translator, is remembered chiefly for the four of her five manuscript diaries edited by Ray Allen Billington and published as *The Journal of Charlotte L. Forten, 1854–1864* (1953).[1] As a young black woman poet reading the *Journal* in the early 1970s, I was put off by the diarist's romantic language, as well as by her class pretensions, and resisted all identification with her.

Years later, when I read Dr. Anna Julia Cooper's typescripts of all five diaries, I began to see them as a series of inter-related texts sustaining progression and development.[2] Restoring Billington's editorial omissions presented a more rounded view of the diarist's day-to-day life, beyond her commentary on matters of political and historical significance; I began to view the published edition of the diaries as a mutilated text. Yet even when I read the typescripts with omissions restored, Forten seemed aloof and distant; she refused to speak with me.

In the hope of improving my relationship with the subject of my interest, I began to read what Forten read: Shakespeare, Blake, Keats, Wordsworth, Lydia Maria Child, Emerson, the Brownings, and the Brontës. And I read what she wrote: "Life on the Sea Islands"; "Personal Recollections of Whittier"; a handful of unpublished essays; the dozen or so poems published during her lifetime; and *Madame Therese, or the Volunteers of '92,* a novel by Emilie Erckmann and Alexander Chartrian, which she translated from the French.[3]

I returned to the Moorland-Spingarn Collection to read the original handwritten diaries for possible omissions, and it was then that Charlotte began to smile on me. When I held the slender, leather-bound volumes, each covered with a graceful marbled paper, and when I read the delicate, faded black-ink handwriting, I could feel the tension of pen against paper, and I could hear a voice. It was, unmistakably, the voice of a poet, struggling to be heard—the voice of Charlotte Forten Grimké.

The first diary covers the period from May 24, 1854, to December 31, 1856, and the second runs from January 1, 1857, to January 27, 1858. These diaries, which Charlotte Forten kept between the ages of seventeen and twenty-one, describe her life as a schoolgirl in Salem, as a young abolitionist, and as an aspiring poet and writer. The third diary covers the span from January 1858 to February 1863, and the fourth dates from February 1863 to May 1864. In these diaries, she records her continuing personal development and her participation in the historic "Port Royal Experiment" on the South Carolina coastal islands during the Civil War. She began her fifth diary in November 1885 and made her final entry in July 1892, twenty-two years before her death in 1914. The final diary remained unpublished until 1988 when it was included in a new collection of Forten's work edited by Brenda Stevenson.[4] This diary presents an intimate view of Forten's thirty-five-year marriage to the Reverend Francis J. Grimké, a distinguished black Presbyterian minister, who was also the nephew of white feminist abolitionists Sarah and Angelina Grimké Weld via their brother, Henry Grimké, and a slave woman, Nancy Weston (Billington, *Journal*, 29).

Taken together, the five manuscript diaries show an intelligent black and female cultural sensibility struggling to balance political, intellectual, and emotional conflicts, and to forge a public voice. Although the diaries were intended to be private, the diarist's autobiographical act relates to the development of a public voice in the move to objectify and take control of experiences through the writer's craft; in the pages of her diaries, she gains distance between herself as subject and object. This chapter examines Charlotte Forten Grimké's use of the diary as a tool for the development of political and artistic consciousness and as a means of self-evaluation; for her, the diaries also represent a retreat from potentially shattering encounters with racism and a vehicle for the development of a black and female poetic identity, a place of restoration and self-healing.

The product of an environment that was both abolitionist and feminist, Charlotte Forten grew up in the Philadelphia home of her paternal grandfather, James Forten, a wealthy and respected free black who advocated abolition and women's rights. The daughter of Mary Wood and Robert Bridges Forten, she was named for her grandmother, Charlotte Forten, who lived to be one hundred years old.[5] In 1837, the year Charlotte was born, her aunts Sarah and Margaretta Forten, both active in the Philadelphia Female Anti-Slavery Society, organized a national convention of black women abolitionists (Billington, *Journal*, 13). The Fortens were cultured and well educated, yet, like other free blacks in the "City of Brotherly Love," they found themselves excluded from museums, stores, ice-cream parlors, and restaurants. Predictably, the Fortens chose a private tutor over a segregated public school education for Charlotte. Stifled by years of living primarily in her grandfather's house and by being shut off from much of the social routine in which other girls participated, Charlotte Forten grew into an intensely introspective adolescent, continually examining and reexamining her intellectual and literary development. Thus she was separated from the dominant culture by race, and from much of the black community by economic and educational privilege.

In 1854, Robert Bridges Forten responded to his daughter's increasing isolation by sending her to the Higginson Grammar School in Salem, Massachusetts, where she lived with the Charles Lenox Remond family. Significantly, Charlotte began her first diary (May 24, 1854–December 31, 1856) with the advent of her stay in Salem, marking the initial separation from her home and Philadelphia. But even in "free" Massachusetts, Charlotte felt the sting of white racism:

> I wonder that every colored person is not a misanthrope. Surely, we have everything to make us hate mankind. I have met girls in the classroom—they have been thoroughly kind and cordial to me,—perhaps the next day met them in the street—they feared to recognize me; these I can but regard now with scorn and contempt. (*Diary* 1, Wednesday, September 12, 1854)

When encounters such as these threaten her sense of self, Charlotte seeks refuge in the pages of her diary, looking back on them from her own perspective and laying claim to her experience in the language of her private diary. Here, she confronts the dominant white culture in small, homeopathic doses, analyzing and gaining psychological distance. On July 17, 1854, she enters, "I am hated and oppressed because God gave me a *dark skin*. How did this cruel, this absurd prejudice ever come to exist? When I think of it, a feeling of indignation rises in my soul too deep for utterance" (*Diary* 1). For young Charlotte Forten, the diary becomes a private (and therefore defensible) "territory" of the mind and a retreat from the racism and sexism of the dominant culture.

The first and second diaries also demonstrate the young poet's quest for literary models. In Salem, Charlotte reads voraciously and attends an impressive number of readings, lectures, and antislavery fairs. Caught in the surge of politics and romanticism of the 1850s, she finds Hawthorne's gothic tales "thrilling" and enjoys walks by the sea and in the moonlight. On Christmas Day 1858, she comes away from Emerson's lecture "On Beauty" "much pleased" (*Diary* 3). The Quaker poet John Greenleaf Whittier, a special friend, seeks her out for nature walks and for talks on farming and spiritual development. Among her favorite writers are Blake, Keats, Wordsworth, Emerson, the Brontës, and Lydia Maria Child. Charlotte apparently accepts Mrs. Child's promotion of "a love of reading as an unspeakable blessing for the American female."[6] Engaged in the quest for literacy and self-respect, Charlotte finds books a means of knowing a world from which she feels excluded, a route to transcendence of her perceived cultural isolation:

> And hence are *books* to us a treasure and a blessing unspeakable. And they are doubly this when one is shut out of society as I am, and has not opportunities of studying those living, breathing, *human* books, which are, I doubt not, after all, the most profoundly interesting and useful study. (*Diary* 3, January 1, 1860)

As a young abolitionist, Charlotte Forten read and reread in 1854 Elizabeth Barrett Browning's powerful feminist–abolitionist polemic, "The Fugitive Slave at Pilgrim's Point," calling it "most suitable to my feelings and the times."

On May 30, 1854, she added this commentary to the diary: "How earnestly and touching does the writer portray the bitter anguish of the poor fugitive as she thinks over all the wrongs and sufferings that she has endured, and of the sin the tyrants have driven her but which they alone must answer for!" (*Diary* 1). Hence, the young black writer identified both with the literary sensibility of the white author of the poem and with the feminine heroism of its narrator, an outraged mother who rebels against her rapist master, murdering the child she has borne by him.

Naturally, Charlotte Forten's heroes and heroines included the fugitive slaves, whose experiences were beginning to come to light not only through polemical poetry and fiction but through firsthand narratives and the camera. One entry in her second diary describes her reactions on being shown

> a daguerreotype of a young slave girl who escaped in a box... My heart was full as I gazed at it; full of admiration for the heroic girl, who risked all for freedom; full of bitter indignation that in this boasted land of liberty such a thing *could occur*. Were she of any other nation her heroism would receive all due honor from these Americans, *but as it is*, there is not even a single spot in this broad land, where her rights can be protected,—not one. (*Diary* 2, July 5, 1857)

Perhaps there is a sense in which the girl in the box can be viewed as a metaphor for Charlotte's own experience of separateness from and isolation within the dominant culture, for although she herself was free, she recognized the interrelatedness of her oppression with the bondage of the slave woman.

Determined to live a full and expansive life, to *live out* herself, she responds to a feeling of restlessness that portends the rise of modernism in black women's writing. "I wonder," she writes on January 2, 1858, "why it is that I have this strange feeling of not *living out myself*. My existence seems not nearly full or expansive enough—This longing for—something, I know not what?" (*Diary* 3). Without her conscious knowledge, what she seeks is, in the words of the critic Margaret Homans, "a return to her proper origins," the place where her identity (and her own subjective voice) resides.[7] Like other black women writing autobiography in nineteenth-century America, Charlotte Forten discussed family, society, her profession, and her duty to her race; she also wrote of her longing for an image of her deceased mother. "How I love to hear of her," she writes. "What a pleasure it would be if I had an image of her, my own dear mother!" (*Diary* 2, April 15, 1858). Lacking such a portrait, she set out to paint her own, and she would create her images with words.

Charlotte Forten's poetry, noted for "its quiet simplicity and controlled tension," might well qualify her as a "literary lady." Although she published no more than a handful of poems, some of them received critical acclaim. Praising her "The Angel's Visit" (1860), William Wells Brown wrote, "For style and poetic diction, it is not surpassed by anything in the English language."[8] "Were she white," Brown commented, "America would recognize her as one of its brightest gems."[9] Although minor poetry in the dominant tradition, Charlotte Forten's poems possess rich descriptive imagery, intense lyricism, and dramatic power.

Given the choice of a public voice or a private one, Charlotte Forten, in a different time and in a culture where she did not bear the dual stigma of race and gender difference, might have blossomed as a poet. By her third and fourth diaries, she has gained the desired distance between self as subject and object, making a clearer distinction between the public and the private voice. During these years, she published more than at any other period, placing "Two Voices" (1858), "The Wind Among the Poplars," "The Slave Girl's Prayer," and "The Angel's Visit" (circa 1860) in the *National Anti-Slavery Standard* and *The Liberator*.[10] In "The Angel's Visit," the poet's angel-mother/muse returns to plant the kiss of tradition and restore a childhood sense of wholeness threatened by the "cruel wrongs" that might destroy the motherless child who drifts from her roots:

A sudden flood of rosy light
  Filled all the dusky wood,
And, clad in shining robes of white,
  My angel mother stood.

She gently drew me to her side,
  She pressed her lips to mine,
And softly said, "Grieve not, my child"
  A mother's love is thine.

I know the cruel wrongs that crush
  The young and ardent heart;
But falter not; keep bravely on,
  And nobly bear thy part.

In this public creative act, the motherless speaker of the poem claims the identity of both poet and daughter, still attempting to come to terms with the vocation of poet, as well as her experience of race and gender difference. The speaker recovers the "material origins" of her "feminine creativity" and creates a vehicle for the potential realization of her black and female poetic identity.

That Charlotte Forten never realized her literary goals may be attributed, in part, to what Margaret Homans has called a pressure "to conform to certain ideas of ideal womanhood, none of which included a poet's vocation."[11] To add that racial conflicts intensified Forten's confusion may be redundant, for as Claudia Tate has written, "Nowhere in America is the social terrain more rugged than where a social minority and a 'weaker' gender intersect."[12]

Providing a testing ground for the development of Charlotte Forten's poetic identity and her public voice, diaries 3 and 4 also narrate her participation in the "Port Royal Experiment" during the Civil War. Forten's attraction to this experiment, which was designed to prove the fitness of former slaves for freedom, may be explained, in part, by her strong sense of duty to her race. Early in 1862, General Rufus Saxon, commander of the military district that encompassed Port Royal and the South Carolina coastal islands, wrote to the

War Department to request instructors to teach former slaves. Charlotte Forten answered the call immediately, but was turned away, ostensibly because she was a woman.[13] Despite the disappointment, she showed her determination to go to Port Royal. Turned down by the Boston Commission, she applied to the Philadelphia Port Royal Relief Association, where she was again discouraged because of the dangers involved in sending a woman to a war zone. John Greenleaf Whittier interceded on her behalf, however, and as she records in her diary on May 27, 1862, Charlotte Forten sailed from New York aboard the steamship *United States* as an accredited agent of the Philadelphia Port Royal Relief Association.[14]

In terms of her inner life, the experiment, viewed romantically as part of her duty to her race (and her transcendental, or higher, purpose), promised a partial solution to her predicament of isolation, a reconciling of intellect, and a sense of Christian duty, with the so-called cult of true womanhood. An inscription written in pencil inside the front cover of diary 4 confirms this interpretation. Speaking of her experience as a teacher of former slaves at Port Royal, she comments, "This is what the women of this country need—healthful and not too fatiguing outdoor work in which are blended the usefulness and beauty I have never seen in women." Forten speaks of her labor as "healthful"; it might also be viewed as *health building* in that it offered her opportunities to work for the sublime balance between usefulness and beauty.

The Port Royal diaries modify the impulse toward self-sufficiency with the Christian ideal of duty and service, as revealed in this reflective entry, made on Charlotte Forten's twenty-fifth birthday:

> The accomplishments, the society, the delights of travel which I have dreamed of and longed for all my life, I am now convinced can never be mine. If I can go to Port Royal, I will try to forget all these desires. I will pray that God in his goodness will make me noble enough to find my happiness in doing my duty. (*Diary* 3, August 17, 1862)

Always something of a self-apologist, she makes use of the apology as a literary strategy, for she does not wish to appear presumptuous or self-serving. Moreover, doing one's Christian duty absolves a woman of the need to conform to the cult of true womanhood and opens up new avenues of identity. Many entries in diaries 3 and 4 have a lyrical, poetic quality. She describes her romantic vision of the voyage to Port Royal in an entry written on white letter paper and headed "At Sea—1862":

> Oh, how beautiful those great waves were as they broke upon the sides of the vessel, into foam and spray, pure and white as new fallen snow. People talk of the monotony of the sea. I have not found it monotonous for a moment, since I have been well. To me there is "infinite variety," constant enjoyment about it.... One of the most beautiful insights I have yet seen is the phosphorescence in the water at night—the long line of light in the wake of the steamer, and the stars, and sometimes balls of fire that rise so magically out of the water. It is most strange and beautiful. (*Diary* 3, October 12, 1862)[15]

Here, once again, the diary becomes a testing ground for the development of a poetic identity, as Charlotte Forten explores her experience in language. Simultaneously, she continues her use of the diary as a tool of personal restoration and self-healing. An entry made on her arrival at Port Royal provides an example of this use. She has "overheard" a conversation between two white Union officers, a conversation she has judged to be deliberately calculated to disturb her:

> The word "nigger" was plentifully used, whereupon I set them down as *not* gentlemen. Then they talked a great deal about rebel attacks and yellow fever, and other alarming things. We saw through them at once. (*Diary* 3, October 28, 1862)

Maintaining an admirable detachment, she finds refuge in the pages of her diary, balancing her encounter with these racists with a lyrical description of the singing black boatmen who rowed her from St. Helena to Port Royal:

> The row was delightful. It was just at sunset—a grand Southern sunset; and the glamorous clouds of crimson and gold were reflected in the waters below, which were as smooth and calm as a mirror. Then as we glided along, the rich sonorous tones of the boatmen broke upon the evening stillness. The singing impressed me very much. It was so sweet and strange and somber. (*Diary* 3, October 28, 1862)

Transforming and transcending, she brings the values of romantic poetry to her text as she comments on the power of black spirituals to "lift [her] out of [her]self."[16] A parallel between the diarist's romantic mode of self-expression and the "transcendental present" of the slave spiritual emerges here, and Charlotte Forten responds to both oral and literary traditions as she seeks her own voice:

> The singing was very beautiful. I sat there in a kind of trance and listened to it, and while I listened looked through the open windows into the grove of oaks with their moss drapery. "Ah w'ld that my tongue c'ld utter the thoughts that arise in me." (*Diary* 3, November 2, 1862)

Yet, despite a sensitivity to black communication styles and the language of feeling, she remains an outsider. From the viewpoint of her own standard English voice, the lyrical quality of the slave spiritual is still foreign to the New England–educated diarist; she stands outside the black folk experience.

Although she generally reserved her diary entries as a record of the growth of her own mind, she did send an excerpt to John Greenleaf Whittier "for private perusal." Whittier submitted "Life on the Sea Islands" to the *Atlantic Monthly*, where it was published in two segments in May and June 1864.[17] The published article, subtly different from the form of the private journal entries, displays more thematic and topical development than the strictly chronological diaries. Also, this account shows more detailed analysis and seems more publicly autobiographical, giving focused attention to her role as a teacher of former slaves. Significantly, she refers to her young scholars as "my children," seeking a public persona that would redeem her in the eyes of the "cult of true womanhood."

By the time she comes to the end of her Port Royal diary, the entries have become less frequent; however, they display the thematic and topical development that distinguishes diary 4 from the earlier diaries. Thus, strictly speaking, diary 4 adheres more closely to the form of what is properly called a journal than any of the earlier diary texts where organization is chronological and based on entries that lack formal continuity.

Oddly, diary 4 omits the diarist's reaction to her father's death. Robert Forten died in Philadelphia in April 1864 after contracting typhoid fever in Maryland, where he was recruiting black troops for the Union Army (Billington, *Journal*, 14).[18] Although the completion of the fourth diary coincides roughly with the death, she makes no comment about it—a very curious omission indeed. After her father's death, she returns to Philadelphia, where she remains for seven years before moving to Washington, D.C.

An interruption of twenty-odd years ensues between the fourth and fifth diaries. During most of these years, Charlotte Forten attempted to support herself as a writer of children's stories and a translator of novels from the French and German. It was a point of honor with her to support herself solely by her own efforts—her literary efforts. In these years, Whittier played an active role as her mentor and protector, but requests for help of various kinds eventually exhausted him. After one of her continuing bouts with illness, Whittier wrote: "I am pained to hear of Charlotte Forten's illness. I wish the poor girl could be better situated—the wife of some good, true man who could appreciate her as she deserves."[19]

In 1878, Charlotte Forten married such a man. Having moved to Washington, D.C., she taught for a year at the Sumner School and later worked as a clerk in the U.S. Treasury Department; she also joined the Fifteenth Street Presbyterian Church. And she married the pastor of this church, the Reverend Francis James Grimké. Called the "black Puritan," Reverend Grimké upheld ideals of black womanhood as well as black manhood, exposing the sexual double standard of the South and attacking it in his sermons.[20] As the son of a slave woman sired by a white master, he was well qualified to do so.

Despite the fact that Charlotte Forten was nearly thirteen years older than her husband, the two were drawn together by the magnetism of like minds: Both Francis Grimké and Charlotte Forten were isolated by the tensions of race and intellect; both faced a "crisis of confidence" that confronted ministers and literary women in mid-nineteenth-century America, as defined by Ann Douglas in *The Feminization of American Culture*. According to Douglas, both literary women and ministers shared a feminizing "impulse toward articulation and change," but they were "confined to the kitchen and the pulpit" and "forbidden to compete in the markets of the masculine world." As a reaction, Douglas argues, these ministers and literary women often stressed illness "as a way ... to dramatize their anxiety that their culture found them useless and wished them no good." They also used their illnesses "as a means of getting attention, of obtaining psychological and emotional power even while apparently acknowledging the biological correlatives of their social and political unimportance."[21] Perhaps this parallel development explains, in part, Grimké's lifelong invalidism, as well as the continual ill health of her beloved husband, Francis; in this sense, her experience reflects that of other literary women of nineteenth-century America who chose to marry ministers.

During the years of her marriage, Charlotte Forten Grimké continued to write poetry, but although her craft improved, her perspective changed substantially with age. Gone is the rebellion and conflict of the early poems; it is replaced by a tone of reflection and contemplation, as seen in her poem "Wordsworth," stylistically reminiscent of that poet's "The Prelude":

> In youth's fair dawn, when the soul, still untired,
> Longs for life's conflicts, and seeks restlessly

> Food for its cravings in the stirring songs,
> The thrilling strains of more impassioned bards;
> Or, eager for fresh joys, culls with delight
> The flowers that bloom in fancy's fair realm—
> We may not prize the mild and steadfast ray
> That streams from thy pure soul in tranquil song
> But, in our riper years, when through the heat
> And burden of the day we struggle on,
> Breasting the stream upon whose shores we dreamed....

No longer the dreaming youth, the poet has entered "the riper years," "breasting the stream" of the dominant tradition, meeting, opposing, and balancing against it at the crest. She has grown, in her own words:

> Weary of all the turmoil and the din
> Which drowns the finer voices of the soul;

and weary of her struggle against the tide. Seeking now "the finer voices of the soul," she turns to the hierophant in his temple, speaking in a neutral voice but embracing symbolic polarities she avoided in her earlier poems.

> We turn to thee, true priest of Nature's fane,
> And find the rest our fainting spirits need,—
> The calm, more ardent singers cannot give;
> As in the glare intense of tropic days,
> Gladly we turn from the sun's radiant beams
> And grateful hail fair Luna's tender light.[22]

Associating the sun with the active "masculine" principle and the glaring heat of the struggle, the poet seeks a retreat into a "feminine" radiance symbolized by "fair Luna's tender light." She retreats into the inner solace of a marriage that will be, for her, a source of renewal and rejuvenation.

Together, the Grimkés braced each other, finding in their marriage a retreat from the anxieties of constant confrontation with the dominant culture. Here Charlotte found the balance, the communion she had achieved earlier only in the pages of her diary. Charlotte Forten Grimké found love, not the glaring love of subordination and domination that passes with the day, but a radiant, tender, and enduring love—a higher marriage.

Although she maintained diary 5 in a bound notebook of 144 pages, she apparently used only 43 of them. Pages 44 to 100 are empty, and unfortunately, pages 1 and 2 have been lost. Had they not been, they might have furnished some insight into the reasons for Forten's return to keeping a diary. We may speculate that she found life with Grimké in "The High Ranks of Afro-America" to be another adventure, or she may have been influenced by watching him keep his own notebook diaries.[23] Yet, it is also possible that she returned to diary keeping to objectify her many personal losses and the separations from her husband occasioned by her ill health. Although the diary runs from January 1885 to July 1892, there are fewer and fewer entries as her health worsens. Most of the entries occur between 1885 and 1889. There are no entries for 1890 and 1891 and only one entry for 1892.

The fifth and final diary has a very different character from that of the first four. This diary represents the work of a mature woman who has become a chronic invalid, but a woman who has also found personal happiness in her marriage with a noble man who apparently possessed all the gentleness and kindness of his slave mother and none of the faults of his white master/father. In this until recently unpublished diary, Charlotte writes of her 1885 move to Florida and her desire "to accomplish something" in "missionary labor" as well as "direct church work... among the lower classes" (*Diary* 5, November 29, 1885). For the Grimkés clearly saw themselves as part of a black elite, and they must set an example.

Although the Grimkés held themselves a bit above many of the less fortunate in the small town in which they lived, they were warmly received in their new parish. One evening, while they were still living at a boardinghouse, they were asked to come to the church and were then escorted to their new home. They found the cottage "beautifully lighted" with a

"sitting room and bedroom very comfortably furnished...
besides a handsome writing table for F's study, and a kitchen
table, plates, and other useful articles." Their home, the
classic "dog-trot" of southern architecture, had been built
with "a hall through the center,—a style I have always
liked,—a study and a bedroom on one side, sitting room and
kitchen on the other. Our pictures and books make the place
very homelike" (*Diary* 5, November 15, 1885). But there was no
study for Charlotte Forten Grimké and no desk either. The
idealized view she presents of her marriage in diary 5 may be
justifiable, but the critic must ask why Charlotte Forten
Grimké never found fulfillment in her own work. Perhaps the
answer lies in the social restrictions placed on her as a
minister's wife or in her reluctance to assume a public voice.

Greatest among the losses sustained by the Grimkés (including the deteriorating health of Whittier and the death of
family members and other friends from the old abolitionist
network) was the death of their only child, Theodora Cor-
nelia, who died less than a year after she was born.[24] On
December 19, 1885, the diarist made this reflective entry:

> We have been married seven years today, —they would have
> been seven happy years had it not been for that one great
> sorrow! Oh my darling, what unspeakable happiness it would
> have been to have her with us to-day. She would be nearly six
> years old, our precious New Year's gift, how lovely and
> companionable I know she could have been. But I must not
> mourn. Father, it was Thy will. It *must* be for the best. I must
> wait. (*Diary* 5)

Already cut off from her primary link to black women's
culture through the early death of her mother, Charlotte
Forten Grimké is further separated from that feminine tradition because the loss of her daughter denies her the possibility of acting out the role of mother. Her reflections center
on the idea that Theodora would have been "lovely and
companionable," a creature balanced in beauty and intellect,
another potential source of identity for the mother herself.

When she writes, "I must wait," Mrs. Grimké, already nearing the end of her biological generativity and still childless, probably does not mean that she must wait for another child. Rather, she must wait *on the Lord* for an understanding of the inherent ironies of her life. She continues to use her diary for restoration and self-healing, a tool for readjusting her psychic balance.

During the Grimkés' many separations, Charlotte's diary is still her best companion and at times her only confidant. In the spring and summer of 1887, she finds it necessary to go north "for her health," spending May in Washington and June and July at Newport. "Beautiful, beautiful Newport!" she writes in July 1887. "In spite of illness I enjoy the sea and the rocks." "If my dear, dear F. were only here to share the happiness with me" (*Diary* 5). The next entry begins, "Back home with my dearest F. How glad I am to see him and find him well. I hope we shall not be separated again" (*Diary* 5, October 1887).

In several entries, she notes that she is "too unwell" to attend evening service. In fact, it was her illness that prevented her from maintaining her diary with any regularity. "I regret having been able to write only at long intervals in my journal. My head and eyes are so bad that I can't use them much of the time" (*Diary* 5, October 1887). She suffered in the Florida heat, complaining of mosquitoes and fleas. "If one could only spend six months here, and the remainder of the year at the North! Sometimes I become dismayed at my almost continual ill health. It unfits me for work, and there is so much to be done here" (*Diary* 5, April 1888).

Although a physician examined her in Newport in July 1888, "he could find no organic disease,—only weakness" (*Diary* 5). This brings us back to Douglas's discussion of the "cultural uses of sickness for the nineteenth-century minister and lady." Certainly, it could be argued that Forten, the invalid, used her ill health to dramatize her anxiety over a culture that found her useless (as the very appellation *invalid* implies). Francis Grimké was affected to a lesser degree; he developed a competent public voice in his highly articulate sermons. But his wife became more and more retiring, publishing less and less, and making fewer entries in her diaries as her headaches increased and her vision dimmed.

There are few entries for 1889, the year Grimké resumed the ministry of the Fifteenth Street Presbyterian Church in Washington, and none for 1890 or 1891. In 1892, his wife would make only one entry, written in Ler, Massachusetts, during July. "The last three years have been full of work and of changes, but on the whole, happy ones," she wrote. "The greatest drawback has been constant ill health, which seemed to culminate this summer, and I was obliged to leave Washington with its intense heat, sewer gas, and malaria, before it was time for Frank to. I was sorry to leave him, but hope he will join me next week" (*Diary* 5, July 1892). This entry, typical of those made by Charlotte during the years of her declining health, proved to be her last. She died of a cerebral embolism in Washington, D.C., on July 23, 1914, twenty-two years after her diaries end.

On his wife's death, Francis Grimké wrote a testament of praise for the years of their marriage. "Not only my love for her, but my highest respect for her remained to the very last," he wrote shakily. "I have always felt that I was very fortunate in being thrown into such close and intimate company with so rare and beautiful a spirit." In thirty-five years of marriage, he wrote, he had never been able to detect anything "little, mean, contemptible, or unbecoming about her." He found his wife "an unusual woman, not only of great strength and character, but also sweet of temper, gentle, loving, full of the milk of human kindness."[25]

The poet Angelina Weld Grimké, daughter of Francis Grimké's brother Archibald, would remember her "Aunt Lottie" with a poem, "To Keep the Memory of Charlotte Forten Grimké." The Grimké poem, published in *The Crisis* in January 1915, attempts to place her aunt's "gentle spirit" in the stream of eternity:

> Where has she gone? And who is to say?
> But this we know: her gentle spirit moves
> And is where beauty never wanes,

Perchance by other streams, mid other groves;
And to us here, ah! She remains
A lovely memory
Until eternity.
She came, she loved, and then she went away.

Wherever she had gone, Charlotte Forten Grimké did not die without leaving her mark on a tradition of black women writing. Her private autobiographical act portends the rise of literary forms less restrictive than most nineteenth-century narratives by black American women, and the diaries offer untold insight into one black woman's search for a poetic identity and a public voice. In her own words, in "Poem," published in *The Liberator* in August 1856:

Knowing this, toil we unwearied.
  With true hearts and purpose high;—
We would win a wreath immortal.
  Whose bright flowers ne'er fade and die.

4
Crusader for Justice:
Ida B. Wells

Who shall say that such a work accomplished
by one woman exiled and maligned by that
community among whom she had so long
and so valiantly labored, bending every effort
to the upbuilding of the manhood and
womanhood of all races, shall not place her
in the front rank of philanthropists, not only
of the womanhood of this race, but among
those laborers of all ages and all climes?

—*G. B. Mossell (1894)*

The importance of black autobiography as literature and
history is well documented. The historian John Blassingame
views black autobiography as "a counterweight to the white
historian's caricature of black life," possessing a "therapeutic
value" for both authors and readers, "a vehicle blacks used to
express their true feelings without having them distorted by
whites." One of the "mainsprings of the black novel," autobiography has also been "one of the major forums of black
protest, a chief source of adequate historical information, and
a link in the black literary tradition."[1] In *The American
Autobiography*, the literary critic Albert E. Stone suggests
that "the best place to start to understand autobiography as a

cultural act is with history," that is to say, "historical consciousness speaks *out* of a singular experience, for some particular social group, to a wider audience. This...articulation is at once an act of perception and creation. Autobiography is, simply and profoundly, personal history."[2]

Like *The Education of Henry Adams* (1907) or *The Autobiography of W. E. B. Du Bois* (1968), Ida B. Wells's *Crusade for Justice* represents a posthumously published autobiography by a well-known public figure. Wells employs the medium of the historical memoir, a subgenre of autobiography dominated almost entirely by men, to create her lasting version of the self.

"The memoir," James Cox asserts, "is a category of autobiography that needs attention," part of the "lost ground" of American literature. "There is a distinct tiresomeness about the ease with which literary critics assure themselves that 'mere' fact has nothing to do with the art of autobiography. The truth or falsity of autobiography is thereby subordinated to the creativity, the design, 'the inner' truth of the narrative." Cox observes, moreover, that "autobiographies devoted to the emotional consciousness of the writer have been much more subject to investigation than the memoir, particularly the memoir of a well-known public figure."[3] Thus, Wells's *Crusade for Justice*, as the memoir of a well-known public figure who is also a black woman, constitutes part of the "lost ground" of Afro-American literary tradition. It does much to establish continuity within black female autobiographical tradition, for this text has distinct characteristics common to both nineteenth- and twentieth-century autobiographies by black American women. The title *Crusade for Justice* refers primarily to Wells's recollections of her public life, but it also borrows from the confessional mode of autobiography to allow Wells the latitude to discuss her experience of marriage and family as it influenced her work and public life. Therefore, the "confessional" aspect is more fully developed in *Crusade* than in most historical memoirs.

In at least one respect, Wells departs from the traditional autobiographical stance of an older person looking back and settling accounts;[4] she is not a wise and paternal elder, some "articulate hero" looking back at the end of a quest fulfilled. In *Crusade*, the outraged mother of the slave narrative emerges in the personal myth of a "fiery reformer, feminist, and race leader."[5] Speaking as the outraged mother who carries her nursing son on an antilynching speaking tour, Wells's autobiographical posture is that of a protector of black manhood and a nurturer and defender of black womanhood. Marked by unpredictable shifts in narrative movement similar to those found in earlier autobiographies by black American women, *Crusade* emphasizes the public sphere more in the first half of the narrative, and home and family life more in the second, with a perceptible break at Chapter 30, "A Divided Duty." Although Stephen Butterfield argues that *Crusade* represents "the slave narrative in its purest and truest light," this autobiography is organized according to more sophisticated principles than the slave narrative, and the sensibility is a broadened one.[6] Although Wells de-emphasizes her personal life in order to focus on her public career and achievements, *Crusade for Justice* qualifies as what James Olney calls a "duplex" autobiography in that Wells gives the reader enough of a view of her domestic sphere to round out what she presents of herself as a public person.

The structure of *Crusade for Justice*, like that of many autobiographies, is chronological rather than thematic or topical. Organized into forty-six short chapters, the memoir has the same "disconnected" quality of many women's narratives.[7] Although it begins with Wells's recounting of her painful adolescence, the autobiographical "I" shifts to the viewpoint of the mature young woman fighting against lynching, then to that of an older woman wise in many ways, looking back on her life, ordering her experience in the recreation of the self.

Part of its intrinsic cultural value is that *Crusade for Justice* presents prime source material for speculation on the role of race and sex in the development of Wells's psychosocial identity and her autobiographical point of view. In his *Life History and the Historic Movement*, Erik Erikson defines the autobiographer's psychosocial identity primarily in relation to "the personal coherence of the individual and the group." Erikson postulates that "one must first ask oneself under what circumstances the memoirs were written, what their intended purpose was, and what form *they assumed*. Only then can one proceed to judge the less conscious motivations, which may have led the autobiographer to emphasize selectively some experiences and omit other equally decisive ones ... to correct what might spoil the kind of immortality he has chosen for himself."[8] Certainly such questions must be asked of Wells's autobiography, which was written toward the end of her career and her life, when she might have been susceptible to such "less conscious motivations." And if Erikson had read *Crusade for Justice*, he might have criticized it as one of those "autobiographies ... written at certain late stages of life for the purpose of recreating oneself in the image of one's method."[9]

Wells began her autobiography in 1928; she died in 1934, leaving her work in midsentence. According to Alfreda M. Duster, her youngest child and editor of the posthumously published autobiography:

> Ida B. Wells really wrote her own autobiography beginning in 1928. Our home had a large dining room with a huge dining table that could be expanded by putting "leaves" where the halves were pulled apart. That table was extended to its fullest length and was covered with papers, notes, books, etc.
>
> She spent most of her days there, except when she was attending meetings, giving lectures, or answering requests for help from people in trouble, which were many.
>
> She wrote the preface and the first three chapters by hand, writing and re-writing, then she secured the services of my brother's secretary, Miss Sinclair, for the rest of the chapters or re-typed at the next session.[10]

Although the editors at the University of Chicago Press supplied the book and chapter titles (since Wells did not), the manuscript was otherwise printed "just as she wrote it," partly because the editor was aware that as Wells's daughter, anything she wrote would be suspect. Thus the text may be regarded as essentially Wells's own, although the published work represents an impressive feat of mother–daughter bonding and personal and political commitment spanning two generations. *Crusade for Justice* is a family and community document as well as the celebration of an individual triumph.

In Duster's words, "My role was a determination to see that this book was published. I knew it was a valuable story—one that should be published by a press which had nation-wide and even international distribution facilities, and I would not settle for less. So I just kept seeking and sending, and when the manuscript was returned, I just kept looking for another publisher." According to Duster, the cycle of rejection started shortly after her mother's death and went on for about thirty-five years. "I knew the story should be told," she wrote in answer to my query. "I knew it had significance, and I wanted it published ... if I'd given up and put the manuscript somewhere and never tried, it would never have been available." But Duster's true role extended beyond a determination to see her mother's autobiography published. For three years after the book was accepted, she worked under the supervision of the historian John Hope Franklin, "reading, travelling all over the country, verifying what mother had written from memory by facts and figures, articles, books, newspapers, correspondence, etc."[11] In his foreword, Franklin attests to Duster's scrupulous editing:

> Although her interest in the subject is understandably deep and her knowledge of the things about which her mother writes is great, Mrs. Duster has not intruded herself into the story that is, after all, the story of Ida B. Wells. She has accurately perceived her role as an understanding and sympathetic editor, scrupulously avoiding the pitfalls of filial subjectivity.[12]

Where an error or discrepancy occurs, Duster includes a note of correction, but her concern with historical accuracy does not intrude; the reader can almost hear Ida B. Wells through the immediacy of the text. This sense of presence represents one of the central paradoxes of *Crusade for Justice*, the dependence of the deceased mother on the living daughter for the revelation and publication of her autobiography.

Presumably, therefore, Duster had some voice in the selection of the title and subtitle, which were not supplied by the autobiographer. The title, *Crusade for Justice*, signals the central concerns and forecasts the dominant metaphors and "necessary fictions" of the text; it also suggests a holy war, a figure of thought that runs throughout Wells's narrative. The subtitle, *The Autobiography of Ida B. Wells*, indicates the intention to minimize the autobiographer's personal life in order to portray her participation in a vast historical drama; *Crusade for Justice* is clearly presented as the story not only of Ida B. Wells but also of her times.

Duster's introduction occupies a crucial position, following the foreword by John Hope Franklin and preceding Wells's own preface. Unlike the authenticating subtexts of nineteenth-century slave narratives, which seem to challenge or undermine the narrator's authorial control, the Duster introduction engages in a kind of literary call and response with Wells's preface and the larger text, resulting in a remarkable resonance between *Crusade for Justice* and its authenticating subtexts. Duster begins her introduction by quoting Norman B. Wood's *The White Side of a Black Subject*:

> God has raised up a modern Deborah in the person of Miss Ida B. Wells, whose voice has been heard throughout England and the United States ... pleading as only she can plead for justice and fair treatment for her people.... we believe God delivered her from being lynched at Memphis, that by her portrayal of the burnings at Paris, Texas, Texarkana, Arkansas and elsewhere she might light a flame of righteous indignation, in England and America which by God's grace, will never be extinguished until a Negro's life is as safe in Mississippi and Tennessee as in Massachusetts or Rhode Island.[13]

Duster asserts that Wood's "was not an unusual description" of Wells, "who was described over and over again as militant, courageous, determined, impassioned, and aggressive."[14] In the remainder of the first paragraph, Duster authenticates her mother's slave birth, her uncommon parentage and upbringing, and much of the factual content of the early chapters of *Crusade*.

But Duster does more than attest to the truth value of her mother's narrative; by quoting a white author who likens her mother to Deborah, a prophetess and judge among the Hebrews of the Old Testament, she participates in the myth-making process. Like the Old Testament heroine, who "arose a mother in Israel" to lead an army against the enemies of her people, Ida B. Wells led the crusade against lynching, full of outrage and indignation, going where men feared to tread. Thus Duster's rhetorical strategy works partly because she directs the reader's attention away from herself as authenticator, and because she contributes to the development of Wells's myth. Near the end of her introduction, Duster forecasts and softens the "strained analogy" that opens her mother's preface, as she supports Wells's personal identification with Joan of Arc:

> In the preface to her autobiography she mentions that a young lady compared her to Joan of Arc. The analogy is, at best, strained, but the odds against [Wells] were in many ways greater. True enough, Joan was a peasant girl in a time when peasants and girls had nothing to say to the ruling class in France. But Ida B. Wells was a black woman born into slavery who began carrying the torch against lynching in the very South bent upon the degradation of the blacks.[15]

The torch of righteous indignation carried in the crusade against the barbaric practice of lynching becomes one of the central metaphors of Wells's text.

Wells's own preface affirms the "holy war" motif as she begins with the reference to Joan of Arc in an indirect advancement of a statement of her autobiographical purpose and intention:

> A young woman recently asked me to tell her of my connection with the lynching agitation which was started in 1892. She said

she was at a YWCA vesper service when the subject for discussion was Joan of Arc, and each person was asked to tell of someone they knew who had traits of character resembling this French heroine and martyr. She was the only colored girl present, and not wishing to lag behind the others, she named me. She was then asked to tell why she thought I deserved such mention. She said, "Mrs. Barnett, I couldn't tell why I thought so."[16]

Wells's identification with Joan of Arc recalls the preface to Sojourner Truth's *Narrative* where Truth evokes the same image; thus Wells revises and recasts Truth's chosen historical metaphor. Wells underscores her historical intention as she builds her personal myth of self:

When she told me she was twenty-five years old, I realized that one reason she did not know was because the happenings about which she inquired took place before she was born. It is therefore for the young who have so little of our history recorded that I am for the first time in my life writing about myself. I am all the more constrained to do this because there is such a lack of authentic race history of Reconstruction times written by a Negro himself. (*Crusade*, 3–4)

Moreover, Wells's preface advances a historical association with Frederick Douglass, an association often reinforced in the text. Wells writes:

We have Frederick Douglass's history of slavery as he knew and experienced it. But of the storm and stress immediately after the Civil War, of the Ku Klux Klan, of ballot stuffing, wholesale murders of Negroes who tried to exercise their new-found rights as free men and citizens, the carpetbag invasion about which the South published much that is false, and the Negroes' political life in that era—our race has little of its own that is definite or authentic. (*Crusade*, 4)

The autobiographer's goal is clearly one of definition, documentation, and authentication; her story is intended not only as her own but as the story of her people and her times. She presents her life as a representative and symbolic one.

Wells's documentary mode is signaled by the form of the "linear narrative," which is heavily influenced by journalism and reportage, and authenticated by quotes from newspapers, letters, and "other verifiable, external records." Yet another clue concerns the autobiographer's "attention to chronology and causes," and her brooding historical consciousness, which seems to pervade every word.[17] In *Crusade for Justice*, Wells attempts to compensate for a public image frequently maligned in the white press. Like the fugitive slaves, Wells feels compelled to tell her story from her own point of view. She wants to set the record straight.

The development of Wells's consciousness resembles the growth of Harriet "Linda Brent" Jacobs's as it unfolds in a series of autobiographical turning points, which might also be viewed as autobiographical "cover memories." A cover memory, according to Erik Erikson, is "a roughly factual event that has come to symbolize in condensed form a complex of ideas, affects and memories...living on in adulthood" as an "account to be settled."[18] The narrative movement of *Crusade for Justice* proceeds from one cover memory to the next; thus, "settling accounts" becomes an important figure of thought and a locus of thematic meaning in the text.

As in many other autobiographies by black women, childhood receives scant treatment; Wells treats her childhood in fewer than fifteen pages. While these memories seem dim, what Wells recalls from childhood prefigures a motif of central importance in the later text: the division between public and private duty. Born into slavery, Wells's "earliest recollections" are of reading the newspaper to her father and "an admiring group of his friends." Of her father, she writes, "He was interested in politics and I heard the words of the Ku Klux Klan long before I knew what they meant. I dimly knew that it meant something fearful, by the way my mother walked the floor at night when my father was at a political meeting." Wells portrays her mother as a "deeply religious woman" who "won the prize for regular attendance at Sunday school" and taught her children "the work of the home" as well as the virtue of literacy as a tool of liberation. "She was not forty when she died, but she had borne eight children and brought us up with a strict discipline that many mothers who had had educational advantages have not exceeded. She used to tell us how she had been beaten by slave owners and the hard times she had as a slave" (*Crusade,* 9). Jim and Lizzie Wells provide for Ida a direct contact with an oppressive slave past. Jim reinforces the connection of freedom, literacy, and struggle, while Lizzie triumphs as nurturer, protector, and defender of her family.

The young Ida B. Wells does not understand the implications of everything that she sees and experiences. The narration in the early pages of the autobiography by the mature Ida B. Wells profits from the child's point of view; although incidents narrated seem randomly chosen, Wells endows each "cover memory" with symbolic significance. The feminist critic Patricia Spacks argues that attitudes of many women autobiographers toward adolescence differ from those of men in that women tend to remember adolescence with a kind of "nostalgic pleasure," but that black women writing autobiography do not fit this model: They typically have tragically short childhoods. The black woman autobiographer typically substitutes a concern for survival for the flirtations and diversions of traditional "white" adolescence.[19]

The death of Wells's parents during a yellow fever epidemic propels the teenage girl into a world of adult reality. Reborn into a world of "Hard Beginnings," Wells is suddenly charged with the responsibilities of an adult. In presenting this experience, the autobiographer employs both the inquiring mind of the historian and the selectivity of the artist. Wells's narration of her conversation with the conductor of the train that took her home develops the myth of the stalwart "Christian soldier," who serves family and community under the most adverse circumstances. She finds ample opportunities for heroism in her everyday life and possesses the courage necessary to fulfill a heroic role:

> It was a freight train. No passenger trains were running or needed. And the caboose in which I rode was draped in black for two previous conductors who had fallen victim to this dreaded disease. The conductor who told me this was sure that I had made a mistake to go home. I asked him why he was running the train when he knew he was likely to get the fever as had those others for whom the car was draped. He shrugged his shoulders and said that somebody had to do it. "That is exactly why I am going home. I am the oldest of seven living children. There's nobody but me to look after them now. Don't you think I should do my duty, too?" (*Crusade*, 12)

In choosing these images and metaphors, Wells, like many other twentieth-century autobiographers, accentuates her adolescent performance. She also conforms to this pattern by diminishing the importance of the actions of her siblings in this crisis. "There were six of us left, and I the oldest, was only fourteen years old. After being a happy, light-hearted schoolgirl, I suddenly found myself at the head of a family" (*Crusade*, 12). Wells's recognition that she will have to rely on personal resources parallels that of Harriet Jacobs. Like the fugitive slaves, Wells achieves self-reliance by facing hardship. Reflecting the values of the slave narrative, Ida struggles to keep her family together, even after well-meaning friends and neighbors offer to take the children in:

> I said that it would make my mother and father turn over in their graves to know their children had been scattered like that and that we owned the house and if the Masons would help find work, I would take care of them. Of course they scoffed at the idea of a butterfly fourteen-year-old schoolgirl trying to do what it had taken the combined effort of mother and father to do....
>
> I took the examination for a country schoolteacher and had my dress lengthened, and I got a school six miles out in the country. (*Crusade*, 16)

In striving for self-sufficiency, the young woman unconsciously oversteps the boundaries of community-sanctioned propriety. The death of Wells's parents and her efforts to keep the family together precipitate an adolescent identity crisis, for Ida rebels against her perceived lack of power and an unwritten code of social etiquette designed to protect young black women from the sexual advances of white men.

For example, after Wells's father had died, the family physician, a friendly white man, had locked up $300 of Jim Wells's money for safekeeping, and sent for Ida, the oldest child. When Ida returned to Holly Springs, the doctor made arrangements to have the money transferred to her. This conscientious act of decency leads to a confrontation:

> But someone said that I had been downtown inquiring for Dr. Gray shortly after I had come from the country. They heard him tell my sister he would get the money, meaning my father's money, and bring it to us that night. It was easy for that type of mind to deduce and spread that already, as young as I was, I had been heard asking white men for money and that was the reason I wanted to live there by myself with the children.
>
> As I look back at it now I can perhaps understand the type of mind which drew such conclusions. And no one suggested that I was laying myself open to gossiping tongues. (*Crusade*, 17)

This negative interaction impresses the young Ida B. Wells with an awareness of her sexual identity as well as her social powerlessness. Here Wells's ingrained concept of duty to family conflicts with the conventional notions of ideal womanhood espoused by her community. By demanding to be allowed to stand as the head of her family, Wells had unintentionally violated the racial and sexual etiquette of her community, which dictated that respectable young black women, white men, and money did not mix. Generally, the community did what it could do to discourage its women from having anything to do with white men; this conservative behavior served to minimize the potential for violence to some degree. Reinforcing the "hometraining" she had received from gentler hands, this incident helped both to form and to transform Ida's identity.

Outraged at the unjust accusation, Wells becomes even more set in her ways. In relating this experience in the pages of her autobiography, Wells introduces the idea of identity formation through conflict, a motif that can be linked to the literary strategy of settling accounts, as the autobiographer moves from one psychological turning point to the next.

The early narrative treatment of another incident, which occurred in 1884, clearly demonstrates the growth of what Erikson might view as a "pattern of analogous events...that combine to suggest a plausible direction."[20] Here a defiant Wells confronts the Chesapeake and Ohio Railroad with regard to its "color policy":

> But ever since the repeal of the Civil Rights Bill by the United States Supreme Court... there had been efforts all over the South to draw the color line on the railroads.
>
> When the train started and the conductor came along to collect tickets, he took my ticket, then handed it back to me and told me that he could not take my ticket there. I thought that if he didn't want the ticket that I wouldn't bother about it and so went on reading. In a little while when he finished taking tickets, he came back and told me that I would have to go into another car. I refused, saying that the forward car was a smoker, and as I was in the ladies car, I proposed to stay. He tried to drag me out of the seat, but the moment he caught hold of my arm I fastened my teeth into the back of his hand.
>
> I had braced my feet against the seat in front and was holding to the back, and as he already had been badly bitten, he didn't try it again by himself. He went forward and got the baggageman and another man to help him and of course they succeeded in dragging me out. (*Crusade*, 18–19)

This "cover memory" contributes to a pattern in the development of Wells's consciousness. The outraged young schoolteacher with her teeth in the back of the conductor's hand is one of the selves of the autobiographer. In *Crusade for Justice*

Wells performs on a historical stage, seeking a larger audience than that of the white "ladies and gentlemen" in the train car. She authenticates her narrative elaborately, quoting one of her many subtexts, a headline from the *Memphis Commercial Appeal* that read: "Darky Damsel Obtains a Verdict for Damages against the Chesapeake and Ohio Railroad—What it Cost to Put a Colored School Teacher in a Smoking Car—Verdict for $500." Eventually, the railroad appealed the case to the state supreme court, which reversed the findings of the lower court, and ordered Wells to pay court costs. Even so, Wells's strategic inclusion of this incident in her "authenticating narrative" strengthened her posture as a crusader for justice.

Never enthusiastic about teaching, Wells found the profession too confining; she felt stifled and isolated. In the chapter titled "Iola," she writes: "The confinement and monotony began to grow distasteful. The correspondence I had built up in newspaper work gave me an outlet through which to express the real 'me' " (*Crusade*, 31). Journalism propels Wells out of teaching, as her outrage flares into another, more public conflict with community leaders. As a writer and editor for the *Memphis Free Speech*, Wells writes an editorial that attacks the morals of Memphis teachers. This sparks a dispute that embarrasses her employers on the Memphis School Board and contributes to the suicide of a black female teacher who had allegedly been involved in an affair with a white lawyer employed by the same board. Wells's public revelations were not news to the rest of the community, but she had disrupted a delicate balance of race relations by revealing a situation about which community leaders had agreed to keep quiet.

Losing her job as a result of the controversy, Wells becomes totally involved in publishing. As an investigative reporter, she continues to define her identity through the adversary relationship. Publishing provides Wells with a wider audience and greater opportunities for identity-defining experiences. Thus, early in *Crusade*, Wells reveals her established pattern of forming her identity through public conflict.

In 1892, the lynching of three black Memphis citizens stirs Wells's moral indignation, and her reaction places her in a position of national prominence. Wells's autobiographical response to the "Lynching at the Curve" proves Robert Stepto's assertion that "personal history may be created through immersion in an elaborately authenticated historical event." By re-creating this historical event as an "act of language," Wells elevates it to the equivalent of metaphor in what Stepto calls "rhetorical usefulness."[21] As an event, the "Lynching at the Curve" lives on in Wells's autobiographical consciousness as a "supreme account to be settled."

> One day some colored and white boys quarreled over a game of marbles and the colored boys got the better of the fight which followed. The father of the white boys whipped the victorious colored boy, whose father and friends pitched in to avenge the grown man's flogging of a colored boy. The colored men won the fight, whereupon the white father and grocery keeper swore out a warrant for the arrest of the colored victors.
>
> Sunday morning's paper came out with lurid headlines telling how officers of the law had been wounded while in the discharge of their duties, hunting up criminals whom they had been told were harbored in the People's Grocery Company, this being "a low dive in which drinking and gambling were carried on: a resort of thieves and thugs." So ran the description in the leading white journals of Memphis of this successful effort of decent black men to carry on a legitimate business. (*Crusade*, 48–49)

Wells used this case as a prime example of the economic motivation behind some lynchings. According to Wells's analysis, the quarrel over the game of marbles was designed to involve black men in a dispute that would cost them their business.

The "Tennessee Rifles," a black militia group, guarded the jail where the black men were held as long as they felt the white "officers" were in danger of dying. When they left their post, after deciding that tensions were easing, a group of white men crept into the jail at night, carried the black prisoners a mile outside the city, and "horribly shot them to death" (*Crusade*, 50). The lynching had a profound effect on Wells. Although she was in Natchez when the incident occurred, she knew all three men personally. That week, in the newspaper *Free Speech*, Wells carried words of advice for Memphis blacks:

> The city of Memphis has demonstrated that neither character nor standing avails the Negro if he dares to protect himself against the white man or become his rival. There is nothing we can do about the lynching now, as we are out-numbered and without arms. There is therefore only one thing left that we can do; save our money and leave a town which will neither protect our lives and property, nor give us fair trial in the courts, but takes us out and murders us in cold blood when accused by white persons. (*Crusade*, 52)

This editorial, which Wells excerpted in her autobiography, precipitated a series of events that led to the smashing of Wells's press and her forced exile. Following Wells's advice, blacks disposed of their property and left Memphis, bringing business to a virtual standstill:

> Music houses had more musical instruments, sold on the installment plan, thrown back on their own hands than they could find storage for. Housewives found a hitherto unknown shortage of help and resorted to the expedient of paying their servants only half the wages due them at the end of the week. (*Crusade*, 53)

The article that led to the final destruction of Wells's press pointed to the root cause of many lynchings. Some few months after the lynching at "the curve," Wells wrote the following in a May 1892 editorial in *Free Speech*:

> Eight Negroes lynched since the last issue of the *Free Speech*. Three were charged with killing white men and five with raping white women. If Southern white men are not careful ... a conclusion will be reached which will be very dangerous to the moral reputation of their women.

In response to this editorial, a white rival paper, the *Memphis Commercial Appeal*, called on "chivalrous" white men to avenge this insult to the honor of white womanhood. As a result, the type and furnishings of Wells's *Free Press* were demolished, and a note was left behind saying that anyone attempting to publish the paper again would be killed. Wells received the information while attending a series of conferences in the Northeast. She had lost her paper, and been threatened and exiled from her home, for telling the truth as she saw it.

This experience, perhaps more than any other, contributed to Ida B. Wells's self-image; it reinforced her sense of self as a black woman who did her Christian duty by decrying the evils of lynching and the moral decay at its root. According to Erikson, "Leadership is prominently characterized by the choice of the proper place, the exact moment, and the specific issues that help" to make a point "momentously."[22] Wells liberated her power to effect change and became a woman of action in response to a given historical moment and a specific issue, lynching. In psychosocial terms, her lifelong struggle against lynching became what Erikson would have called a defense against "identity confusion."

As an investigative reporter, Wells published several booklets on lynching. The first of these, *Southern Horrors, Lynch Law in All Its Phases*, originally appeared as an article in the June 25, 1892, issue of T. Thomas Fortune's *New York Age*, the paper on which Wells worked after her forced departure from Memphis. In *Southern Horrors*, Wells established the falseness of the rape charge as an alleged cause of lynching and exposed many of these "rapes" as mere cover-ups for interracial love affairs between black men and white women. She also pointed to a deeper irony:

> The miscegenation laws of the South only operate against the legitimate union of the races; they leave the white man free to seduce all the colored girls he can, but it is death to the colored man who yields to the force and advances of a similar attraction in white women. White men lynch the offending Afro-American, not because he is a despoiler of virtue, but because he succumbs to the smiles of white women.[23]

Decrying the sexual double standard at the root of America's race war, Wells recognized the issue as one embedded in cultural and sexual stereotypes of black men, as well as conventional (and often false) notions of white womanhood. Although lynching proved an effective sanction against sex between black men and white women, white men were rarely punished for their sexual exploitation of black women. Such interracial liaisons degraded not only black women but white women, who perceived the features of a husband or a brother in a young mulatto face.

It was during this early part of her public career that the "Sage of Anacostia" became interested in Wells's work:

> Frederick Douglass came from his home in Washington to tell me what a revelation of existing conditions this article had been to him. He had been troubled by the increasing number of lynchings, and had begun to believe that there was an increasing lasciviousness on the part of Negroes. He wrote a strong preface to the pamphlet which I afterward published embodying these facts. This was the beginning of a friendship with the "Sage of Anacostia" which lasted until the day of his death, three years later. I have never ceased to be thankful for this contact with him. (*Crusade*, 72–73)

Despite Wells's assertion and Douglass's authentication of her life and work, there is no known evidence to suggest that he ever believed "there was an increasing lasciviousness on the part of Negroes." The above passage illustrates a certain self-serving behavior that is characteristic of Wells's autobiographical persona, a form of posing that, when manifested in life, did not endear her to the leadership that moved forward to fill the void left by Douglass's passing. Even though the Wells assertion may be true, a more modest estimation of her contribution to Douglass's ideas would have been more persuasive to the cautious reader.

Douglass's preface to *Southern Horrors*, written at Wells's request, emerges as yet another key subtext in the interpretation of Wells's authenticating strategy. On October 17, 1892, Wells queried Douglass on stationery from the *New York Age*. "Dear Mr. Douglass," she wrote, "I take the liberty of addressing you to ask if you will be so kind as to put in writing the encomiums you were pleased to lavish on my article on Lynch Law published in the June 25 issue of the Age."[24] Wells wrote that she was "revising the matter for a pamphlet" and asked for a letter she could use as an introduction; the pamphlet later appeared as *Southern Horrors*. In 1895, Wells recycled Douglass's letter as an introduction to *A Red Record: Tabulated Statistics and Alleged Causes of Lynching in the United States, 1892–1893–1894.*

Douglass's letter authenticated Wells's "moral sensibility" and the bravery of her response to the "persistent infliction of outrage and crime against colored people." He also affirmed the significance of Wells's investigative reporting when he wrote, "There has been no word equal to it in convincing power. I have spoken, but my word is feeble in comparison. You give us what you know and testify from actual knowledge. You have dealt with the fact, and cool, painstaking fidelity and left those naked and uncontradicted facts to speak for themselves."[25] In the view of many veterans of the antislavery movement, the struggle against lynching was a continuation of the fight for a freedom that would never be secure until blacks were able to exercise full civil rights without fear of reprisal. A spirit of black resistance metamorphosed into a budding nationalist consciousness, uniquely Afro-American in character. A contemporary of Booker T. Washington, W. E. B. Du Bois, Francis E. W. Harper, Anna Julia Cooper, and Mary Church Terrell, Ida B. Wells contributed to the development of this black political awareness. In this endeavor, race, not sex, served as Wells's point of departure, for she knew that black women were oppressed primarily because they were black and not because they were women.

Continuing in her role as outraged mother and defender of the race, Wells produced *A Red Record*, her most substantial and best-known antilynching book. For this work, Wells collated only undisputed reports of lynching previously published in the reputable *Chicago Tribune*. Her analysis showed that a large percentage of the men and women lynched were innocent of any crime. She reported that blacks were lynched for wife beating, hog stealing, quarreling, "sassiness," and even for no offense.

In her autobiography, Wells returns to the rape myth and gives the history of several cases that discredit it. One of the cases Wells cites is that of Edward McCoy, who was burned alive in Texarkana, Arkansas, after being accused of assaulting a white woman. "He was tied to a tree, the flesh cut from his body by men and boys, and after coal oil was poured over him, the woman he assaulted gladly set fire to him, and 15,000 persons saw him burn to death." In this case, the woman involved was known to have been intimate with the man for "more than a year previous." As she lit the pyre, McCoy "asked her if she would burn him after they had 'been sweethearting' so long." Ironically, Wells writes, a "large majority of the 'superior' white men" responsible for the lynching were "reputed fathers of mulatto children" (*Crusade*, 93). Thus the McCoy case is paradigmatic of the lynching phenomenon and the sexual double standard at its root.

Often instigated by the alleged rape of a white woman, lynching assumed cruel and atrocious forms of murder and "slow death," including mutilation, castration, and burning alive. As Wells systematically demonstrated, many of the men lynched were innocent of any crime. Conscious recognition of this fact and its culturally symbolic significance led Wells to a course of action that assured her rise to national and international prominence. She had seized upon the issue, time, and place.

Although the *New York Age* was on an exchange list with many white periodicals, Wells maintained that none of them commented on her investigative reporting. Initially, it seems, very little attention was paid to Wells in the white press; her support came from the black community. In 1892, the black women of Brooklyn and New York City gave Wells a testimonial that called immediate national attention to her anti-lynching activities. This event marked the beginning of

Wells's public speaking career. Nowhere is Wells more modest in her autobiography than she appears in the chapter entitled "The Homesick Exile," as she looks back on her first public speech:

> When the committee told me that I had to speak I was frightened. I had been a writer, both as a correspondent and editor for several years. I had some little reputation as an essayist from schoolgirl days.... But this was the first time I had ever been called on to deliver an honest-to-goodness address.
>
> After every detail of that horrible lynching affair was imprinted on my memory, I had to commit it all to paper, and so got up to read my story on that memorable occasion. As I described the cause of trouble at home my mind went back to the scenes of the struggle, to the thought of the friends who were scattered throughout the country, a feeling of loneliness and homesickness for the days and the friends that were gone came over me and I felt the tears coming. (*Crusade*, 79)

Wells dates this 1892 testimonial as the beginning of the black women's club movement, thus asserting a founding role. She describes her early work in establishing clubs in New York, Boston, Providence, Newport, and New Haven. Following addresses by Wells in these cities, black women met to organize clubs such as the Women's Era Club of Boston and the Twentieth Century Club of New Haven. Wells's involvement in the black women's club movement should not be diminished, for it involved the active fusion of powerful influences: black feminism and black nationalism. The result of this fusion was the development of a race-centered, self-conscious womanhood in the form of the black women's club movement. Whereas the white woman's movement reflected her commitment to temperance and suffrage, the black woman's movement was born in the outrage of the slave mother and the struggle against lynching. Racial oppression, not sexism, was the primary issue. For an Ida B. Wells or a Frances E. W. Harper, a blow at lynching was a blow at racism and at the brutally enforced sexual double standard that pervaded the South. It was a defense of the entire race.

Through her antilynching activities, Wells made a unique contribution. The historian Gerda Lerner assesses Wells's leadership role in this way:

> In the 1890's, under the leadership of Ida B. Wells, who initiated an international crusade against lynching, Negro women's clubs launched a national campaign against this evil, and challenged white club women to support them. An early example of the now familiar pattern of the white liberal, accused of racism by black friends, grew out of this anti-lynching campaign and involved Frances Willard, the president of the Women's Christian Temperance Union, whose earlier abolitionist convictions and interracial work were a matter of record. Mrs. Willard was hesitant and equivocal on the issue of lynching and defended the Southern record against accusations made by Ida B. Wells on her English speaking-tour. Severe attacks on her in the women's press and a protracted public controversy helped to move Mrs. Willard to a cautious stand in opposition to lynching. Black women continued to agitate this issue and to confront white women with a moral challenge of their confessed Christianity.[26]

The conflict between Wells and Frances Willard recalls an earlier confrontation between Frederick Douglass and Susan B. Anthony over the passage of the Fifteenth Amendment, which (theoretically) guaranteed black men the right to vote with white men, but which, in effect, continued to deny the vote to women of any color. Douglass had been elected one of three vice-presidents of the American Equal Rights Association, founded with the aim of gaining suffrage for black men and for all women. When it became apparent what the ultimate outcome of the Fifteenth Amendment would be, Anthony led white women in withdrawing their support for the organization.

At the 1866 Albany convention of the association, Douglass had a serious clash with Anthony and Elizabeth Cady Stanton, who accused him of "pushing one reform at the expense of another," and the women began to talk of actively opposing any amendment that did not grant suffrage to women. With the enfranchisement of black men, the tentative alliance between profeminist black abolitionists and proabolition feminists dissolved into confusion. Douglass saw a need for continuing equal rights agitation and sought to extend the life of both the American Anti-Slavery Society and the American Equal Rights Association until all blacks and women were granted full suffrage. Nevertheless, the 1866 convention ended in the dissolution of the American Equal Rights Association and in the formation of the National American Women's Suffrage Association (NAWSA), which did not address itself to black rights.

In the chapter of *Crusade* titled "Susan B. Anthony," Wells takes up some of her arguments with NAWSA and the Women's Christian Temperance Union (WCTU). Although a member of NAWSA, Wells believed that the vote would change neither "women's nature nor the political situation" of the South (*Crusade*, 230). She also believed that white women would continue to vote the way their husbands did. Wells viewed a feminism that confirmed white women's racist attitudes as not only invalid for black women but as a dangerous threat to the entire race. Through the women's club movement and its antilynching campaign, Wells began to renew an old alliance with white women and to clarify the terms under which such cooperation would be acceptable to black women.

During this year, 1892, Wells began to receive what she interpreted as the "loyal endorsement and support" of the black press, but she was disappointed that the white press remained virtually untouched by her campaign. Through Peter Still, the black former Underground Railroad agent, she met Catherine Impey, editor of the *Anti-Caste* of Somerset, England, who was visiting with Quaker relatives in Philadelphia. Their meeting, Wells writes, "resulted in an invitation to England and the beginning of a worldwide campaign against lynching" (*Crusade*, 82). As Wells relates in her autobiography, she was visiting in the Washington home of Frederick Douglass when the invitation to go to England arrived. Her metaphor for this opportunity reaffirms her relationship to the narrative tradition of the fugitive slaves:

It seemed like an open door in a stone wall. For nearly a year I had been in the North, hoping to spread the truth and get moral support for a demand that those accused of crimes be given a fair trial and punished by law instead of by mob. Only in one city—Boston—had I been given a meager hearing, and the press was dumb. I refer, of course, to the white press, since it was the medium through which I hoped to reach the white people of the country, who alone could mold public sentiment. (*Crusade*, 86)

Wells made two trips to England, one in 1893 and one in 1894, on both occasions seeking a larger, more receptive audience. She lectured throughout England and Scotland, and during the 1894 trip she served as overseas correspondent for the *Inter-Ocean* newspaper. Her lectures were well attended, and she generally received good coverage in the English press. Thus Wells internationalized her movement.

Employing the strategy of authentication used throughout the text, Wells quotes the *Birmingham Daily Gazette* of May 18, 1893, to describe a meeting of that same date:

Having given some particulars showing flimsy evidence on which people who afterwards were proven innocent were lynched, Miss Wells said that when the woman was black and the man who assaulted her was white the offender was not even punished by law. The white men of the South had forgotten entirely that in the war when their fathers and brothers were away the white women of the South had been in charge of the black men, against whose freedom their masters were fighting and not one black man was accused of betraying his trust. (quoted in *Crusade*, 97)

Conscious of her historical connection with the abolition movement, "Miss Wells argued from the result of the antislavery agitation that British public opinion if properly aroused would have good effect on the people of the United States, and strengthen the hand of those in America who were desirous of putting an end to these cruel proceedings" (quoted in *Crusade*, 97–98). Wells knew that one way to get American papers to comment on lynching was to arouse public opinion abroad. Black abolitionists and former slaves had provided early models for this strategy. Wells simply followed the route of fugitive slaves, who used English public opinion to bring about an end to the cruelty and brutality of slavery. In fact, she was even received as the "honored guest" of Ellen Richards, the woman who had previously purchased the freedom of Frederick Douglass and William Wells Brown.[27]

In her public speeches and lectures in England, Wells continued to attack the racial and sexual myths believed by many Americans who condoned lynching, and she articulated the roots of the American race war. Additionally, she pointed out that women as well as men were lynched, often for violating the unspoken code of racial etiquette:

> It is true they had read of lynchings and while they thought them dreadful had accepted the general belief that it was for terrible crimes perpetrated by Negro men upon white women. I read the account of that poor woman who was boxed up in a barrel and rolled down a hill in Texas, and asked if that lynching could be excused on the same ground. (*Crusade*, 154)

Through this and similar examples, Wells demonstrated the cruelty and brutality of lynching and defeated the "threadbare notion" that whites lynch blacks because they rape white women. Moreover, Wells attested, some white women were "willing victims":

> I found that white men who had created a race of mulattoes by raping and consorting with Negro women were still doing so whenever they could; these same white men lynched, burned, and tortured Negro men for doing the same thing with white women; even when the white women were willing victims. (*Crusade*, 71)

It took courage for Wells to publish these radical statements, for here she attacked the heart of southern racial mythology. Wells's attitude toward interracial sexual relationships was determined by her belief that these relationships could not exist on a basis of social parity with same-race relationships.

Rightly or wrongly, she viewed black men who accepted sexual favors from white women as "weak." Relationships between black women and white men she viewed as one-way exploitation.

In Europe, Wells continued her established pattern of seeking and defining her identity through public conflict. In a chapter titled "An Indiscreet Letter" Wells treated the controversy surrounding her 1893 trip; she continued to settle "accounts outstanding." Catherine Impey, one of Wells's English sponsors, made the mistake of sending an unsolicited love letter to an East Indian physician working in the anti-caste movement in England. The horrified doctor gave the letter to Fyvie Mayo, who edited the *Anti-Caste* newspaper with Impey. Mayo reacted strongly, banishing Impey from the movement. Wells writes that her dismay increased when Mayo "insisted on the destruction of the entire issue of *Anti-Caste* which had their names jointly as editors and demanded that I quit Miss Impey and go with her in an effort to carry on the work" (*Crusade*, 104). Although Wells agreed that Impey had been indiscreet, she saw no need to publicize the incident. She could not agree with Mayo's assessment "that Miss Impey was the type of maiden lady who used such work as an opportunity to meet and make advances to men" (*Crusade*, 104). The final blow came when "Dr. Ferdinands himself wrote and strongly condemned Wells for staying with Miss Impey" (*Crusade*, 105). Settling her account with Ferdinands, Wells notes, "Although I did not answer his letter I often wonder if he realized his mistake in passing on the offending letter instead of destroying it" (*Crusade*, 104). Had Ferdinands simply destroyed the letter, Wells asserted, the controversy could have been avoided.

In a chapter titled "A Regrettable Interview," Wells treats the controversy that disrupted her second trip to Europe. Because she continued to assail the indifference of the WCTU and other "Christian and moral influences" in the United States toward lynching, Wells became very unpopular with some of Frances Willard's English friends. When Wells reprinted an interview from the *New York Voice* in which

Willard condoned lynching in the influential British magazine *Fraternity*, Lady Henry Somerset countered with a new
interview with Willard intended to cast doubt on Wells and
her mission. In this interview, Willard, for the first time,
expressed a cautious stand against lynching.

Still showing her concern for setting the record straight,
Wells documents this chapter with quotes from both the
Somerset interview and her editorial response to it, which
appeared the next day in the same publication, the
Westminster Gazette. Wells's editorial represents a written
equivalent of Harriet Brent Jacobs's "sass":

> Sir:
>
> The interview published in your columns today hardly merits
> a reply, because of the indifference to suffering manifested.
> Two ladies are represented sitting under a tree at Reigate, and,
> after some preliminary remarks on the terrible subject of
> lynching, Miss Willard laughingly replies by cracking a joke.
> And the concluding sentence of her interview shows the object
> is not to determine best how they may help the Negro who is
> being hanged, shot and burned, but "to guard Miss Willard's
> reputation."
>
> With me, it is not myself nor my reputation, but the life of
> my people which is at stake, and I affirm that this is the first
> time to my knowledge that Miss Willard has said one single
> word in denouncing lynching or demand for law. The year
> 1890, the one in which her interview in *The Voice* appears, had a
> larger lynching record than in any previous year, and the
> number and territory of lynching have increased, to say
> nothing of the number of human beings burned alive.

Here Wells asserts her relation to the unifying symbol of her
autobiography and her life, and to a personal myth of self that
reflects the outraged mother defending the life of her people.
This is accomplished through the "crusade" motif that
provides the central metaphor for Wells's experience in the
same way that "education" serves for Henry Adams. The
extensive use of quotes in the chapter on Wells's experiences

in England serve as part of the text's "historicizing parapher-
nalia." The quotes authenticate both the text and the author's
image of self, as they signal the historical intention in Wells's
autobiographical impulse. Unfortunately, they also contribute to the eclectic quality and choppiness of form that
characterize the text as a whole, especially the fourteen
chapters on Wells's experiences as an antilynching lecturer
abroad.

White newspapers in the United States, receiving marked
copies of the articles from the British press, attempted to
defame the crusader, providing another account to be settled.
Wells's old enemy, the *Memphis Daily Commercial*, referred to
her as a "Negro Adventuress." Defending her autobiographical stance in the chapter "You Can't Change the Record,"
Wells quotes an article from the June 13, 1894, *Liverpool Daily
Post* that showed British reaction to the article published in
the *Memphis Daily Commercial*: "If we were to convey an idea
of the things said we should not only infringe upon the libel
law, but have every reason to believe that we would do a
gross and grotesque injustice." In the "Ungentlemanly and
Unchristian" chapter, Wells writes about how she met the
editor of the *St. Louis Republic* while speaking against lynching in that city in 1894: "He remarked that he had been to
great pains in sending persons throughout the south where I
had lived in an effort to get something that he could publish
against me. 'Well,' he answered, 'you were over there giving
us hail columbia, and if I could have found anything to your
discredit I would have been free to use it on the ground that
all is fair in war' " (*Crusade*, 234). The effect of these attacks,
the autobiographer argues, was to increase public interest in
her cause: "The *Brooklyn Daily Eagle* said it would pay
Memphis to send for me and a salary to keep me silent; that
as long as I was living in Memphis and publishing only a 'one
horse' newspaper few people outside my district knew about
me" (*Crusade*, 221).

"With help from her detractors," writes the cultural historian Paula Giddings, "Wells' British tour was a personal
triumph, and in the end had a great impact on the antilynch-

ing campaign.... English opinion had also broken the silence of many prominent American leaders. No longer could they afford to ignore 'the talented schoolmarm,' and such influential people as Richard Gilder, editor of *Century* magazine, Samuel Gompers, the labor leader, and yes, Frances Willard eventually lent their names in support of the campaign."[28] In some sense, Wells seems to have understood and appreciated the dynamics of confrontation and identity formation as it functioned in her life and work, as well as the importance of choosing the proper time, public place, and issue for speaking out and assuming leadership. Never before had a black woman so publicly articulated the roots of the immediate oppression of her people or mounted an international campaign against the horror that oppression implied. Ironically, Wells's exile from Memphis gave her the opportunity to have an impact of greater magnitude. Yet this impact would be felt in Memphis as much as elsewhere. Giddings argues that the decrease in lynchings in 1893 and each year thereafter "can be directly attributed to the efforts of Ida B. Wells" and that "the effect of Wells' campaign was aptly demonstrated" in her "home city" of Memphis. "Memphis exported more cotton than any other city in the world, and Wells' assertions had been especially damaging to its image. So, as a direct result of her efforts, the city fathers were pressed to take an official stand against lynching—and for the next twenty years there was not another incident of vigilante violence there."[29]

After her first trip to England in 1893, Ida B. Wells returned to Chicago and a position on the *Chicago Conservator*. On June 27, 1895, she married Ferdinand L. Barnett, one of the founders of the *Conservator*. Wells's courtship coincides with a noticeable gap in her narrative; yet this is not surprising when one considers that *Crusade for Justice* is primarily a story of Wells's public life. She says only that Barnett proposed before she went to England the second time and that, when she returned, they married. Some of the details of their courtship are available from Alfreda Duster, who reports that her parents met "in the work." After the death of his first wife,

Barnett, the father of two small sons, was often asked if he would marry again: "He wasn't interested in just anybody, he was looking for a certain type of woman who would mean something to his life and career. And evidently Mama fit that pattern. He pursued and married her."[30]

When Wells "came back the second time, she went across the country, trying to organize anti-lynching leagues...and while she was touring the country, her itinerary was known and wherever she stopped there would be a letter from my father. And so they had a long distance correspondence courtship and I understand—I never saw one—but I understand my father could write a beautiful love letter."[31] According to her daughter, Wells was delighted to have found a man who believed in, and would agitate for, the same principles. At the time of their marriage, Wells began using the hyphenated surname Wells-Barnett. She was then thirty years old. "So far as her perception was concerned," says Duster, "she was continuing her work. She was continuing in journalism because she took over the editorship of the *Conservator* within a week after they married. She wrote and she didn't want to lose the identity of Ida B. Wells."[32]

A perceptible change in Wells's autobiographical focus and the direction of her narrative occurs in the chapter entitled "A Divided Duty." Thereafter, the text concentrates more on local affairs and on Wells's private life, the "rounding-out possibility" of the domestic sphere. Wells's treatment of the early years of her marriage explores the tension between the roles of public crusader and private woman—a theme introduced early in the autobiography and further developed in the written re-creation of her first speaking engagement in New York. Having returned from Europe and married Barnett, Wells purchased the *Conservator* from her husband "and others who owned it," embarking on "A Divided Duty": "I decided to continue my work as a journalist, for this was my first, and might be said, my only love" (*Crusade*, 242). Immediately following her marriage, Wells "took charge of the *Conservator* office." "My duties as editor, as president of the Ida B. Wells Woman's Club, and speaker in many white women's clubs in and around Chicago kept me pretty busy. But I was not too busy to give birth to a male child the following 25 March 1896" (*Crusade*, 244–245).

Ida Wells-Barnett remained active. She named her first-born Charles Aked Barnett, after the Reverend C. F. Aked of Liverpool, one of her English antilynching allies. Shortly after the child's birth, she undertook an antilynching speaking tour: "And so I started out with a six month old nursing baby and made trips to Decatur, Quincy, Springfield, Bloomington, and many other towns. I honestly believe that I am the only woman in the United States who ever travelled with a nursing baby to make political speeches" (*Crusade*, 244). Perhaps one of the greatest moments of her life came at the founding meeting of the National Association of Colored Women (NACW). Present were Rosetta Sprague, daughter of Frederick Douglass, Ellen Craft, daughter and namesake of another famous slave narrator, Frances Ellen Watkins Harper, and "General" Harriet Tubman, the "Moses" who had led hundreds of fugitive slaves to freedom. Harriet Tubman, "the grand old woman" of the convention and the oldest member in attendance, "arrived to a standing ovation." Charles Aked Barnett, the youngest in attendance, was named "Baby of the Association." Thus, with the founding of the NACW, a symbolic torch was passed to a new generation, proclaiming both the emergence of "Black women into the forefront of the struggle for Black and women's rights" and the launching of "the modern civil rights movement."[33]

The latter portion of *Crusade for Justice* alternates between the activities of the political organizer and the life of hearth and home. The following anecdote symbolizes Wells's life of "divided duty" and demonstrates the complex practical problems facing a public figure who is also a mother:

> When the time came for me to speak I rose and went forward. The baby, who was wide awake, looked around, and failing to see me but hearing my voice, raised his voice in angry protest. Almost unconsciously I turned to go to him, whereupon the

chairman, who instantly realized the trouble, put someone
else in the chair, went back to the back of the platform, and
took the baby out into the hall where he could not hear my
voice and kept him there until I had finished my task. (*Crusade*,
245)

Ida Wells-Barnett soon discovers the demands of motherhood: "I found that motherhood was a profession by itself,
just like schoolteaching and lecturing, and that once one is
launched on such a career, she owed it to herself to become as
expert as possible in the practice of her profession" (*Crusade*,
255). Even though she writes that she had not "entered into
the bonds of holy matrimony with the same longing for
children that so many other women have," she believes that
the creator has given woman "a wonderful place in the
scheme of things" and revels in "having made this discovery"
for herself. She writes that she is happy to have rejected
birth-control information on her wedding night (*Crusade*, 241).

On the birth of her second son, Herman K. Barnett, in
1897, Wells-Barnett resigned the editorship of the *Conservator*
and gave up the presidency of the Ida B. Wells Woman's Club
in order to give full attention to raising her children. For the
next fifteen years, motherhood was her primary occupation.
Wells's autobiographical reticence about her private experiences in marriage reinforces the public nature of her narrative, as well as its authenticating structure. Apparently,
many in the antilynching movement felt that Wells had
"deserted the cause" by taking up her new "profession of
motherhood." In "Divided Duty," Wells narrates an encounter
with Susan B. Anthony:

> She said, "I know of no one in all this country better fitted to do
> the work you had in hand than yourself. Since you have gotten
> married, agitation seems practically to have ceased. Besides,
> you have a divided duty. You are here trying to help in the
> formation of this league and your eleven-month-old baby
> needs your attention at home. You are distracted over the
> thought that maybe he is not being looked after as he would be
> if you were there, and that makes for a divided duty."

> Although it was a well-merited rebuke from her point of view, I could not tell Miss Anthony that it was because I had been unable, like herself, to get the support which was necessary to carry on my work that I had become discouraged in the effort to carry on alone. (*Crusade*, 255)

So "carry on alone" becomes a central motif of the autobiography. When Wells married Barnett, she felt her own people censured her for having "abandoned the struggle." From her point of view, "they were more outspoken because of the loss to the cause than they had been in holding up my hands when I was trying to carry a banner" (*Crusade*, 241). The passage cited above reflects a tone of conciliation affected by Wells's autobiographical persona from time to time. By telling the reader that some feminist leaders criticized her for diverting her energy away from her active public role into the private maternal sphere, and by registering her disappointment in not receiving more support from the black community for her crusade, Wells wins our sympathy for her difficult role of "carrying on alone." Through the use of the earlier quotation attributed to Susan B. Anthony, Wells suggests that the overall success or failure of the antilynching campaign depended, at this time, largely on her individual effort. There is considerable validity to her claim. In the estimation of the historian August Meier, "Later on, after World War I, the NAACP entered upon the anti-lynching campaign, but at the turn of the century opposition to this vicious practice was essentially one and the same with the activities of Ida Wells-Barnett."[34] Dedicated to both motherhood and activism, Wells refused to sacrifice either the public or the private role, but motherhood increased the enormity and complexity of her task.

In a later chapter, "Illinois Lynchings," Wells relates her reluctance to continue the antilynching work after the birth of her children. In addition to the charge that she has "deserted the cause," she also has been "accused by some of our men of jumping ahead of them and doing work without giving them a chance" (*Crusade*, 311). For these and other reasons, she writes, she has become less willing to do the hard and "thankless" work of investigating lynchings. But she *did* go, with the encouragement and blessing of her husband and family. Wells's "duty" absolves the "true woman" of the need to be politically quiescent:

> I thought of that passage of Scripture which tells of wisdom from the mouth of babes and sucklings. I thought if my child wanted me to go I ought not to fall by the wayside....
>
> Next morning all four of my children accompanied my husband and me to the station and saw me start on the journey. (*Crusade*, 311–312)

As a result of her efforts, Wells contends, the governor issued a statement that outlawed lynching in Illinois. And he refused to reinstate the Cairo sheriff who had cooperated with the mob that took the life of "Frog" James. Wells writes: "That was in 1909, and from that day until the present there has been no lynching in the state. Every sheriff, whenever there seem to be any signs of the kind, immediately telegraphs the governor for troops" (*Crusade*, 346). Of course, many lynchings went unreported. Despite the lack of a clear causal relationship between the actions of Wells-Barnett and those of the governor, her investigation did exercise a significant influence on public opinion.

In her role as wife and mother, Ida B. Wells fulfills the dream of Harriet Brent Jacobs—the dream of having a legitimate relationship with a man who will cherish and protect her. Ferdinand L. Barnett offered Wells this security, as well as a degree of financial independence and unlimited "moral" support for her mission. In the pages of her autobiography, Wells diminishes her personal importance to emphasize the importance of "the work," the crusade of the outraged mother. On the other hand, she highlights the relationships she shared with her dependent children, for they help illustrate her life of "divided duty." With the support of her dynamic mate, Wells-Barnett was able both to raise a family and to carry on her struggle against lynching. Barnett pushed her ahead, and in the folk idiom of Zora Neale Hurston, he propped her up on "every leanin' side."

A look at the interview with Alfreda Duster on record at the Black Women's Oral History Project at Harvard University yields some of the personal information missing from the text. To the young Alfreda, Ida B. Wells-Barnett was "just mother," a homemaker active in civic life. Duster remembers that her father did most of the cooking and that it was her job to have the potatoes cooked and ready for dinner when her father came home; she also remembers that her mother took an active part in the educational life of her children, often visiting teachers at school.[35] Like her own dear parents, Wells-Barnett stimulated in her children a love of reading and an appreciation for the importance of a good education. The archetypal outraged mother, Wells-Barnett was both protective and strict with her children. When her daughters were young, she established a rule that they must play in plain sight of the front door at all times. Discovered out of view in a friend's house, young Alfreda received a spanking.[36]

Wells never grew quiescent. Despite the responsibilities of motherhood, she remained active in the struggle against lynching, the women's club movement, and the formation of the NAACP. Even when she had given up her work at the *Conservator* and the presidency of the Ida B. Wells Club, she remained active in the city where she founded the Negro Fellowship League and the Alpha Suffrage Association. She was also a charter member of the National Negro Committee, a forerunner of the NAACP. In her work with the Alpha Suffrage Association in Chicago in 1914, Wells organized black women to canvass their neighborhoods and report their progress:

> The women at first were very much disappointed.
> They said that the men jeered at them and told them that they ought to be home taking care of the babies. Others insisted that the women were trying to take the place of men and wear the trousers. I urged each one of the workers to go back and tell the women that we wanted them to register so that they could help put a colored man in the city council. (*Crusade*, 346)

Black men's reluctance to support female suffrage was under-standable in the light of the racist attitudes of some white suffrage leaders and segregation within the suffrage move-ment. In fact, some southern white women hoped suffrage would offer "a means to the end of securing white su-premacy."[37] But Wells continued to attack racism within the movement as she organized the black community. In the end, her appeal to the black men of Chicago was successful.

Overall, Wells's work with the Alpha Suffrage Association would seem to indicate that black men who were reluctant to support women politically overcame that reluctance when presented with sound arguments about black women's suf-frage. Many black men agreed with the analysis of W. E. B. Du Bois: "Votes for women means votes for Black women." The consensus of masculine opinion, in the words of Paula Giddings, was that "political empowerment of the race re-quired the participation of Black women."[38] Thus Wells advanced the cause of the race through advancing the cause of black women and challenging publicly, at every oppor-tunity, the racism of white suffragists. But always, even in this endeavor on behalf of women, the interests of the race came first.

If Du Bois was correct when he asserted that the Afro-American is a kind of seventh son gifted with double con-sciousness of himself as a black and an American, then Wells acquired a triple consciousness of herself—as an American, a black, and a woman. For Wells, existence was a phenomenon in which belief and action could not be separated. She believed, and therefore she acted, attaining an escape from the South that liberated her for an even greater potential. Her autobiography reflects a model of "antislavery" expression. Because lynching was one of the tools by which whites hoped to reduce blacks to their previous condition of servitude, antilynching agitation was truly antislavery agitation in the hearts and minds of its supporters. Despite the enormity of her task, Wells forged a legitimate black feminism through the synthesis of black nationalism and the suffrage movement, providing a useful model with race, not sex, as a point of departure. Her work established not only the ideological basis for later antilynching work by the NAACP but also for similar work done by the Association of Southern Women for the Prevention of Lynching, a white group headed by the Texas feminist Jessie Daniel Ames. This Wells accomplished either because of, or in spite of, her racial and sexual identity.

In *Crusade for Justice: The Autobiography of Ida B. Wells*, the intelligence and sensibility of the narrator far exceed that of the unlettered slave. Here an aging author "confront[s] and connect[s] nineteenth and twentieth century experience" by placing herself at the center of a "repossessed past."[39] Yet this twentieth-century autobiography possesses distinct formal attributes that help to identify its place in a tradition of black women writing autobiography. Wells's autobiographical consciousness alternates between the confession and the historical memoir, allowing the autobiographer the necessary latitude to discuss both her public and her private duty. This Wells required in order to demonstrate her development, not only as a political activist, but as a wife and mother. Throughout the autobiography, the concept of extended family reaches out to others in "the work." In this way, *Crusade for Justice*, Wells's historical memoir, looks forward to the modern political autobiographies of Ann Moody, Shirley Chisholm, and Angela Davis. It represents an important link between the old and the new, part of the "lost ground" of Afro-American literary tradition.

Part III
Claiming the
Afra-American Self

The 1940s were years of transition as millions of blacks left the South for better opportunities in the industrial North and attempted to come to terms with life in Washington, Baltimore, Harlem, and Chicago. Some of the feeling of this period is captured in Richard Wright's *Twelve Million Black Voices* (1941), a pictorial history of this "Great Migration," and Margaret Walker's *For My People* (1942), a celebration in verse that won the Yale Younger Poets Competition. The 1940s also saw the rise of modernism in black autobiography—a great change had occurred, both in the spirit of the autobiographers and the form of their works. Although black women did not publish much autobiography during the Great Depression, the 1940s ushered in a new era. Responding to a sense of geographic and cultural displacement, black women gained access to the literary tools of Western culture generally reserved for whites and

men, and found the writing of autobiography to be a refuge of identity and a route of
potential wholeness. In 1940, Jane Hunter
published *A Nickel and a Prayer* and Mary
Church Terrell published her well-known *A
Colored Woman in a White World*, a formidable historical and personal memoir closely
related to the Ida B. Wells type, but
demonstrating a broader cultural sensibility
and a wider range of knowledge. In 1942,
Laura Adams published *Dark Symphony*, and
Zora Neale Hurston published *Dust Tracks
on a Road*. Era Bell Thompson's remarkable
American Daughter appeared in 1946, the
year after Richard Wright's *Black Boy*, and
in 1945, Syble Everett published *Adventures
With Life: An Autobiography of a Distinguished Negro Citizen*, the life story of a
public school teacher.

In Chapter 5, I have chosen *American
Daughter* and *Dust Tracks on a Road* to
represent the autobiographies by black
American women published during the
1940s. In comparison to *Black Boy* and other
autobiographies written by black men during the same period, many of them in the
protest mode, these women autobiographers
portray resilient and self-sufficient individuals rather than victims of their culture. The
authors are, in short, survivors. For them,
there was nothing tragic about their blackness; some might even criticize Thompson
and Hurston for not focusing clearly enough
on racial issues. In fact, each is notable for
the ways in which she responds to potential
sources of identity confusion by returning, in
the writing of autobiography at least, to a
kind of "middle age" of childhood that
serves as a bulwark of identity.[1] Although

Thompson's autobiography is more traditional than Hurston's (which is more frag-
mented and less balanced in its narrative
proportions), the texts are similar in their
use of portraiture, humor, rhythmic, and
almost poetic language, as well as in their
narrators' closeness to the land. Each text
seeks to fulfill a special vision of wholeness,
and though Thompson is more successful in
sustaining this vision (and the coherent
voice it requires), the kinship of the texts is
obvious. Taken together, they forecast the
major literary events that will occur in this
tradition for the next two decades. Though
Era Bell Thompson and Zora Neale Hurston
feel anger, they temper and direct it according to their lights, holding out the possibility of a better day.

No major work of "pure" autobiography
was published during the 1950s, but Pauli
Murray's family memoir, *Proud Shoes* (1952),
echoed the themes of the past while looking
toward the future. Murray, a lawyer and
civil rights activist, wrote: "It had taken me
almost a lifetime to discover that true
emancipation lies in the acceptance of the
whole past, in deriving strength from all my
roots, and in facing up to the degradation as
well as the dignity of my ancestors."[2] Other
autobiographies by black women published
during the 1950s included Marian Anderson's
My Lord, What a Morning: An Autobiography
(1956), Leila Mae Barlow's *Across the Years:
Memoirs* (1959), Ella Earls Cotton's *A Spark
for My People: The Sociological Autobiography
of a Negro Teacher* (1954), Helen Day
Caldwell's *Color Ebony* (1951) and *Not
Without Tears* (1954), Katherine Dunham's
sensitive *A Touch of Innocence* (1959), Althea

Gibson's *I Always Wanted to Be Somebody* (1958), Ruby Goodwin's *It's Good to Be Black* (1953), Estelle Hicks's *The Golden Apples: Memoirs of a Retired Teacher* (1959), Eartha Kitt's *Thursday's Child* (1956), and the coauthored *Lady Sings the Blues* (1956) (by Billie Holiday with William Dufty), and *In Person: Lena Horne* (1950) (as told to Helen Arstein and Carlton Moss).

In the 1960s, the New Social History and autobiography as a genre emerged as source material for the study of groups whose history had remained unwritten. The fact that the advent of this discovery coincides with the civil rights movement and the women's movement underscores the close relationship of the autobiographical genre to the political and historical moment; in fact, the political movements of the 1960s fostered an interest in and an attitude of receptivity toward the publication of autobiography by black Americans. In 1961, James Baldwin published *Nobody Knows My Name*, marking, as Stephen Butterfield notes, a period of reawakened consciousness in black autobiography. These turbulent years saw the publication of Claude Brown's *Manchild in the Promised Land* (1965), *The Autobiography of Malcolm X* (1965), Gordon Parks's *A Choice of Weapons* (1966), and James Meredith's *Three Years in Mississippi* (1966). The times had changed, and circumstances that encouraged the publication of these books by black men also made possible the publication of autobiographies and memoirs by black women. In 1962, Daisy Bates published *The Long Shadow of Little Rock*, and Septima Clark published *Echo in My Soul*. In 1964, Anna Hedgeman published

The Trumpet Sounds: A Memoir of Negro Leadership, Martha Moore produced *Unmasked: The Story of My Life on Both Sides of the Color Barrier*, and Eva Rutland's *The Trouble With Being a Mama* was published. Lena Morton published *My First Sixty Years: Passion for Wisdom* in 1965.

Commenting on the favorable reception her work had received, Maya Angelou, in a 1975 interview, attributed the improved publishing climate "directly to the protest movements of the 1950s and 60s."[3] And on finally achieving success after almost four decades of trying to publish *Crusade for Justice: The Autobiography of Ida B. Wells* (1970), Alfreda Duster remarked, "The times had changed in my favor."[4] Critics of many races and nationalities began to speak simultaneously of "the coming of age" of autobiography as a genre, as well as a "renaissance" in black women's writing heralded by the advent of such writers as Maya Angelou, Nikki Giovanni, Alice Walker, June Jordan, Toni Cade Bambara, Sonia Sanchez, Lucille Clifton, and Toni Morrison. Writing in many genres—fiction, poetry, autobiography, and screenplay— these women were viewed by an enthusiastic and admiring audience as the consummate flowering of a long tradition that began in America in the eighteenth century. This renaissance in black women's writing, coupled with developments in the field of literary criticism generally, engendered black feminist literary criticism as a recognized field of scholarly endeavor suited specifically to the works of women who, in the words of the critic Barbara Smith, "experience both racial and sexual oppression at the same time."[5]

5

Motherless Daughters and the Quest for a Place: Zora Neale Hurston and Era Bell Thompson

My grandmothers are full of memories
Smelling of soap and onions and red clay
With veins rolling roughly over quick hands
They have many clean words to say
My grandmothers were strong.
Why am I not as they?

> —*Margaret Walker,*
> *"Lineage"* (1942)

The autobiographies of Era Bell Thompson and Zora Neale Hurston turn away from the restrictions and limitations of the slave narrative and extend the quest for a dignified and self-defining identity to include a search for personal fulfillment. These women represent the first generation of black women autobiographers that did not continually come into contact with former slaves. Their texts reveal a growing sense of displacement that is geographic, cultural, and social; it is accompanied by a reevaluation and rejection of the traditional female role. As formal literary enterprises, these autobiographies vary in coherence, wholeness, orderliness, and artistic achievement, as individual works in any genre will do. More significant, for my purpose of looking at them at a particular stage in the development in black women's auto-biographical tradition, are the shared female bonding and conformity to a "female" narrative mode—Thompson's narrative of isolation and transcendence, and Hurston's narrative of vision and power. Both use portraiture and the depiction of lyrically suspended moments of consciousness, or autobiographical "cover memories," that serve as narrative turning points.

In a study of three hundred autobiographies by creative thinkers from many eras and cultures, Edith Cobb asserts that "the child's primary aesthetic adaption to childhood may be extended through memory in a lifelong renewal of the early power to learn and evolve ...the psychobiology of genius suggests the perception of wholeness has been characteristic of all individuals who have thought more closely with the instrument of the body." "What a child wanted most of all," she states, "was to make a world in which to find a place to discover the self." Examining "statements made by adult geniuses about their own childhood" and comparing them "with references to the child in myth and religion," Cobb claims a "widespread intuitive understanding that certain aspects of childhood experience remain in memory as a psychological force, an elan, which produces the pressure to perceive creatively and inventively."[1] Such a force is characteristic of both *Dust Tracks on a Road* and *American Daughter.* Moreover, Hurston's and Thompson's autobiographies parallel Richard Wright's *Black Boy,* the most widely written about and best-known black American autobiography of the 1940s. Applying Cobb's theory to *Black Boy,* Albert Stone argues that "most autobiographers ... achieve self-consciousness through a kind of *metanoia.* They write as if, and after, some transforming event or inner crisis has occurred. Visions and conversions are in this sense simply models for several sorts of experiences through which changes and continuities in identity are dramatically realized."[2] Stone's insights apply here as well: Zora Neale Hurston and Era Bell

Thompson are visionaries who experience inner crises and write as if they are transformed by them. Each must overcome the sense of displacement she faces when the death of her mother shatters her preadolescent world. In response, each develops a special vision of wholeness: Hurston the vision of a perfect marriage, and Thompson the vision of a united America. Both visions are central to the psychic wholeness of young women deprived of their connection with the primary source of their black and female identity.

Zora Neale Hurston

Zora Neale Hurston remains one of the most enigmatic and elusive figures in black American literary history. The author of four novels (*Jonah's Gourd Vine* in 1934, *Their Eyes Were Watching God* in 1937, *Moses, Man of the Mountain* in 1939, and *Seraph on the Suwanee* in 1948), two book-length anthropological studies (*Mules and Men* in 1935 and *Tell My Horse* in 1938), the autobiography *Dust Tracks on a Road* in 1942, and numerous articles, poems, and plays, Hurston was often at the center of controversy, the object of resentment by her peers. Hurston, a native of Eatonville, Florida, was the only one of the Renaissance writers of the 1920s who was really "of the folk." She alone had been raised in the rural South amid the folk culture and oral traditions that formed the basis of the spiritual and cultural flowering that attracted otherwise mostly middle-class writers to Washington, D.C., Harlem, and other urban cultural centers.

As the critic E. Edward Farrison wrote in his 1943 review of Hurston's *Dust Tracks on a Road*, "This is not a great autobiography, but it is a worthwhile book."[3] While *Dust Tracks* fails to sustain the spontaneous "creative imagination of childhood," there are momentary glimmers of what Edith Cobb would call "individual genius" experiencing "a sense of discontinuity, an awareness of [her] own unique separateness and identity and also a continuity." Part of this "renewal of a relationship with nature as a process" is exhibited in Zora's sitting in the chinaberry tree, her contemplation of the horizon, and her childhood race with the moon.[4] Lyric glimpses of the Hurston home and the interior spaces of domestic life in Eatonville and young Zora's enchantment with the natural landscape fill the early parts of the book. The artist's relationship with her mother might also be viewed as part of that revitalization, yet Hurston rejects the socially maintained dependence that characterizes her mother's relationship to her father.

The text portrays strong bonding between the mother and her daughter. Hurston writes: "The most interesting thing that I saw was the horizon. Every way I turned, it was there, and the same distance away. Our house then, was the center of the world."[5] Hurston's mother mediates explosions of the Hurston temper between Zora and her father: "My mother was always standing between us. She conceded that I was impudent and given to talking back, but she didn't want to 'squinch my spirit' too much for fear that I would grow up to be a mealy-mouthed rag-doll by the time I got grown. Papa always flew hot when Mama said that. He predicted dire things for me. . . . Somebody was going to blow me down for my sassy tongue" (*Dust Tracks*, 21).

Literally and metaphorically, then, Lucy Potts Hurston stood at the center of the Hurston household and young Zora's world. The mother sowed the seeds of liberation, and she protected them; in the guise of the peacemaker she was subversive, undermining the forces that would "squinch the spirit" of her daughter. This, too, is female tradition, for the outraged mother who cannot confront directly, operates indirectly to secure the safety and security of her child. And so Zora Neale Hurston learned both a subversive principle of indirection and the use of language as a means of self-defense by observing her "sassy" mother.

When her mother dies, these ties are cut, and Hurston's link with place and tradition is broken; the magical inner world of Eatonville is destroyed. "That hour began my wanderings. Not so much in geography, but in time. Then not so much in time as in spirit. Mama died at sundown and changed a world. That is, the world that had been built out of her body and her heart" (*Dust Tracks*, 89). After the mother's death, the family is dispersed and Zora is sent to boarding school in Jacksonville, where she is practically abandoned. The destruction of her world is complete, creating a profound inner crisis: "I was deprived of the loving pine, the lakes, the wild violets in the woods and the animals I used to know. No more holding down first base on the team with my brothers and their friends. Just a jagged hole where my home used to be" (*Dust Tracks*, 95). Although the remainder of the book treats a variety of subjects, it is essentially concerned with retrieving Hurston's childhood perception of wholeness and well-being.

Hurston applies imagination and intuition to a natural landscape to create a psychic one, whereby the real-world Eatonville is transformed into fiction, autobiography, and "anthropology." She puts herself at the center of this world, and thus at the center of human experience as she knew it. Like the slave narrator, Zora Neale Hurston, in her attempt to make something permanent from the elusive "dust" of life, attaches deep significance to her experiences, addressing both spiritual and personal issues: "As early as I can remember, I was seeking and questing. It was not that I did not hear" (*Dust Tracks*, 266). The autobiography purports to be arranged around a series of visions, but as the critic and biographer Robert Hemenway has noted, Hurston's use of the visions raises structural expectations that the text of *Dust Tracks* does not satisfy. "Although meant to explain Hurston's life, the visions do not successfully structure the autobiography. They fade into insignificance as the story unfolds. Although visions one and two serve as chapter headings, vision three is given only a single sentence. We encounter no further visions until Zora suddenly announces that six visions have now passed. There is no mention of the eighth." The ninth, a meeting with her patron, Mrs. Mason, "is not identified as such in the published text," although presented very clearly in the manuscript. Visions ten, eleven, and twelve are "nowhere in sight."[6] Nevertheless, as the narrative rambles, it unfolds a vivid psychohistory of the artist. Visions and dreams are vital sources of information for Hurston. In the chapter "The Inside Search," she writes of her first experience of visions:

> I do not know when the visions began. Certainly I was not more than seven years old, but I remember the first coming very distinctly.... I saw a big raisin lying on the porch and stopped to eat it, and soon I was asleep in a strange way. Like clearcut stereopticon slides, I saw twelve scenes flash before me, each one held until I had seen it well in every detail, and then replaced by another. There was no continuity as in an average dream.... I knew that they were all true, a preview of things to come, and my soul writhed in agony and shrunk away. But I knew that there was no shrinking. These things had to be. (*Dust Tracks*, 56–57)

Zora writes of "a feeling of difference" that sets her apart from other people at an early age and of a terrible "cosmic loneliness": "I had a feeling of difference from my fellow men and I did not want it to be found out. Oh, how I longed to be just as everybody else! But the voice said No. I must go where I was sent. The weight of the commandment laid heavy and made me moody at times.... It gave me a terrible feeling of aloneness" (*Dust Tracks*, 58–59). After the death of her mother, Hurston's second vision is realized: "So my second vision picture came to be. I had seen myself homeless and uncared for. There was a chill about that picture that used to wake me up shivering. I had always thought I would be in some lone, arctic wasteland with no one under the sound of my voice. I found the cold, the desolate solitude, and earless silences, but I discovered that all that geography was within me. It only needed time to reveal it" (*Dust Tracks*, 115). This "desolate solitude" forecasts the "desolate freedom" Era Bell Thompson feels, first on the death of her mother and, later, when her father dies. The resulting feelings of emptiness and displacement shatter the insular natural world created out of the protective bond between the nurturing parent and the child. Once Lucy Hurston dies, Zora feels adrift in a world of "earless silences." But Hurston will strive to re-create the perfect world of her childhood in autobiography, fiction, and anthropological works where she serves as fictional narrator; she will destroy silence with song, especially the spirituals, sung in the true voices of her people, with all their "jagged harmony" and "dissonances."

Richard Wright, Alain Locke, Sterling Brown, and others have criticized Hurston for not depicting racial oppression and interracial conflict, for not "telling the whole story," but she felt justified in her chosen view. For as Robert Hemenway has observed, "As a dedicated Harlem Renaissance artist Zora Neale Hurston searched hard for a way to transfer the life of the people, the folk ethos, into the accepted modes of formalized fiction. She knew the folkloric content better than any of her contemporaries and this led to a personal style that many did not understand." She was, in Hemenway's estimation, "struggling with two concepts of culture."[7]

Dust Tracks reveals these inner conflicts; like many other women autobiographers, Hurston affects a tone of conciliation in her autobiography, and she is not sufficiently concerned with narrative development and proportion. Although the narrative takes us through her years as a student at Howard University, her migration to New York, and her subsequent meetings with Fannie Hurst, Franz Boaz, and Ruth Osgood Mason, its style seems too controlled; it withholds and defends. Although *Dust Tracks* comes relatively late in Hurston's publishing career, she spends little time discussing her life as a writer or her participation in the Harlem Renaissance movement. Hurston's conciliatory tone necessitates silence about some of the crucial matters in the life of the artist, such as the problem of white patronage, the controversy surrounding her friendship with Langston Hughes, and the dispute over the play *Mule Bone*. Hurston is also largely silent about her sexual awakening, nor does she reveal her true feelings about men and white folks. The chapter titled "Love" does not tell the reader anything: "Don't look for me to call a string of names and point to chapter and verse. Ladies do not kiss and tell anymore than gentlemen do" (*Dust Tracks*, 249). Hurston's text, like her self, is "well defended": She does not reveal too much; that is, she does not open herself to criticism or love for the fear of losing her hard-won self. The comment "ladies don't kiss and tell" is a way of thumbing her nose at reader expectations with a glib self-defense reminiscent of her mother's sass. It is also a tipoff that she has made some decisions about what she wants to keep private. Such self-imposed constraints help explain the discontinuity of form and voice in *Dust Tracks*.

Unfortunately, Hurston also makes concessions to her publisher that effectively shatter the text's narrative proportion and development and undercut her subversive racial humor. Robert Hemenway describes the editorial process *Dust Tracks* was subjected to at the publishing firm of Lippincott, which deleted many of Hurston's views on race and international politics, especially her criticism of American foreign policy in Japan and Mexico: "The completed manuscript (now in the James Weldon Johnson Collection at Yale University) carries with it a note in Zora's own hand: 'Parts of this manuscript were not used for publisher's reasons.' " One of the greatest contributions of the 1984 edition prepared by Hemenway is an appendix that restores much of the original manuscript and provides "a better feeling for Hurston the writer, who obviously did not feel that her international opinions were 'irrelevant' to her autobiography ... or that her views on her people needed to be filtered through an editorial process."[8] The Hemenway edition includes three chapters either omitted from the 1942 edition or published in a much altered form: the manuscript version of the chapter that became "My People! My People!" in the first edition, along with "The Inside Light—Being a Salute to Friendship" and "Seeing the World as It Is," both of which were omitted from the 1942 edition.

In the manuscript version of "My People! My People!" Hurston speaks out on such controversial racial issues as "passing." Although she protests that "this passing business works both ways" and that there are "white folks among us who pass for colored," she goes on to catalogue seven ways to identify blacks by characteristic behavior, "signifying" on those who would deny their Afro-American heritage. For example, "If you look at a man and mistrust your eyes, do something else and see if he will imitate you right away. If he does, that's My People. We love to imitate. We would rather do a good imitation than any amount of something original. Nothing is half so good as something that is just like something else."[9] The implication, of course, is that the black man would rather be an "imitation" white man than an "original" black man. Beyond this comment, Hurston does not indicate how to identify whites passing for blacks.

On another controversial topic in the same chapter, she says that she cannot complain of " 'Tomming'—if it's done right." "Tomming," she writes, "is not an aggressive act ... but it has its uses like feinting in the prize-ring."[10] In "Seeing the World as It Is," Hurston attempts to "wash [herself] of race pride and repudiate race solidarity." "And why should Negroes be united?" she asks. "Nobody else in America is.... In other words, I know I cannot accept responsibility for 13 million people. Every tub must sit on its own bottom regardless." "Race Pride," she writes, is not "a virtue but rather a 'sapping vice.' ... It has caused more suffering in the world than religious opinion, and that is saying a lot."[11] After the Japanese attacked Pearl Harbor in 1941, the editors at Lippincott found Hurston's comments about American imperialism too inflammatory for publication:

> The United States being the giant of the Western World, we have our responsibilities. The little Latin brother south of the border has been a trifle trying at times. Nobody doubts that he means to be a good neighbor. We know his intentions are the best. It is only that he is so gay and fiesta-minded that he is liable to make arrangements that benefit nobody but himself. Not a selfish bone in his body, you know. Just too full of rumba. So it is our big brotherly duty to teach him right from wrong. He must be taught to share with big brother before big brother comes down and kicks his teeth in.[12]

This is *not* the language of a woman who intends to stay in her place. Hurston had an international analysis. She also saw an analogy between the spread of Western imperialism and race relations at home:

> There is a geographical boundary to our principles. They are not to leave the United States unless we take them ourselves. Japan's application of our principles to Asia is never to be sufficiently deplored. We are like the southern planter's wife when he kissed her the first time.
>
> "Darling," she fretted, "do niggers hug and kiss like this?"
>
> "Why, I reckon they do, honey. Fact is, I'm sure of it. Why do you ask?"
>
> "You go right out and kill the last one of 'em tomorrow morning. Things like this is too good for niggers."[13]

Hurston was "Tomming," using her humor "like feinting in the prize-ring." Lippincott struck these and other examples of Hurston's subversive humor and her outright criticism of America's national and international politics from the original edition of *Dust Tracks*.

In addition to the material expurgated from the original edition of *Dust Tracks*, there are other places where Hurston's authentic voice may be heard, especially her folklore studies. Elements of Hurston's autobiography may be found in *Mules and Men* (1935) and *Tell My Horse* (1938). Representing Hurston's personal and symbolic reminiscences of her experience as a professional anthropologist working within the veil of the black folk experience, these volumes are in some ways more successful as forms of symbolic memory than *Dust Tracks*. Hurston's narrative voice reveals enthusiasm, if not passion, when she talks about her research. Speaking of her collecting trips in the South, Hurston wrote of a "particular ceremony where I became blood brother to the rattlesnake. We were to aid each other forever. I was to walk on the storm and hold my power, and to get my answers to life and things in storms. The symbol of lightning was painted on my back. This was to be mine forever." In another ceremony, Hurston had to "sit at the crossroads in complete darkness and meet the Devil, and make a compact," but "the most terrifying was going to a lonely glade in the swamp to get the black cat bone." Of this ceremony, she writes, "The magic circle was made and all the participants were inside. I was told that anything outside that circle was in deadly peril."[14] This passage reflects Hurston's struggle to remain inside the magic cultural circle within the veil of blackness. Yet she seeks to transcend its limitations by documenting and interpreting the black folk experience from the scientific point of view as an anthropological participant–observer. It proved difficult for Hurston to maintain any degree of detachment in these ventures, for her "magic circle," like Frye's *temenos* (or a mother's love), is a world of specified language, references, and allusion, closed to all but the initiated.

In Jamaica, Hurston recorded the rituals through which virgins were prepared for marriage: "These specialists are always women. They are old women who have lived with a great deal of subtlety themselves. Having passed through the active period and become widows, or otherwise removed from active service, they are re-inducted in an advisory capacity." Here Hurston depicts an aspect of the black experience reserved for women alone. She records not only the ritual but also her reaction to it as part of her changing environment. Hurston speaks again of a magic circle of black and female tradition: "People not inside the circle know nothing about what is going on."[15] Hurston attempts to assume the role of the passive observer–recorder, subduing her narrative voice. As an initiate, however, Hurston must sometimes speak as an observer–practitioner, and when she does, her work assumes a tone that is clearly autobiographical, even when there is no assertion of autobiographical intent.

Although *Dust Tracks* suffers because of editorial sacrifices Hurston might not have made if she had put the manuscript away and come back to it a few years later, the autobiography offers an invaluable view of her interior and imaginary landscape, her spiritual vision, and the recurring themes and images in her other works. Autobiographical elements figure prominently in Hurston's novels, especially *Jonah's Gourd*

Vine (1934), a fictionalized treatment of Hurston's early years in Eatonville. The narrative ends on a note of female bonding at the end of Chapter 16, which treats the death of Lucy Pearson, mother of Isis, Hurston's fictional persona. Lucy, a spirited woman, rebels against her husband John's life style, "bigmouthing" him from her sickbed, and getting slapped for her just reproval of his indiscretions: "Ah ain't goin' tuh hush nothin' uh de kind. Youse livin' dirty and Ahm goin' tuh tell you 'bout it. Me and mah chillun got some rights. Big talk ain't changin' what you doin'. You can't clean yo' self wid yo' tongue lak a cat."[16]

Later, in the scene before Lucy's death (which closely parallels the death of Hurston's real mother, portrayed in *Dust Tracks*), the two share a moment in which the mother–daughter bond is cemented: "Stop cryin', Isie you can't hear what Ahm sayin', 'member tuh get all the education you kin. Dat's de onliest way to keep out from under people's feet." This outraged black mother gives Isie her last piece of advice: "Don't you love nobody better'n you love yo'self. Do you'll be dying befo' yo' time is out."[17] And so the feet of the little Isis, like those of the young Zora, are put on the road to literacy, freedom, and the path to self-fulfillment with the admonition "Don't you love nobody better'n you love yo'self." This goes some distance toward explaining Hurston's "matraphobia"; Hurston does not want to die like her mother, before her time is out. She rejects the role of the woman who sacrifices everything to love a man and raise a family, while her husband goes about with other women. When the relationship of the fictional John and Lucy Pearson is superimposed on that of the real John and Lucy Hurston, it amplifies and rounds out the critique of black male–female relationships implicit in *Their Eyes Were Watching God*. This issue Hurston felt comfortable broaching in fiction, but she avoided it in her autobiography by employing a strategy of submersion and subversion.

Their Eyes has a profound relationship to black female autobiographical tradition, not only as autobiographical fiction but as the fictional autobiography of Janie Starks. Hurston begins the narrative with a blueslike note, comparing the life of men with the life of women, thus announcing the central concerns of the narrative:

> Ships at a distance have every man's wish on board. For some they come in with the tide. For others they sail forever on the horizon, never out of sight, never landing until the Watcher turns his eyes away in resignation, his dreams mocked to death by Time. That is the life of men.
>
> Now, women forget all those things they don't want to remember, and remember everything they don't want to forget. The dream is the truth. Then they act and do things accordingly.[18]

The opening forewarns the reader that Hurston/Starks will omit what she wants to forget and relate only the story she wants (the reader) to remember. In *Dust Tracks*, the dream is the truth—at least in the mind of the autobiographer.

Formally speaking, *Their Eyes* is a circle, which begins and ends on a note of sisterly bonding between Janie and her friend Pheoby. Janie has just returned to Eatonville from the Everglades, where she has been picking beans with her young husband, the good-timing, guitar-strumming "Teacake." As Janie eats from a heaping plate of mulatto beans and rice that Pheoby has thoughtfully prepared, she begins her personal narrative of a quest for self-fulfillment, a classic story of isolation and transcendence, intimately connected with the slave narrative tradition. Janie narrates her grandmother's escape from slavery as an outraged mother, and the sexual exploitation and abuse of her own mother, Leafy, by the black schoolmaster. Janie than goes on to reject Nanny's survival-oriented values and mores, leaving her first husband, Logan Killicks, after he begins to exploit her as a laborer. Eventually, Janie rejects "Nanny's way," Logan's way, the mask of "Mrs. Mayor Starks," and all the other limitations of her environment. At a crucial point in the narrative, Janie engages in verbal warfare with her second husband, Mayor Jody

Starks, and wins. Jody feels that he has been poisoned. Her "sass," it seems, sends him to his grave.

In *Their Eyes*, Hurston treats the sexual awakening of a young woman that, considering the apparent frankness of her expression in other respects, seems so conspicuously absent from *Dust Tracks*. In this work, Hurston's narrator rediscovers her "perceptual unity" with nature while lying on her back under a pear tree:

> She was stretched on her back beneath the pear tree soaking in the alto chant of the visiting bees, the gold of the sun and the panting breath of the breeze when the inaudible voice of it all came to her. She saw a dust-bear bee sink into the sanctum of a bloom; the thousand sister-calyxes arch to meet the love embrace and the ecstatic shiver of the tree from root to the tiniest branch creaming in every blossom and frothing with delight. So this was marriage! She had been summoned to behold a revelation. Then Janie felt a pain remorseless sweet that left her limp and languid.[19]

Janie Starks, like Zora Neale Hurston, seeks self-fulfillment. "Matraphobic," she achieves liberation through a rejection of traditional maternal images, and through a visionary view of love and marriage expressed in terms of her perceptual unity with nature. But nature also has a malevolent destructive power, as evinced by the storm that destroys the happiness Janie and Teacake, her third husband, find together on the muck. This is the work of the same Zora Neale Hurston who (for the sake of her anthropological studies) became blood brother to the rattlesnake and learned answers to things in storms, questioning with the same intensity as Janie, Teacake, and Motor Boat seek to question God during the cosmic storm in *Their Eyes*. In the images of the storm and the pear tree, Hurston taps what are, for her, personally, sources of self-knowledge and self-renewal. In *Their Eyes*, the adult retelling of Janie's autobiographical chronicle, Hurston's heroine draws upon these same natural images in an almost erotic involvement and finds the self-fulfillment she is seeking when she works *beside* her man, down in the natural world of the muck. Thus, in *Their Eyes*, Hurston provides Janie with what she was unable to give herself in *Dust Tracks on a Road*, a sustained natural environment in which to discover (and rediscover) the self.

Era Bell Thompson

Although Era Bell Thompson is a relative unknown compared to many other black autobiographers, some may remember her as associate editor of Johnson Publications (1947–1951) and later as managing editor of *Ebony* magazine (1951–1964), as well as the author of an autobiography, *American Daughter* (1947), and a memoir, *Africa, Land of My Fathers* (1956). In 1976 she received North Dakota's Theodore Roosevelt Roughrider Award, and in 1977 her portrait was hung in the North Dakota Hall of Fame. A much more successful effort at autobiography than Hurston's *Dust Tracks*, Thompson's *American Daughter* is not mentioned in Butterfield's *Black Autobiography* and only briefly discussed in Rebecca Chalmers Barton's *Witnesses for Freedom*, published in 1948. Not so well known as either Hurston's *Dust Tracks* or *Black Boy*, Wright's powerful narrative of ascent, *American Daughter* is a modern autobiography of the isolation and transcendence type that borrows from the best of black female autobiographical tradition and looks forward to Ruby Lee Goodwin's *It's Good to Be Black* and Maya Angelou's *I Know Why the Caged Bird Sings*, later autobiographies that successfully tap "adult memories of childhood ... to renew the ability to perceive as a child and to participate with the whole bodily self in the forms, colors, motions, and sights and sounds of the external world of nature and artifact."[20] Thompson's assertion of blackness as a badge of honor and personal courage contains the seeds of political and social vision expressed by Goodwin and Angelou.

The author's acknowledgment indicates that "this book was made possible by the grant of a Fellowship in Midwestern Studies," signaling the author's intention to tell the story of a *different kind* of black childhood—a midwestern one. Unlike *Black Boy, American Daughter* contains the possibility of personal fulfillment: Thompson recognizes racism, but she is not crushed by it. In *American Daughter,* she sustains the childhood sense of wholeness that eludes most of Hurston's *Dust Tracks on a Road. American Daughter* recreates the enchanted childhood of an exceptionally creative individual who found in autobiography a place to restore and reinvent the self.

Arranged in sixteen chapters, *American Daughter* presents the life of a woman in transition. More than any other autobiography published in the 1940s, Era Bell Thompson's embodies the black woman's continued quest for self-fulfillment and a self-defining identity—for recognition as an *American Daughter.* Like *Incidents in the Life of a Slave Girl, American Daughter* conforms to the basic structure of the narrative of isolation and transcendence, moving through successive stages of isolation, illumination, conviction, and finally, action. Thompson's autobiographical persona engages in a great deal of "sassy" or defiant behavior, and she uses a defensive mode of verbal discourse similar to sass in Chapter 7. The movement of the text follows Era Bell from her birth and early childhood in Iowa through her middle childhood in North Dakota, her early attempts at publishing, her college years at the otherwise all-white University of North Dakota and Dawn College, and her experiences as a maid and a clerk in Chicago. She achieves her transcendence by following a geographic and symbolic search for *her* America that takes her into the South, the Far West, the Northwest, and British Columbia via train, bus, and boat.

Era Bell Thompson grew up among the few black people living in North Dakota, yet she enjoyed the consolation of family and brotherhood. Of one dinner party, she observes, "Now there were fifteen of us, four percent of the state's entire Negro population."[21] This sense of physical and psychological isolation, shared with forebears in black female autobiographical tradition, leads Era Bell to perceive her difference and to attempt to transcend externally imposed limitations:

"Out there in the middle of nowhere, laughing and talking and thanking God for this new world of freedom and opportunity, there was a feeling of brotherhood, or race consciousness, and of family solidarity that I have never since felt. For the last time in my life, I was part of a whole family, and my family was a large part of a little colored world, and for a while no one else existed" (*Daughter*, 67). Because of her regional attachments, this autobiography of a midwestern farm girl in the quest for her identity as an *American Daughter* stands as unique. Although she constructs a landscape of relative racial harmony, Thompson, unlike Hurston, never seems to affect demeaning racial stereotypes—although she sometimes parodies them through glimpses of the "black humor" of the Thompson household. Thompson captures the flavor of the tale-telling sessions of Tom, Dick, and Harry, her three older brothers, in a distinctly Afro-American language style—a strange "conglomeration of Negrowegian and horse-talk" (*Daughter*, 75). Hurston performs for the audience, whereas Thompson allows the reader a privileged peek into a private world. The early chapters of the autobiography introduce the reader to Thompson's family, their background, aesthetics, humor, and most importantly, their involvement with the land.

As in Wright's *Black Boy*, the autobiographer's style appears effortless. The first page sets the tone and assembles what Butterfield calls "the ingredients" of autobiography.[22] But unlike Richard, the hero of *Black Boy*, Era Bell knows that her freedom from the feelings of difference imposed on her by an outside world will be achieved by an inward search. She begins her first chapter, "Go West, Black Man," in just this way:

> "My Lord, it's a girl!" Pop stumbled blindly out into the kitchen, slumped down into a chair, and again said, "Oh, my Lord!"
>
> Now, my Lord had heretofore been very good to my father, for he had three sons: Tom, Dick, and Harry.
>
> There had been another girl a long time before, a girl with fair skin and blonde hair. My father and mother said she "took

back." Our white neighbors were taken aback, too. They didn't blame the iceman, exactly, but they strongly suspected something in the Thompson woodpile besides a Negro—and there was.

In father's mulatto veins flowed the blood of a Dutchman, a Frenchman, and a couple of Indians. Pop had to claim two Indians to make up for the Cherokee chief who was my mother's grandfather, and to cover up that touch of Chinese he couldn't account for. (*Daughter*, 1)

To account for her father (and herself), Thompson looks to the past and the history of the slave. The story of the Thompson family began on a plantation in Virginia where Era Bell's father, Tony, was born the son of a free black woman and a white slaveholder. Though not a slave, Tony Thompson participates in the quest for freedom and literacy: "He was still a Negro, with all his blond hair, and, as such, could not attend school; but his white half-sisters taught him from their books, and, by the time he was ten, he was teaching grown men and women to read and write" (*Daughter*, 2). Like Hurston's father (and like the fictional John Pearson of *Jonah's Gourd Vine*), Tony Thompson, the outcast son of a white man, seeks a place in the black world. Like other black women autobiographers, Era Bell Thompson uses portraiture, creating strong images of her family, especially her father: "The large oval picture that hung on our living-room wall was the bust and apron strings of Pop. The starched white cap sat at a rakish angle, the small black mustache didn't quite cover the confident smile, and the bright eyes twinkled mischievously. A much larger edition of the same picture for many years graced the side of an Illinois hotel in the town where he married my mother, a nursemaid for a wealthy family and also a Virginian" (*Daughter*, 2). The intense bonding she shares with her father is atypical of most autobiographies by black American women. Unlike John Hurston, Tony Thompson does not send his daughter off to boarding school when her mother dies. Instead, he attempts to fulfill the nurturing role himself, raising his daughter to be an independent and high-spirited young woman.

Closeness to the land and involvement with nature contribute to the lyric imagery and sensibility of *American Daughter*, becoming a structural component. Like other gifted autobiographers fascinated with form, Thompson manipulates time and space relations. In the second chapter, "God's Country," Thompson begins her descent into isolation on the train ride from Iowa to North Dakota: "As the train sped along through amber fields of corn dotted with ripe, yellow pumpkins and bright, orange squash, through the mellow haze of an Iowa autumn, Harry and I sat glued to the windows, entranced by the passing panorama, enthralled by the miracle of locomotion" (*Daughter*, 15). This involvement with nature continues in Chapter 3, "Testing Ground." Like Wright, Thompson employs selection and method "to make language such a perfect vehicle for content that the two are indistinguishable."[23] Thompson's summary catalogues, reminiscent of the poetry of Whitman and Sandburg, are probably even less intrusive than those found in *Black Boy*. In describing the Thompson farm in North Dakota, the narrator's highly eroticized interaction with nature achieves a poetic quality: "Pale-gray sage and dull buffalo grass flecked the fields, and here and there red brown patches of stiff buck-brush sheltering a coyote's den. In the slough at the north end of the pasture was long, dry marsh grass, flat from the recent weight of snow. Purple crocuses blossomed reluctantly on thick furry stems among the rocks and boulders" (*Daughter*, 31–32). Thus, like Janie Starks in Hurston's *Their Eyes Were Watching God*, and like the mature Richard Wright looking back on his life in *Black Boy*, Era Bell Thompson expresses much of her autobiographical impulse in terms of her perceptual unity with nature. Era Bell's "middle childhood" is knit of the life of the farm—haying, harvesting, plowing, breaking wild horses, and listening to the song of the meadowlark.

But nature is not necessarily benign. As in *Their Eyes Were Watching God*, nature has a more oppressive aspect. Of the prairie heat, Thompson writes: "There were days, silent, hot motionless days when not a blade of grass stirred, not a stalk of grain moved." Thompson understands these periods as part of the natural cycle and responds appropriately: "You didn't talk much then, you hated to break the prairie silence, the magic of its stillness, for you had that understanding with nature, that treaty with God. There was no need for words. The silence wore hard on those who did not belong" (*Daughter*, 41). In "Blizzard Bound," Thompson brilliantly describes the coming of winter: "Huge Russian thistles, ugly and brittle now, free of their moorings, rolled across the prairie like silent, gray ghosts, catching in fence corners, piling up in low places, herded and driven mercilessly on by the cold wind that whistled down from the far North. Days grew thin and worried, gray and colder, erasing the boundaries that separated them from night" (*Daughter*, 58).

"Broken Dreams," the chapter that narrates the events preceding and immediately following the death of Era Bell's mother, relates them primarily in terms of nature. Mary Thompson, a woman who was "hardly ever sick," dies during a February chinook or warm spell, which brings "sudden, unseasonable spring to the Dakotas" (*Daughter*, 87). It is as if nature has played a cruel trick on the Thompsons, destroying their family unity: "They lowered my mother into the frozen earth at the close of day, as the sun sank behind the snow-blotched hills. We stood on the brink of the grave, listening to the clods of dirt fall upon her bier while the neighbors sang 'Nearer My God to Thee.' And for the last time, there were six of us" (*Daughter*, 90). In the early chapters of the autobiography, Thompson establishes an enchanted landscape in which to restore the self; the death of her mother destroys that enchantment. Yet Thompson is spared the devastation that Hurston experienced because of Thompson's strong and supportive father.

There is another important difference, a thematic one. The common dangers of frontier life—brush fires, coyotes, blizzards, and starvation—made common friends of blacks, Norwegians, and German Americans. Unlike Hurston, who escaped race prejudice (to a large degree) because she lived in an all-black town, Thompson lived in a region where there were so few Afro-Americans that little stigma attached to blackness. When the Thompsons run out of food and credit, a white neighbor, Carl Brendel, brings them a hundred pounds of flour, "canned goods and staples, meal and lard," as well as jelly beans for Era Bell, all completely unsolicited. When Era Bell's father explains that he does not then have the money to pay for these goods, Brendel retorts, *"Nein, nein!* I vant no money. Ven you get it you pay me if you vant. I got money, I your neighbor, I help you. Dot iss all" (*Daughter*, 46). This interracial cooperation is what Arthur C. Davis sees as "the unconscious thesis of the book, and the secret of the work's fascination." Black and white Americans share "the same problems and above all the same human kindliness." For Davis, therefore, Thompson's book represents "something new under the sun" and a breath of fresh air.[24]

The first real intrusion of racial strife occurs in the chapter "Our Land" when Era Bell comments on her reaction to an article from the *Chicago Defender* that her brother Dick sent back to North Dakota during the Chicago riots of 1919. The article contained an account of a southern lynching. Thompson reveals her feelings about the South and her own regional identification and sense of place:

> For a long time I could see the lifeless body hanging from the tree. To me it became a symbol of the South, a place of hate and fear. And Dick's civilization was a riot where black and white Americans fought each other and died. I wanted never to leave my prairies with white clouds of peace and clean, blue heavens, for now I knew that beyond the purple hills prejudice rode hard on the heels of promise and death was its overtaking. I wondered where was God. (*Daughter*, 109–110)

These "prairies with white clouds of peace and clean, blue heavens" represent an interior world insulated from the race hatred of the South and violence of northern cities. For Era Bell, Chicago was a far-off battleground of black and white and the South a place of hate and fear.

Thompson chronicles her developing consciousness of race throughout the narrative, but seems to have suffered little of the racial horror that southern black autobiographers like

Richard Wright, Maya Angelou, and Ann Moody found so familiar. Because Thompson lived in an environment relatively free from racial conflict, and because of her competitive spirit, she made friends easily among both races. When she was twelve years old, she made her debut in the custom of the country, "clad in blue crepe de Chine, riding a brown pony" (*Daughter*, 110). The occasion was a basket social, and Era Bell's basket was bought by a loud nineteen-year-old Swede: " 'Look who's robbing the cradle!' they yelled, and Knut called them flat-chested Polacks or square-headed bohunks and mildly suggested that they were jealous" (*Daughter*, 112). This, Era Bell writes, was the first time she had eaten alone with a man. At this important moment in her life, Era Bell had come a mighty long way from the Virginia culture that shaped the master–slave relationship of her paternal grandparents. The incident is evidence of social as well as geographic progress—by escaping the South and moving to the West, blacks found increased social freedom, but also social ambiguity.

Thompson develops the themes of independence and self-reliance in the second half of the narrative. In the ninth chapter, "Where the West Begins," "the West" becomes a metaphor for these two virtues. A third, unspoken virtue might be the heroic trait of personal courage, or "spunk," a trait shared with Hurston and her "sassy" predecessors in black female autobiographical tradition. Determined to get an education, Thompson sets out "for a strange town in North Dakota" to work her way through college "with nothing but [her] hands" (*Daughter*, 163). At first, she attends the University of North Dakota in Grand Forks by living on small sums of money sent to her by her family, but later she wins a track-and-field scholarship. Since there is no on-campus housing available for black students (only one black student had attended the university previously), she finds a job as a live-in babysitter working for Sol and Opal Block. During these early years of her college career, Thompson breaks five North Dakota records in track, and she overcomes her aversion to Opal's swearing. Later in the narrative, Opal leaves her husband and child to pass into black society as Opal Brown, a light-skinned black. When Opal and her black boyfriend run into Era Bell at a carnival in St. Paul, Opal actually attempts to pass Era Bell off as a long-lost cousin.

In the chapter "Disaster," Thompson narrates some of her minor misadventures as well as some of her great misfortunes. Incidents in which she and another female friend are out with a dining-car cook who is arrested for carrying a pistol in his pocket, and in which she and two other friends hop a freight and get more adventure than they bargained for, merely foreshadow the real disasters, especially her bout with pneumonia. This illness costs Era Bell a career as a runner and almost brings about the end of her college career. "No more physical education, the nurse said, but if I couldn't run and play anymore, what was the good of remaining in school" (*Daughter*, 186). She comes home for the holidays, but decides not to return to college. In the language of the slave spiritual, Thompson finds a void "so big I couldn't go around it, so deep I couldn't wade through it, so high I couldn't see over it; so I tried to build another castle to shape a new future, one without college and athletics" (*Daughter*, 191).

Obsessed with an urge to wander, Era Bell moves to Chicago, where she is awed by crowds of black people: "All around me now were black people, lots and lots of black people, so many black people I stared when I saw a white person" (*Daughter*, 193). At the doors of the YWCA, Thompson learns that "if the W meant white in Grand Forks, the C could mean colored in Chicago" (*Daughter*, 193). Thompson's YWCA experience is a significant one for her, for here at the Y she has her first experience of being a black woman among black women, of whom she seems surprised to find that "no two were exactly alike. Some were dark with a black-brown velvetness, two were white with gray eyes and auburn hair, in between were all the shades of brown, all different textures of hair, kinds of features. They were intelligent, well-mannered girls, with good schooling, from good homes" (*Daughter*, 194). In time, Era Bell will develop a strong bond with these women: "Like myself they were new to Chicago, coming from all over the United States, even from Africa and the West Indies, seeking better jobs and further education in the big city. Most of them were still in their teens, away from home for the first time, bewildered and a little awed. It was perhaps this common bond that quickened friendships, for in time they forgave me for being from North Dakota and took me in" (*Daughter*, 194).

For Thompson, "Chicago was a city of splendor and squalor, excitement and disappointment." She "saw city slums, black slums, black poverty, and black prosperity side by side, for the streets of the Black Belt were dotted with Negro business houses, from imposing banks to greasy lunch counters, and in between were the white food stores, foul with the smell of rotting vegetables and live poultry; clothing stores displaying cheap, gaudy merchandise, encouraging credit" (*Daughter*, 194, 195). Thus, in Thompson's psychic landscape, dense with oppositions, between the black worker and the black bank stands a white merchant class living parasitically on the community, draining it of the economic resources necessary for its growth and development. Although she enjoys the "cultural atmosphere" of the Y, the recitals, concerts, classes, and lectures deplete her funds. Desperate for work, she accepts a stenographer's position for which she is not qualified; then, after several false starts, she finds a job in a magazine office. Writing book reviews, "histories of familiar hymns and an occasional editorial," she "learn[s] more about writing than [she] could ever have learned in school" (*Daughter*, 197–198). But independence is costly.

When a telegram arrives saying that her father is ill and that she "should come home at once," Era Bell does not "have the price of the ticket." Stunned by the realization that her father is an old man and that he might die, she waits for train fare from relatives. Her thoughts reveal her alienation from the natural world with which she was at home as a child. She recalls a caged coyote she saw while on assignment at the Lincoln Park Zoo: "I watched a coyote in his artificial home behind iron bars, walking back and forth on a stone floor, never giving up, ever seeking escape from his man-made prison. I wondered what it was I had sought to escape, running back and forth from prairie to city, trying to find myself, looking for my people, only to lose my father: not

seeing the forest for the trees" (*Daughter*, 198). Tony
Thompson's loss becomes the greatest "Disaster" of all, for
now the one person Era Bell had always been able to depend
upon is gone, and Era Bell is truly alone. "ALONE, THIS TIME, I
STOOD AT THE GRAVE. DRY DUST. DEATH. EMPTINESS. Then a
merciful numbness crept over me, stifling unwept tears"
(*Daughter*, 200). Era Bell Thompson gives the death of her
father the same emphasis that Hurston gives the death of her
mother, and both women react in a similar fashion, Era Bell
speaking of her "desolate freedom": "Between two deaths I
stood at prairie eventide, the last vestige of family lay lifeless
at my feet; gone too were the bonds and obligations, and in
their stead stood bereftness, a desolate freedom. My life now
was my own choosing, and there could be no more coming
home" (*Daughter*, 200).

"Secondhand Girl" narrates Thompson's successful effort
to pay off her father's debt and bills, her fight against
depression and suicide, and her rejection of Joseph, a young
white man and would-be suitor. "Our side of the family didn't
believe in miscegenation," she writes (*Daughter*, 208). When
she has sold the last piece in her father's second-hand furniture store, she goes to work in her uncle's furniture business. Era Bell manifests her creativity in writing and design:
"Through a trade magazine I submitted a name for a new coil
spring, winning twenty-five dollars, and I was paid another
dollar for a poem describing the spring. My interest in
furniture increased" (*Daughter*, 209). When a Twin City bed-
ding house accepts drawings of a Thompson-designed bed
"with all its crudeness," Thompson is offered her "choice of
the bed or its wholesale equivalent" in cash. She takes the $15
and treats herself to Grand Forks and the University of North
Dakota, her old school. In Grand Forks, she meets a white
minister, Dr. Riley, who promises to help her get back into
school. Here she experiences a kind of illumination: "All at
once an education seemed awfully important; I wanted to go
back to school, for an education this time." Thompson returns
to college to pursue education for its own sake and for its
value as a tool of survival.

When Dawn College, a Methodist school in Lawrence, Iowa, asks Dr. Riley to become its president, he accepts with the understanding that Era Bell be allowed to matriculate as a student there. As the "President's Daughter" she enjoys a position of special privilege. At Dawn College, for brief periods of time, she transcends both white racism and her feelings of difference. She does so spontaneously, as on one occasion when she is asked to join "a howling, writhing snake dance that weaved itself in and out of the business section of sedate Dawn, coming at last to a halt in a confectionery store." "Somebody," she writes, "I never knew who, paid for my sundae" (*Daughter*, 234–235).

In the company of her white classmates, Era Bell displays "sassy" or defiant behavior, creating small acts of what might be seen as "protest theater," flouting racial prejudice. On one occasion, she shops with a handsome male student, Ronny, and the Rileys' young son Jan, playfully creating the impression that they are an interracial family, enjoying the impact on white shoppers, who are shocked by what they see. Era Bell also integrates the white YWCA, and a private lakefront club whose posted sign reads "No Jewish trade solicited." And she attends the traditional Dawn College mother–daughter banquet with Susan Riley, "the prettiest mother there," their interracial appearance obviously a first in the history of Dawn College (*Daughter*, 246–248).

Despite Era Bell's apparent acceptance into the college community, her social existence remains an isolated one, especially since she refuses to consider white men as romantic prospects. This position sometimes forces the autobiographer into a defensive verbal posture, a variation of the slave girl's use of language as a weapon of self-defense. In "President's Daughter," a handsome white male student confronts Era Bell as she parks the Riley car after a student outing:

> "What will you do when you are ready to marry?"
> "Well, get married, that's all." I stepped on the starter.
> "You'll have to marry a white man, won't you?" I killed the engine. "Why?"

"Well, where will you find a colored man to marry, one that is educated like you?" (*Daughter*, 241)

Although her sensibility is bruised by this question, Era Bell responds coolly, understating her outrage. She sassily informs the young man that many of the black train porters and bellhops he has seen in city hotels are college men, "working to make money to finish their education." "A whole lot more you didn't see are educated, are professional people with jobs and offices like the people you know. Right here in Lawrence there is a doctor, a dentist, and a lawyer; all of them and their wives are college people" (*Daughter*, 241–242). Era Bell, a modern heroine, "caps" this verbal duel with an ironic gesture and the rhetorical use of understatement, framed by roses and moonlight that help parody or "signify" conventional and/or "white" notions of romance. Leaning against the rose arbor, she quips, "My problem isn't where I'll find an educated colored man.... But where will one find me?" (*Daughter*, 242). As Era Bell succeeds in the white world of Dawn College, she finds herself more and more removed from black people, a dilemma she shares with other twentieth-century autobiographers. In Lawrence, Iowa, she is separated from the masses of Afro-Americans, a well-educated young black woman making progress in a world practically devoid of other black people—black people to pray with, black men to court. Old attractions prevail, and Era Bell makes up her mind "to go to Chicago again," attempting to bridge the gap.

She goes to Chicago "seeking work and a home among my people" (*Daughter*, 251). Yet "The Life of Riley's" had been a healing experience for Era Bell, who "rode away from Lawrence that night, away from the love and shelter, the kindness and democracy of the Rileys, eager and anxious, confident now that I could make my way among the peoples of the world, both black and white" (*Daughter*, 250). Her womanly courage and "spunk" serve her well, and her experiences with her surrogate family at Dawn College allow her to replenish her childhood sense of racial harmony and personal wholeness. Era Bell can continue the quest for "work and a home among [her] people," defining "[her] people" in any way that she chooses.

As a college-educated black woman in Chicago during the depression, Era Bell finds her employment possibilities severely limited. Determined to maintain her self-sufficiency, she supports herself with odd jobs—"a little typing, bussing dishes at the Loop Y," and so on. Whenever a chance for Thompson to work as a domestic occurs, she seizes it.

Unlike Hurston, Thompson does not back away from talking about whites or expressing her ambivalence about some blacks. "Weighing" the segregated world in which she finds herself "on white scales," comparing it "with white standards," she finds it "wanting." Thompson is in a bind of identity confusion, "hating the common Negro who had recently migrated from the South without the benefit of freedom or education." "I hated his loud, coarse manners, loathed his flashy clothes and ostentatious display of superficial wealth, yet by his standards all of us were judged for his actions, all condemned and imprisoned in a black ghetto, separated from all the other people of the city by the covenants of prejudice and segregation" (*Daughter*, 256). Obviously, Thompson does not consider herself "the common Negro." On the contrary, she is, in her mind, quite an *un*common Negro. "Little wonder" then, she observes, that some blacks "passed over to the other side," becoming "borderline people, Negroes who pass, on the job, for economic reasons, but remain black socially." When Thompson moves into the home of such a couple, the Burtons, she begins "to feel uneasy, to feel a color line within the color line, boundaries within black boundaries: the bigger the city, the smaller the world" (*Daughter*, 256). The boundaries are both tangible and intangible, physical and metaphysical. Sometimes they are emotional and spiritual as well.

One of Era Bell's first recognitions of the cultural gap between herself and other black people comes at a storefront church service. On this difference, she remarks, "Their blood flowed in my veins, their color, their features were mine, but not their God, for theirs was a faith beyond anything I had experienced." And Thompson, a stranger to the old "church of emotion" in which Hurston grew up, "sat tense and tight, trapped in the hard shell of [her] white folks' religion" (*Daughter*, 260). Like the Burtons, Thompson has become a "borderline" person, although her skin is black. She feels trapped, like the coyote in its cage.

Thompson proceeds steadily in her quest for identity, but that quest is not without hindrance or confusion. She must face one "double bind" after another. Finding a job at the Illinois Occupational Survey, she quickly learns "that mentioning a degree during a depression was like waving a red flag in front of a bull; that a Negro girl with a degree was like waving the bull" (*Daughter*, 262). When interviewing relief clients for the survey, "There were those [blacks from the South] whose meekness and humbleness angered me, for I did not know then that that was a thing they had learned in the South—and more recently, from some of the sharp-tongued northern case workers, so exalted by their power to give or deny" (*Daughter*, 263). The other side of Thompson's anger is dramatically understated in her commentary on her white co-workers' acquiescence to segregation in a public restaurant:

> As the staff grew, the number of Negro workers increased— and the proprietor of the little Greek restaurant on the corner refused to serve us further. Not that he cared, he explained, but his customers were complaining. His customers were a few employees from a near-by factory and quite a few drunks and loafers. Our white co-workers boycotted the place for a while, but, one by one, they returned, and we pretended not to notice. (*Daughter*, 263)

Although Era Bell would not tolerate segregation at Dawn College, she finds it wise to do so in Chicago. Like Frederick Douglass, she learns that "a still tongue makes a wise head." Like Richard Wright, she finds that maintaining a job in Chicago during the depression demands the practice of such wisdom.

Two days after Thompson becomes assistant supervisor, the Illinois Occupational Survey ends. A month later, still out of work, she moves from the Burtons' to a cheaper place. "I moved to a cheaper room, closer inside the Black Belt topographically and racially. This time there was no mistaking my landlord and landlady's nationality" (*Daughter*, 264). Thompson hears the loud parties and the "angry voices of men and women fussing and cursing," and eventually she moves back to the Chicago YWCA, a cultural "buffer zone" and a haven for middle-class black girls seeking work in Chicago.

Five main elements seem to contribute to Thompson's survival as a whole person during these depression years: work, education, writing, travel, and friendship. "I found a real friend in a colored woman who operated a real estate business. She gave me a couple of days' typing each week; she didn't have enough work to keep me busy even then, so she sent me on unnecessary errands and spent a lot of time taking me out to lunch" (*Daughter*, 265). Finally, Thompson finds another full-time job, this time with the Chicago Department of Public Works as a "senior typist," which pays $90 a month. Thompson writes, "So began the temporary job that turned out to be the longest job I ever had. For five years I worked from one payday to the next amid a wave of layoff rumors and layoffs that weren't rumors." Most of the black women were fired in the first layoffs.

"During peak periods typists were loaned to the filing department, but not without protest, for no one wanted to work for the blonde bomb, Silver." After a change in Thompson's work load, she moves to the filing department permanently. There she comes to know "a different Silver, a quiet, subdued girl, hungry for small talk, for knowledge and a place in the world." After having dinner at Silver's, Thompson comes away "marveling at the nice apartments available to white girls for the same price I paid for a shabby little room at the end of a dark hall" (*Daughter*, 269).

Segregated housing, like work, remains a problem. After an unsuccessful interim stay with a white family, Era Bell finds a more suitable place to live with a "prosperous and intelligent" black couple who "didn't like white people." "I found that out the day I brought Silver home with me. We were met with a cold, hostile silence, far more eloquent than words. I was surprised at first; somehow I had never thought of Negroes being prejudiced, that they could return hate with hate, and hate with far more justification" (*Daughter*, 270). When Gwyn Doyle, a white friend from high school and college, comes to Chicago for a visit, Era Bell does not repeat the error of taking her home. She also wants to take her friend to a "nice cafe in the Loop," but these establishments exclude blacks. Only in nature are Era Bell and Gwyn free to relive their high school and college days without the intrusion of "a shadow of race." "Remembering my landlady, I took Gwyn to lunch at a corner drugstore and found a shady knoll in Washington Park where we could sit on the cool grass and talk, where, under the pure blue sky, under the whispering trees, no shadow of race would come between us" (*Daughter*, 271). Chicago's "pure blue sky" brings back Era Bell's childhood sense of a wholeness symbolized by her perceptual unity with nature and the blue skies of her North Dakota girlhood. Nevertheless, Gwyn's visit heightens Era Bell's experience of isolation and her feelings of difference. "When Gwyn left that night," Thompson writes, "I walked away from the depot feeling I was fighting the world alone, standing in a broad chasm between the two races, belonging to neither one" (*Daughter*, 271).

Through work and friendship, Era Bell finds the pathway to a better understanding of black people and their culture. Friends, many of them white, help Era Bell to close the "culture gap" somewhat. At the Works Progress Administration (WPA), Esther, a Jewish stenographer, tells Era Bell about Marian Anderson: "That night I went to her home, and a Jew, a Scotchman, and a Negro sat on the floor and listened to a phonograph while a colored girl sang. The more they talked, the more conscious I became of my ignorance of Negroes, and the more anxious they were to help me, so they loaned me books and took me to concerts and lectures, dance recitals and forums" (*Daughter*, 271–272). With Esther and her

Scottish husband, Era Bell "could talk freely about people and races, for they understood black hate and knew white prejudice"; and as she talks with them, "the chasm narrowed." Thus she portrays her friends, both black and white, as an extended family in support of her quest for an authentic cultural identity.

After a layoff, Era Bell returns to work as a junior clerk and turns her attention once more to areas of her quest, especially journalism and writing. Travel becomes an important metaphor for Era Bell's search for *her* America, and it leads her in different directions: east, west, north, and south. "By vacation time," Era Bell writes in the chapter "My America, Too," "I had saved a travel fund of fifty dollars, enough to go East, for I had to see more of America" (*Daughter*, 279). In New York, she "climbed inside the Statue of Liberty, went through the liner 'Queen Mary,' waded in the Atlantic Ocean, mounted every observation tower and monument, and few were the things I didn't see, didn't do." "The last thing I did," Thompson writes, "was to visit a colored newspaper and apply for a job. I wanted to hear 'No' and know it didn't matter" (*Daughter*, 281–282). From New York, Thompson goes to Washington where she experiences her first contact with southern-style prejudice: "While ascending the narrow stairs of the Capitol on my way to the dome, I was caught between two groups of southern white people who outaccentuated Amos and Andy, and I thought my lynching days had come" (*Daughter*, 282). Here again, Era Bell feels trapped within her culture, as symbolized by the Capitol building. Despite the fiction of law, southern whites are free to harass a black girl in the very sanctuary of democracy. Thompson uses humor and understatement to soften the force of her criticism, but the irony is apparent. She takes a more serious tone when she talks about Maryland, "beautiful Maryland with its velvet hills and its red clay roads, which I was ready and willing to leave long before I did, for it was at a little bus stop in the middle of the night, high in the Cumberland Mountains that I was initiated into Jim Crow, southern style." Refusing to eat in "a corner of the kitchen," she "put the sandwich back on the rack, left the cup of coffee on the counter and walked out. Alone in the empty bus...the awful stories...of the South loomed big and terrible. I had defied a white man: black men and women had been lynched for less." For Thompson, "It was a sour ending to a lovely trip" (*Daughter*, 238).

Later, Thompson uses an extra week's leave to cover commencement exercises at Philander Smith College on a journalistic assignment for the Methodist Board of Education. Once again, she faces a double bind: "I was thrilled at the prospect of visiting my first Negro school, but Philander was in Little Rock, and Little Rock was in the South—much farther south than Maryland." In St. Louis, Thompson changes to a "Jim Crow car, about half the size of a regular coach," another image of restriction. Here her confusion is compounded by the attentions of "the man across the aisle— was he a light colored man trying to be friendly, or a dark white man trying to be fresh?" She turns away from this scene of potential exploitation to the "out of the window South, which was equally baffling." Where Thompson expects "cotton blossoms and magnolia trees," she sees only "vast areas of inundated land and raging torrents caused by spring rains." She cannot identify with the South, and always she speaks as a proud westerner. "If this was spring in the South, I thought, give me North Dakota" (*Daughter*, 284–285). Nevertheless, going to the South for a working vacation proves a positive experience for Thompson, affirming both her independence and her ability as a journalist. Although she is not at ease with the geography or the cultural restrictions of the South, she completes her assignment successfully, combining work, travel, and journalism in her quest for an authentic American identity.

Travel helps Era Bell Thompson further to define that identity. In 1939, she sets out alone "to see the West, or as much of it as $200 and seventeen days would permit." In the chapter "Bypassing the Twin Cities," Thompson rides "through the pleasant greenness of Minnesota into the bright-blue autumn of my Dakota, through the sun-burned prairie grasses and the fields of threshing grain." She sees "familiar things, the town, the highways, red elevators, windmills with spangles gleaming in the sun, discarded railroad ties, grazing stock in endless pastures, farmers grouped around the cream cans at tiny stations, waving at the train. And blue sky stretching out to the purple bluffs and distant buttes" (*Daughter*, 288–289). Using this Whitmanesque catalogue, Thompson expresses her identification with the North Dakota landscape, a contrast to the images of isolation and restriction that typify her experiences in Chicago and the Jim Crow South. When she sees Gwyn in Jamestown, North Dakota, there is no trace of the double bind they faced together in Chicago: "Arm in arm we walked up and down the tracks, and this time there was no strain, no shadow between us. When the train pulled out, I waved goodbye to my friend and retired to the ladies' lounge, where I could sit facing the big window, looking out at God's country. And it was good" (*Daughter*, 289). Instead of the limitations of a tiny Jim Crow car and the confusion of a baffling southern landscape, North Dakota affords her a safe, comfortable seat and a consoling view of "God's country." Here Era Bell renews her childhood sense of personal wholeness, expressed in terms of her perceptual unity with nature. She bears no apparent stigma of racial difference.

Thompson travels to Seattle by train without incident, then by ship to British Columbia, spending "all day under the British flag" (*Daughter*, 291). That evening, she returns to Seattle via the same route. Once again she expresses her proud identification with the western landscape:

> It was cold on the water. Snow-tipped mountains rose up from the mainland, smoke-blue and hazy; lazy white clouds caught in the crevices, spilt down their mighty sides. As the sun settled down into the pale waves like a great red ball, streaking the firmament with a bloody blast, a girl standing at the rail began to sing "God Bless America." Others stood up to join her, facing the setting sun, their voices swelling with the waves.

Era Bell sings too:

> I could see her mountains, I knew her prairies well, all around me was the ocean white with foam. For a brief day I had been away from America, and yet my heart thrilled, my eyes blurred, as I looked out across the water toward my country, my home. (*Daughter*, 292)

Thompson discovers her feelings for her country, which becomes a source of identity for her.

On her return to Chicago, Thompson's job picture takes "a sudden change for the better." As a state civil service worker, she is able to afford "a home of [her] own, a place where all [her] friends were welcome, both white and black" (*Daughter*, 298). Moreover, she enjoys her job as an occupational counselor and employment officer. These changes contribute to the development of a spirit of optimism that helps to override her earlier disappointments. In her work in "this employment business in Chicago," Era Bell perceives that "in the struggle for jobs, class, racial and religious prejudice comes quickly to the fore" (*Daughter*, 288–289). Yet she retains a plasticity of response to her environment, something she learned in her North Dakota girlhood, and she is inspired when she sees white Americans transcend their racial prejudice. She envisions a united America, strengthened by its diverse heritage. She sees herself as a part of a larger American family, and she is pleased with the image:

> When a young kid comes in to tell you that he's still on the job you gave him and that his company this very day is being awarded the Navy E. And he's so proud and happy, he tells the little colored girl next in line where she can find a job—the same place where his sister works.
>
> And the employer at the other end of the phone says: "I like you; I like the way you talk. You sound like a real American girl."
>
> Then I know there is still good in the world, that, way down underneath, most Americans are fair; that my people and your people can work together and live together in peace and

happiness if they but have the opportunity to know and understand each other.

The chasm is growing narrower. When it closes, my feet shall be on a united America. (*Daughter*, 301)

Thus Era Bell conquers her feelings of racial and sexual difference to find work and a home among "her people," and this is where her narrative ends, with the hoped-for vision of a united America.

Visions of Wholeness

Era Bell Thompson and Zora Neale Hurston really do write as if some great change has occurred, both within themselves and within the larger culture. As recent immigrants to large northern cities, they can envision a world where black women no longer bear racial and sexual differences as a stigma, and they act accordingly. Unlike their own mothers (and their predecessors in black female autobiographical tradition), they reject the role of mother and race leader to seek their own self-fulfillment. The texts reflect this movement, in part, in a quest for individual and personal language: Thompson's "Negrowegian" and Hurston's folk idioms and dialogue. In these texts, Era Bell Thompson and Zora Neale Hurston experiment freely with the limitations and the possibilities of the autobiographical form. Both attempt a kind of psychic return to the carefree "middle age" of childhood along with its accompanying sense of wholeness.

Thompson's text retains this vision of personal wholeness somewhat better than Hurston's, partially because Hurston cannot sustain her dual roles as participant and observer. In addition, Hurston's attempt to structure the major events of her life around a series of twelve visions stands as a bold one, but she weakens it when she indulges in a literary game of hide-and-seek with the reader and when she allows the publisher to expurgate sections of her narrative. Thompson's book profits from her use of a more conventional structure. In 1946, it is no longer possible to write an autobiography like the one Hurston published in 1942, for every black American autobiography published after *Black Boy* bears the influence of Richard Wright. In a poetic style reminiscent of Wright and Whitman, Thompson sings her "Song of Myself," furnishing details of her childhood more completely than any of her female predecessors in the tradition of black American autobiography, whereas Hurston withholds and defends. Through language, however, both Hurston and Thompson seek to recreate and sustain the same "perceptual unity with nature" by returning to the "middle age" of childhood. The autobiographies of both women are very different from that of Richard Wright, however. While Wright also portrays a "perceptual unity with nature," he identifies primarily with the violent southern landscape, whereas Hurston returns to her relatively harmonious Eatonville childhood and Thompson identifies with the western United States, which she views as an island of relative racial harmony. Both *Dust Tracks on a Road* and *American Daughter* are more attempts at analysis and self-direction than an expression of rage against racial oppression. While each is aware of the contradictions inherent in their chosen identities, each clings to the vision of wholeness.

6
A Song of Transcendence:
Maya Angelou

Maya Angelou's *I Know Why the Caged Bird Sings* (1970) and Ann Moody's *Coming of Age in Mississippi* (1968) appeared at the end of the civil rights movement of the 1960s, and they carry with them the bitter and hard-won fruit of this era. Angelou and Moody know the harsh realities of life in the Deep South in the mid-twentieth century—in Arkansas and Mississippi, respectively. As the critic Roger Rosenblatt has asserted, "No black American author has ever felt the need to invent a nightmare to make [her] point."[1] As Maya Angelou writes of her childhood: "High spots in Stamps were usually negative: droughts, floods, lynchings and deaths."[2] Touched by the powerful effects of these destructive forces, Maya Angelou and Ann Moody hold themselves together with dignity and self-respect. They move forward toward a goal of self-sufficiency, combining a consciousness of self, an awareness of the political realities of black life in the South, and an appreciation of the responsibility that such an awareness implies. For this chapter, I have selected *I Know Why the Caged Bird Sings* as representative of autobiographies written by black women in the post–civil rights era.

In the Arkansas South of Maya Angelou's childhood, recognized patterns of etiquette between the races asserted white

superiority and black inferiority.[3] This etiquette served as a
form of social control that pervaded the daily experiences of
blacks, who negotiated narrow paths of safety:

> Momma intended to teach Bailey and me to use the paths of
> life that she and her generation and all the Negroes gone before
> had found, and found to be safe ones. She didn't cotton to the
> idea that white folks could be talked to at all without risking
> one's life. And certainly they couldn't be spoken to insolently.
> In fact, even in their absence they could not be spoken of too
> harshly unless we used the sobriquet "They." If she had been
> asked to answer the question of whether she was cowardly or
> not, she would have said that she was realist. (*Caged Bird*, 39)

Throughout the course of *Caged Bird*, Maya Angelou moves
toward this same realism, which is not only a practical
political philosophy but also one of the dominant modes of
the autobiography. *I Know Why the Caged Bird Sings* distills
the essence of the autobiographical impulse into lyric imagery touched by poignant realism. Angelou once said, "I speak
to the black experience, but I am always talking about the
human condition—about what we can endure, dream, fail at,
and still survive."[4] In this spirit, she faithfully depicts her
home ground as a version of the universal human experience.

This chapter undertakes the task of defining the characteristics that identify the text in terms of a tradition of black
women's writing. George Kent has argued that *I Know Why
the Caged Bird Sings* "creates a unique place within black
autobiographical tradition ... by its special stance toward the
self, the community, and the universe, and by a form exploit-
ing the full measure of imagination necessary both to beauty
and absurdity."[5] In *Caged Bird*, we witness the full outward
extension of the outraged mother. Although, in some sense,
this text seems yet too close to be explicated adequately, the
availability of criticism outweighs the problem of dealing
with a recent text, for as James Olney has noted, "Here we
have an autobiography by a black woman, published in the
last decade (1970), that already has its own critical literature."
Not only does the preponderance of criticism herald "full

literary enfranchisement" for "black writers, women writers, and autobiography itself," but it indicates the importance of the text to black autobiographical tradition.[6]

Although I have selected *Caged Bird* because of the availability of criticism and because it covers a wider span of time than Angelou's subsequent autobiographies, one of the added advantages in considering this particular volume is that it can be read in relation to Angelou's other autobiographical works. In 1974, *Gather Together in My Name* followed *Caged Bird*, and *Singin' and Swingin' and Gettin' Merry Like Christmas* appeared in 1976, followed by *The Heart of a Woman* in 1981 and *All God's Children Need Traveling Shoes* in 1986. Additionally, Angelou has published several collections of poetry; almost all this poetry has some autobiographical content, and through much of it, Angelou celebrates her dark womanhood, as in "Woman Me":

> Your smile, delicate
> rumor of peace.
> Deafening revolutions nestle in the
> cleavage of
> your breasts
> Beggar-Kings and red-ringed Priests
> seek glory at the meeting
> of your thighs
> A grasp of Lions, a Lap of Lambs.[7]

Thus Angelou's autobiographical impulse manifests itself in lyrical forms as well as the prose narrative.

In *Black Autobiography*, Stephen Butterfield compares the dramatic structure, setting, and content of *I Know Why the Caged Bird Sings* with that of Richard Wright's *Black Boy* and concludes that "Maya Angelou's complex sense of humor and compassion for other people's defects ... endow her work with a different quality of radiance." Elements of humor and compassion contribute greatly to the effect, but this "different quality of radiance" actually derives from *Caged Bird's* special relationship to a tradition of black women writing autobiography. When Butterfield writes, "Ida Wells created the identity of mother and protectress: Maya Angelou in *I Know Why the Caged Bird Sings* inspires the urge to protect," he both demonstrates his respect for and betrays his ignorance of the black female autobiographical tradition.[8] The identity of the mother and protectress is already firmly established in Harriet Brent Jacobs's *Incidents in the Life of a Slave Girl* of 1861. Angelou extends and enlarges that identity.

I Know Why the Caged Bird Sings treats themes that are traditional in autobiography by black American women. These include the importance of the family and the nurturing and rearing of one's children, as well as the quest for self-sufficiency, self-reliance, personal dignity, and self-definition. Like Ida B. Wells, Maya Angelou celebrates black motherhood and speaks out against racial injustice; but unlike Wells, she does so from a unified point of view and in a more coherent form. This derives, in part, from Wells's identity as a public figure and Angelou's identity as an artist. As a creative autobiographer, Angelou may focus entirely on the inner spaces of her emotional and personal life. In *I Know Why the Caged Bird Sings*, the mature woman looks back on her bittersweet childhood, and her authorial voice retains the power of the child's vision. The child's point of view governs Angelou's principle of selection. When the mature narrator steps in, her tone is purely personal, so it does not seem unusual that Angelou feels compelled to explore aspects of her coming of age that Ida B.Wells (and Zora Neale Hurston) chose to omit.

Here emerges the fully developed black female autobiographical form that began to mature in the 1940s and 1950s. Like Zora Neale Hurston and Era Bell Thompson, Maya Angelou employs rhythmic language, lyrically suspended moments of consciousness, and detailed portraiture. Her use of folklore and humor help to augment the effect she creates as tale-teller *par excellence*. Maya Angelou takes the genre of autobiography to the heights that Zora Neale Hurston took the novel in *Their Eyes Were Watching God*. If *I Know Why the Caged Bird Sings* reads like a novel, it carries the ring of truth.

Speaking in terms of its literary merits, it is perhaps the most aesthetically satisfying autobiography written by a black woman in this period.

Necessarily, analysis begins with the title *I Know Why the Caged Bird Sings*, which originally appeared in the poem "Sympathy" by the great black poet, Paul Laurence Dunbar:

> I know why the caged bird beats his wings
> Till its blood is red on the cruel bars
> For he must fly back to his perch and cling
> When he would fain be on the bough aswing
> And a pain still throbs in the old, old scars
> And they pulse again with a keener sting—
> I know why he beats his wings!
>
> I know why the caged bird sings, ah me,
> When his wing is bruised and his bosom sore,—
> When he beats his bars and would be free
> It is not a carol of joy or glee,
> But a prayer that he sends from his heart's deep core,
> But a plea, that upward to Heaven he flings—
> I know why the caged bird sings![9]

The sentiment of this poem, one of Dunbar's best lyrics, presages the tone of Angelou's autobiography, and some of the feeling of her struggle to transcend the restrictions of a hostile environment. Clearly, Angelou is in "sympathy" with the "real" Dunbar, the bleeding bird behind the mask. And it seems likely that Dunbar would have been in "sympathy" with Angelou as well. For like the Dunbar poem and the spirituals sung by southern blacks, *I Know Why the Caged Bird Sings* displays a tremendous "lift" and an impulse toward transcendence. And like the song of the caged bird, the autobiography represents a prayer sent from the "heart's deep core," sent from the depth of emotion and feeling. The autobiographer prays that the bird be released from the cage of its oppression to fly free from the definitions and limitations imposed by a hostile world.

Development occurs on multiple levels in *I Know Why the Caged Bird Sings*. As in the autobiographies considered in the previous chapter, a maturation of consciousness parallels geographical movement (South to North and East to West). Sidonie Ann Smith argues that Angelou's narrative strategy in *Caged Bird* "itself is a function of the autobiographer's self-image at the moment of writing, for the nature of that self-image determines the pattern of self-actualization [she] discovers while attempting to shape [her] past experiences. Such a pattern must culminate in some sense of an ending, and it is this sense of an ending that informs certain earlier moments with significance and determines the choice of what [she] recreates, what she discards.... Ultimately, then, the opening material assumes the end, the end the opening movement."[10]

In *Caged Bird*, Maya Angelou does not progress only from a state of semi-orphanhood to one of motherhood; she develops through various stages of self-awareness. At the beginning of the narrative, Angelou depicts her arrival in Stamps, Arkansas, as a "tagged orphan."

> When I was three and Bailey four, we had arrived in a musty little town, wearing tags on our wrists which instructed—"To Whom It May Concern"—that we were Marguerite and Bailey Johnson, Jr., from Long Beach, California, en route to Stamps, Arkansas, c/o Mrs. Annie Henderson. (*Caged Bird*, 3–4)

The autobiographer, receptive rather than active in her early childhood, absorbs the "hometraining" and humble teachings of her grandmother, Annie Henderson, a self-sufficient woman who provides for her two grandchildren and her crippled son, Marguerite's Uncle Willie. "Momma" owns a store that seems to cater to and survive on the support of poor blacks; Mrs. Henderson also owns some of the land rented by the "poor white trash." She is the only colored woman in Stamps whom the whites refer to as "Mrs."—a clear mark of respect. Throughout the autobiography, her mother and grandmother play an important role, both as protective and nurturing figures, and as models for Marguerite, who, at the end of the narrative, has become a mother herself and assumed a positive, if still somewhat problematic, identity.

For critic Myra K. McMurry, *Caged Bird* is "an affirmation ... Maya Angelou's answer to the question of how a Black girl can grow up in a repressive system without being maimed by it."[11] As in the autobiographies of Era Bell Thompson, Zora Neale Hurston, and Laura Adams, *I Know Why the Caged Bird Sings* reveals the autobiographer's sense of geographic, cultural, and social displacement. "If growing up is painful for the Southern black girl," Angelou writes, "being aware of her displacement is the rust on the razor that threatens the throat. It is an unnecessary insult" (*Caged Bird*, 3). Once again, the quest is not only for survival but also for an authentic, self-defining black female identity, one that evinces care and concern for others. Angelou's treatment of the theme of limitation and restriction resembles Dunbar's treatment in the poem "Sympathy." Like the caged bird, the young Marguerite Johnson feels removed from the larger world. Marguerite is "big, elbowy and grating"; her playmates describe her as being "shit color." Her hair, she thinks, is like "black steel wool" (*Caged Bird*, 17). Still, Angelou finds "hope and a hope of wholeness" in the love and support received from Momma, Bailey, and Uncle Willie. Never considered attractive by the standards of her community, Marguerite develops her intellect:

> During these years in Stamps, I met and fell in love with William Shakespeare. He was my first white love. Although I enjoyed and respected Kipling, Poe, Butler, Thackeray and Henley, I saved my young and loyal passion for Paul Laurence Dunbar, Langston Hughes, James Weldon Johnson and W. E. B. Du Bois' "Litany in Atlanta." But it was Shakespeare who said, "When in disgrace with fortune and men's eyes." It was a state with which I found myself most familiar. (*Caged Bird*, 11)

Later she will become acquainted with Gorky, Dostoyevsky, Turgenev, and other writers who influence her choice of form and style, but during her childhood, Shakespeare and Dunbar speak directly to her dilemma—the problem of developing a positive self-image in a culture whose standards of beauty are uniformly white, and the problem of finding a place for herself in that culture.

The strongest portraits, the strongest images in *Caged Bird*, are the respected figures of Marguerite's mother and grandmother. She celebrates her grandmother's feminine heroism, wisdom, and unselfishness in much the same way that Harriet Brent Jacobs celebrates similar qualities in her own dear grandmother. George Kent argues that "Grandmother's religion gives her the power to order her being, that of the children, and usually the immediate space surrounding her. The spirit of the religion combined with simple, traditional maxims shapes the course of existence and rituals of facing up to something called decency."[12] Mrs. Henderson nurtures Marguerite through her Stamps childhood and beyond, doing what she can to protect her son's young children from frequent intrusions of "white reality." Such painful confrontations can occur at any time, and can be instigated by whites from any age group or social class. Mrs. Henderson is even insulted by the poor white trash children whose parents rent land from *her*. The autobiographer writes of this as "the most painful experience I ever had with my grandmother":

> For an awful second I thought they were going to throw a rock at Momma, who seemed (except for the apron strings) to have turned into stone herself. But the big girl turned her back, bent down and put her hands flat on the ground—she didn't pick up anything. She simply shifted her weight and did a hand stand.
>
> Her dirty bare feet and long legs went straight for the sky. Her dress fell down around her shoulders, and she had on no drawers. The slick pubic hair made a brown triangle where her legs came together. She hung in the vacuum of that lifeless morning for only a few seconds, then wavered and tumbled. The other girls clapped her on the back and slapped their hands.
>
> Momma changed her song to "Bread of Heaven, feed me till I want no more."
>
> I found that I was praying too. (*Caged Bird*, 25–26)

Through this depiction of her experience, Maya Angelou praises her grandmother's courage. It is from her grandmother and from people who raise and nurture her that Maya learns to use and develop this courage, which she views as the most important virtue of all. "Without courage," she had said, "you cannot practice any other virtue with consistency" (*ODU*).

There were ample opportunities for the development of courage in Maya Angelou's young life, and the fine edge of this virtue was honed in facing the commonplace dangers of life in Stamps, such as lynching. Lynching constituted a real danger and hence a legitimate fear in the minds of Arkansas blacks. The terror of lynching persists as a theme throughout the sections of the autobiography set in Arkansas. Early in the narrative, we are told how Mrs. Henderson hid a would-be lynch victim and provided him with supplies for a journey, even though she jeopardized her own security to do so. On another occasion, it is necessary to conceal Uncle Willie one night after an unknown black man is accused of "messing with" a white woman. Angelou forcefully conveys the emotional and psychological impact of the threat of lynching as she experienced it:

> Even after the slow drag of years, I remember the sense of fear which filled my mouth with hot, dry air, and made my body light.... We were told to take the potatoes and onions out of their bins and knock out the dividing walls that kept them apart. Then with a tedious and fearful slowness Uncle Willie gave me his rubber-tipped cane and bent down to get into the now enlarged empty bin. It took forever before he lay down flat, and then we covered him with potatoes and onions, layer upon layer, like a casserole. Grandmother knelt praying in the darkened store. (*Caged Bird*, 14–15)

Like Aunt Marthy in *Incidents in the Life of a Slave Girl*, Mrs. Henderson, "Momma," fulfills the archetypal role of the outraged mother by concealing her innocent child. Angelou succeeds in communicating a sense of the frustration and humiliation her family feels in these encounters. Without polemics, she shows the absurdity of lynching: Why should a crippled old man be forced to spend the night in a bin full of potatoes and onions in fear of his life because some unnamed black man has been accused of an unnamed crime?

Unlike Ida B. Wells, Maya Angelou speaks about lynching from a personal point of view, articulating her experience and her pain. On one occasion, Momma, Marguerite, and Uncle Willie wait for Bailey, who is late returning from the theater in town. Momma's apprehension, Angelou writes, "was evident in the hurried movements around the kitchen and in her lonely fearing eyes" (*Caged Bird*, 95). Later in the narrative (after the return from St. Louis and just before the permanent move to California), Bailey sees the body of a lynch victim whose "things had been cut off and put in his pocket and had been shot in the head, all because whitefolks said he 'did it' to a white woman" (*Caged Bird*, 30). These are harsh experiences for young children to endure, but Bailey and Marguerite survive, due in no small measure to the protection and sense of security they receive from their grandmother. Through Momma, Marguerite absorbs values and concepts that make it possible to maintain and replenish a sense of self-worth. Through Momma, Marguerite learns to pray.

An important theme throughout the autobiography, religion represents a sustaining force in the life of Mrs. Henderson, who derives spiritual sustenance and fortitude from the "Bread of Heaven." When threatened, Momma turns to her faith, which is clearly a source of her personal power. The early religious experiences of Maya Angelou resemble those of Zora Neale Hurston more nearly than those of any other autobiographer studied here; like Era Bell Thompson and Laura Adams, Maya Angelou displays the old "church of emotion," but unlike them, she is no stranger to it. Mrs. Henderson, a respected church elder, requires that Bailey and Marguerite participate fully in church activities and in the religious life of the community. Angelou's regard for black spirituality and black religion does not exempt the church from criticism. Like Wright, she finds comedy in the Sunday performances of "sisters" possessed by the spirit, and she ridicules the greedy minister when he eats more than his fair share of the fried chicken at Sunday dinner. But unlike Wright, she evokes this ridicule and paints this portrait without condescension—still recognizing the solvency of the basic spiritual trust.

Respecting her grandmother's homespun teaching, Maya became a part of the fabric of her culture, absorbing both literary and folk influences through observation, study, and loving imitation. Of the sermons and the spirituals, Angelou has said, "they run through my veins like blood." From her point of view, literature includes written as well as oral tradition, and she sees the spirituals as American classics; "to deny it [the spirituals as unwritten literature] is to spit upon your grandfather's grave. Like all art, it belongs to everyone who appreciates it" (*ODU*). *Caged Bird* shows the influence of myriad folk forms, including the sermon, the ghost story, the preacher tale, the tale of exaggeration, a children's rhyme, and secular and religious songs. The use of these oral forms, together with folk language, contributes to the unique tone, texture, and style of the autobiography. Their presence also helps identify the autobiographer in a relationship with her community and culture.

In *Caged Bird*, as in *American Daughter* and *Dust Tracks*, closeness to the land and continual involvement with nature are essential to the mood and imagery of the autobiography. Marguerite notes the passage of time by watching "the field across from the Store turn caterpillar green, then gradually frosty white. She knew exactly how long it would be before the big wagons would pull into the front yard and load on the cotton pickers at daybreak to carry them to the remains of slavery's plantations" (*Caged Bird*, 5). This mood is enhanced by the use of portraiture, rhythmic language, and the careful depiction of lyrically suspended moments of consciousness.

> In the dying sunlight the people dragged rather than their empty sacks....The sounds of the new morning had been replaced with grumbles about cheating houses, weighted scales and dusty rows....In cotton-picking time, the late

> afternoons revealed the harshness of Black Southern life,
> which in the early morning had been softened by nature's
> blessing of grogginess, forgetfulness and the soft lamplight.
> (*Caged Bird*, 7)

The entire "black community of Stamps," Sidonie Smith
argues, is itself caged in the "social reality of racial subordination and impotence." Marguerite's "personal displacement is counterpointed by the ambiance of displacement
within the larger black community."[13]

Because she works in her grandmother's store, Marguerite
has no direct experience of the intense labor of picking cotton,
but she observes the workers as they go out into the fields and
return. She has "seen the fingers cut by the mean little cotton
bolls" and "witnessed the backs and arms and legs resisting
any further demands" (*Caged Bird*, 7).

The use of portraiture and the feeling of being close to
nature and the land contribute to the lyric sensibility of *Caged
Bird*, but unlike the earlier autobiographies by Thompson
and Hurston, *Caged Bird* admits harsh and painful aspects of
the southern black experience before the civil rights era—the
economic oppression and racial violence that Thompson and
Hurston either knew little about or chose to ignore. This
awareness lends Angelou's lyric imagery the knife-sharp edge
of realism, something contributed to black female autobiographical tradition through the Richard Wright school of the
1940s and 1950s. Thematic and structural similarities between
the autobiographies of Wright and Angelou result from their
common descent from the slave narrative and from the
influence of Russian writers, which both read. Another common denominator between Wright and Angelou concerns
their view of the "Great Migration," of which both were a
part. They depict themselves as participants in a vast historical drama—the movement of rural blacks from the Deep
South to the urban centers of the North, hoping to improve
their economic and social horizons by escaping the racism
and exploitation of the South. Although Wright's tone seems
more political than Angelou's, they respond to the same
historic moment.

Afro-Americans who participated in the Great Migration can be compared with Europeans who emigrated to America only to find "identity problems in their mental baggage." As Erik Erikson has observed of the European-American group, "Emigration can be a hard and heartless matter, in terms of what is abandoned in the old country and what is usurped in the new one. Migration means cruel survival in identity terms, too, for the very cataclysms in which millions perish open up new forms of identity to the survivors."[14] From her autobiography and her life work, Angelou has emerged as a survivor, a "whole" person, with her identity, her sense of humor, her dignity, and her style intact.

One of the important early turning points in the autobiography centers on Marguerite's move to St. Louis. Initially more of a change in geographic location than the beginning of a change of consciousness, the move precipitates profound problems of identity. After four years of living happily with Momma and Uncle Willie in Stamps, Marguerite and Bailey become aware of the impending move during Christmas. Having received presents from their mother and father, they conclude that their parents are about to come and get them. This occurrence raises strong emotions in the two young children, who have come to regard Stamps as their home:

> The gifts opened the door to questions neither of us wanted to ask. Why did they send us away? And what did we do so wrong? So Wrong? Why, at three and four, would we have tags put on our arms to be sent alone from Long Beach, California, to Stamps, Arkansas, with only the porter to look after us? (Besides, he got off in Arizona.) (*Caged Bird*, 43)

A year later, Bailey, Sr., arrives in Stamps without warning. And in a relatively short time the children are on their way west, headed for California or so they think. En route, their father tells them that they are actually going to St. Louis to visit their mother. In Pig Latin, Marguerite asks Bailey, Jr., "Ooday ooyay inkthay isthay is our atherfay, or ooday ooyay inkthay atthay eeway eeingbay idkay appednay?" Her father chuckles and responds, "Oohay oodway antway ootway idkay appnay ooyay? Ooday ooyay inkthay ooyay are indlay ergbay ildrenchay?" Angelou writes that hearing her father speak Pig Latin "didn't startle me so much as it angered. It was simply another case of the trickiness of adults where children were concerned. Another case in point of the Grownups' Betrayal" (*Caged Bird*, 49).

For the young Marguerite Johnson, fresh from Stamps, Arkansas, "St. Louis was a foreign country." "In my mind," writes Angelou, "I only stayed in St. Louis a few weeks" (*Caged Bird*, 58). In St. Louis, Marguerite endures the most shattering experience of her childhood when she is raped by her mother's boyfriend, Mr. Freeman. The experience is a brutal one and necessitates the child's hospitalization:

> Then there was the pain. A breaking and entering when even the senses are torn apart. The act of rape on an eight-year-old is a matter of the needle giving because the camel can't. The child gives, because the body can, and the mind of the violator cannot.
> I thought I had died. (*Caged Bird*, 65)

She feels physical and psychological pain as a result of the rape and guilt from exposing Freeman, who meets a violent death at the hands of "persons unknown," but presumably Marguerite's tough St. Louis uncles (*Caged Bird*, 71–72). The rape precipitates a period of intense identity crisis for Marguerite, who, after Freeman's death, stops speaking to everyone but her brother, Bailey: "Instinctively, or somehow, I knew that because I loved him so much I'd never hurt him, but if I talked to anyone else that person might die too" (*Caged Bird*, 73). As a result of Freeman's death, Marguerite becomes a voluntary mute. Although this temporary solution suits Marguerite, her St. Louis family grows weary of her muteness, which they interpret as insolent sullenness: "For a while I was punished for being so uppity that I wouldn't speak; and then came the thrashings by any relative who felt himself offended" (*Caged Bird*, 73). Marguerite loses much of her innocence during this "perilous passage," which cuts her childhood painfully short. She feels betrayed by adults in general, and she withdraws from their way of life into a world of silence. Although Marguerite longs to be free from her guilt, sadness, and the feeling that she is different from others, she cannot extricate herself from the burdens inflicted by her environment.

Soon Marguerite and Bailey find themselves on the train going back to Stamps, which provides the obscurity the eight-year-old craves "without will or consciousness." Not knowing the exact origin of Marguerite's unwillingness to talk, the blacks of Stamps sympathize with her, as she was known for being "tender-hearted." "Southern Negroes used that term to mean sensitive and tended to look upon a person with that affliction as being a little sick or in delicate health. So I was not so much forgiven as I was understood" (*Caged Bird*, 77). And because the sickness is acknowledged, the healing can begin. Marguerite Johnson returns to Stamps (the source of her strength) to begin rebuilding the identity shattered by her enforced migration and subsequent rape.

After a year of voluntary muteness, Marguerite "met, or rather got to know" Bertha Flowers, "the aristocrat of Black Stamps." This represents another important turning point in the development of the autobiographer's consciousness. Angelou writes of Flowers as "the lady who threw my first life line," and the portrait she paints shows her high regard for the woman (*Caged Bird*, 77).

> She had the grace of control to appear warm in the coldest weather, and on the Arkansas summer days it seemed she had a private breeze which swirled around. Her skin was rich black that would have peeled like a plum if snagged, but no one would have thought of getting close enough to Mrs. Flowers to ruffle her dress, let alone snag her skin. She didn't encourage familiarity. She wore gloves too.
>
> The action was so graceful and inclusively benign. (*Caged Bird*, 77–78)

From Flowers, Marguerite receives her "lessons in living."

> She said that I must always be intolerant of ignorance but understanding of illiteracy. That some people, unable to go to

school, were more educated and even more intelligent than college professors. She encouraged me to listen carefully to what country people called motherwit. That in those homely sayings was couched the collective wisdom of generations. (*Caged Bird*, 83)

The value of Flowers's benign maternal influence should not be underestimated. Her model of black gentility takes root in the young girl's consciousness, and she remains for the mature narrator "the measure of what a human being can be" (*Caged Bird*, 78). Flowers makes tea cookies for Marguerite, reads aloud to her from *A Tale of Two Cities*, and teaches her to recite poetry. Flowers fulfills the role of teacher and healer, providing the traumatized youngster with a process through which to tap internal creative resources for self-healing: These "lessons in living" constitute part of the extensive preparation Marguerite receives for life as a mature black woman. Marguerite needs the values and beliefs these "lessons" contain in order to anchor her identity. The knowledge and wisdom passed down through generations supplement what she reads in books. She *needs* the strength that this knowledge imparts, and from this knowledge she gains power.

The patterns established in *Caged Bird* continue in Angelou's subsequent autobiographies, *Gather Together in My Name* (1974), *Singin' and Swingin' and Gettin' Merry Like Christmas* (1976), *The Heart of a Woman* (1980), and *All God's Children Need Traveling Shoes* (1986). The narrator adapts to her situation creatively, replenishing her sense of self in difficult circumstances, discovering her sexuality, and learning to play the role of nurturer–protector. Because of the loving protection, encouragement, and direction provided to Marguerite by her mother, her grandmother, and Flowers, she is better able to survive later confrontations with white society.

A specific encounter with racial violence motivates Momma to send her grandchildren to California. When whites force Marguerite's brother to help recover the sexually mutilated body of a lynching victim accused of "messing with" a white woman, Bailey begins to ask disturbing questions that his grandmother and uncle are not prepared to answer:

> His experience raised the question of worth and values, of aggressive inferiority and aggressive arrogance. Could Uncle Willie, a Black man, Southern, crippled moreover, hope to answer the questions, both asked and unuttered? Would Momma, who knew the ways of the whites and wiles of the Blacks, try to answer her grandson, whose very life depended on his not truly understanding the enigma? Most assuredly not. (*Caged Bird*, 168)

The enigma, of course, is the dialectical relationship between white hatred and black fear, which governed racial relationships in Stamps. Mrs. Henderson tried to protect Bailey and Marguerite by limiting their knowledge and by forbidding their discussion of certain topics (including "white people" and "doing it"), but the effectiveness of this method waned as her grandchildren approached young adulthood (*Caged Bird*, 30). Eventually, the two would unravel the enigma for themselves, based on observation and evidence.

Recognizing her inability to shelter her adolescent grandson and protect him from the routine racial violence that befell blacks in Stamps, Arkansas, Mrs. Henderson prays and begins making plans to relocate the children with their parents in California. Looking back on this experience in *Gather Together in My Name,* the autobiographer allows her grandmother to express a point of view she withholds in *I Know Why the Caged Bird Sings*. She says, "I never did want you children to go to California. Too fast that life up yonder. But then, you all's their children, and I didn't want nothing to happen to you, while you're in my care. Jew was getting a little too big for his britches." Mrs. Henderson views California as a land of opportunity for Bailey and Marguerite, "a place where lynchings were unheard of and a bright young Negro boy could go places. And even his sister might find a niche for herself."[15]

Maya Angelou's celebration of self derives essentially from her celebration of the black women who nurtured her. She reveres not only the qualities of the individual women but also the tradition in which they participated and the way in which they prepared her, as best they could, to cope with the realities of being black and female. In *I Know Why the Caged Bird Sings*, Momma conforms to the Jungian archetype of the Great Mother, protecting, nurturing, sheltering; Marguerite's own mother, Vivian Baxter, presents another representation of this same archetype. In "the transition from mother to grandmother," Jung wrote, "the archetype is elevated to higher rank."[16] So it is with Marguerite's transition from childhood to motherhood; she is both initiated and reborn, becoming herself the carrier of the archetype.

In California, Marguerite comes under the primary care of her mother, a woman of great personal power, resourcefulness, and hypnotic beauty. "To describe my mother," writes Angelou, "would be to write about a hurricane in its perfect power. Or the climbing, falling colors of the rainbow. People she accepted paddled their own canoes, pulled their own weight, put their own shoulders to their own plows, and pushed like hell" (*Caged Bird*, 49). From her mother, Marguerite learns increased self-reliance; she grows out of the passive stage and begins to think for herself, asserting herself through action, and forging an identity and testing the perimeters of her cage through brief encounters with exploratory flight.

The motif of flight captures the spirit of Marguerite's adventurous attempts to transcend the limitations and restrictions imposed on her. Caught between her father's indifference and his jealous girlfriend when she goes to visit them in Southern California one summer, Marguerite runs away and lives for about a month in an abandoned junkyard with a financially independent and racially mixed group of youthful runaways. This experience has a positive effect in Marguerite's identity-building process:

> The unquestioning acceptance by my peers had dislodged the familiar insecurity. Odd that homeless children, the silt of war frenzy, could initiate me into the [brotherhood of man]. After hunting down unbroken bottles and selling them with a white

girl from Missouri, a Mexican girl from Los Angeles, and a Black girl from Oklahoma, I was never again to sense myself so solidly outside the human race. (*Caged Bird*, 216)

Another positive identity-building experience occurs in the world of work. Marguerite is determined to become a "conductorette" on the San Francisco streetcars, even though no blacks have been hired previously. She visits the Market Street Railway Office with "the frequency of a person on salary" until she is hired, breaking the color barrier previously imposed against blacks and achieving a degree of independence (*Caged Bird*, 228).

The most significant area of challenge facing Marguerite is also the most intimate—that of self-image and sexuality. Considered less than attractive and not very well developed physically, Marguerite begins to harbor fears of being a lesbian after reading Radclyffe Hall's *Well of Loneliness*. Her heavy voice, large hands and feet, undeveloped breasts, and smooth armpits all seem clear indicators. A talk with her mother does nothing to alleviate her fear. Ironically, this irrational fear of lesbianism leads to Marguerite's pregnancy. What she needs, she decides, is "a boyfriend. A boyfriend would clarify my position to the world and, even more important, to myself. A boyfriend's acceptance would guide me into that strange and exotic land of frills and femininity." But in her social group, there are "no takers": "The boys of my age and social group were captivated by the yellow- or light-brown-skinned girls, with hairy legs and smooth little lips, whose hair 'hung down like horses' manes.' And even those sought-after girls were asked to 'give it up or tell where it is' " (*Caged Bird*, 238). Women deemed unattractive, Angelou writes, are "called upon to be generous" only if pretty girls are unavailable. Aware of this fact, Marguerite, like "Linda" in the Harriet Brent Jacobs narrative, plans the seduction of a handsome young man who lives in her neighborhood. Finding herself pregnant after the act (her first truly voluntary encounter with sex), she suffers feelings of "fear, guilt, self-revulsion" (*Caged Bird*, 241). She successfully conceals her pregnancy from her family for over eight months, managing to finish high school before revealing her secret to her mother.

The narrative itself ends, not with the birth of Guy, but with a poignant lesson taught by Marguerite's own mother. Though Marguerite could create a baby, she was herself still dependent on the protection and guidance of her mother. She lacked confidence in handling her child, her "total possession." "Mother handled him easily with the casual confidence of a baby nurse, but I dreaded being forced to change his diapers. Wasn't I famous for my awkwardness? Suppose I let him slip, or put my fingers on that throbbing pulse on top of his head?" (*Caged Bird*, 245).

One night, Marguerite's mother brings the three-week-old baby in to sleep with Marguerite, who protests vigorously, fearing that she will be "sure to roll over and crush out his life or break those fragile bones" (*Caged Bird*, 245). But her mother is insistent. In the night, she awakes to her mother's brisk but whispered command, ordering her to wake up but not to move. When she wakes up, she sees the infant sleeping peacefully by her side. "See," says her mother, "you don't have to think about doing the right thing. If you're for the right thing, then you do it without thinking" (*Caged Bird*, 246). Liliane Arensberg suggests that "Vivian Baxter, as a confident and compassionate mother lovingly bending over her daughter's bed...consummates Maya's growing sense of herself as an adult, life-giving woman."[17]

As George Kent argues, *Caged Bird* "makes its public and political statements largely through generalizing statements which broaden individual characters into types: Grandmother Bailey into the Southern mother; Maya into the young black woman, etc."[18]

Through her depiction of this nocturnal scene, Maya Angelou asserts her identity as both mother and daughter, as well as her relation to the maternal archetype. Her own mother, Vivian, still in the role of teacher–protector, is "elevated to a higher rank," becoming herself the grandmother or "Great Mother."[19] Momma, of course, is elevated still higher. So having a baby was "the right thing to do" in that it opened new avenues of identity, not only for Marguerite, but for her mother and grandmother as well. Even though she was a young woman of only seventeen years who could not recognize the maternal instincts and imperatives that operated within her consciousness, she did, in fact, possess the necessary resources to raise and nurture her son. Through motherhood, she discovered new possibilities in her relationship with her mother and grandmother. In the words of Sidonie Smith, Marguerite "has succeeded in freeing herself from the natural and social bars imprisoning her in the cage of her own diminished self-image by assuming control of her life and fully accepting her black womanhood."[20] And like her archetypal models, she would support her own child with ingenuity and inventiveness.

Maya Angelou has said that she is one of "a generation of women writers, writing in desperation to identify themselves and their times, to provide encouragement and direction" and to have a say in the definition of "what's really happening" (*ODU*). For her, the writing of autobiography is a conscious assertion of identity, as well as the presentation of an alternate version of reality seen from the point of view of the black female experience. Near the end of *I Know Why the Caged Bird Sings*, Angelou summarizes that point of view:

> The Black female is assaulted in her tender years by all those common forces of nature at the same time that she is caught in the tri-partite crossfire of masculine prejudice, white illogical hate and Black lack of power.
>
> The fact that the adult American Negro female emerges a formidable character is often met with amazement, distaste, and even belligerence. It is seldom accepted as an inevitable outcome of the struggle won by survivors and deserves respect if not enthusiastic acceptance. (*Caged Bird*, 231)

Like Era Bell Thompson, Maya Angelou speaks with the triple consciousness of the *American Daughter*. And she speaks, as do many other black autobiographers, both male and female, as a survivor. She knows why she has survived and what the source of her strength has been. She has chosen to honor that source even as she celebrates the emergence of her indeed "formidable character."

A Circle
Closing and Expanding

Our knowledge of the literary traditions of
black American women has been, historically
speaking, so limited that a study of this nature is doomed to raise more questions than
it can answer. Yet these texts themselves are
partially the answer to Alice Walker's question, "How was the creativity of the black
woman kept alive, year after year and century after century?" Think how little we
know of Mary and Nancy Prince, of Jarena
Lee, Rebecca Jackson, and even Charlotte
Forten, whose work has yet to receive the
critical attention that it merits. And what of
the lost work? How many literary parallels
to our great singers, Bessie Smith, Billie
Holiday, Roberta Flack, Ethel Waters, and
Leontyne Price, lived and died in obscurity?
They too "might have been Poets, Novelists,
Essayists and Short-Story Writers (over a
period of centuries)."[1] Their agony is our
agony.

In the same way, we should consider the
strengths of our sisterhood and the existing
texts that easily might have been lost:

Harriet Jacobs's *Incidents in the Life of a Slave Girl: Written by Herself* might never have been published without the patient efforts of Lydia Maria Child; Charlotte Forten Grimké's diaries were published in great part through the efforts of her sister–friend, Dr. Anna Julia Cooper; and Wells's *Crusade for Justice* was published only after her daughter's perseverance of thirty-five years. So the texts that come down to us are largely the products of cooperation and/or collaboration. Indeed, the times have changed; if Maya Angelou (née Marguerite Johnson) had lived and written *I Know Why the Caged Bird Sings* a hundred years earlier, it, too, might have been published pseudonymously with the help of a white editor, or, as is more likely, it might not have been published at all. It might have been one of those great silent spaces that remain, as yet, unpenetrated. Thus collectivity, cooperation, collaboration, and celebration become the watchwords of a tradition that is still defining itself, a tradition that by its very existence questions the notions of genre and canon.

Like most Americanists, critics of black autobiography have tended to settle on what Phyllis Cole and Deborah Lambert see as "a single myth, that of the solitary but representative male figure on the physical or metaphysical frontier of the new world."[2] What this study proves, I think, is that there is no single myth, no single representative hero. Where we once saw a single "mainstream," we now see many. Exploring the "history, styles, themes, genres and structures" of the autobiographical tradition of black American women, the preceding chapters constitute what Elaine Showalter might call an effort in "gynocriticism."[3] Such gynocritical perspective offers the possibility of a more inclusive vision of black autobiography, a vision in which the outraged mother stands beside the articulate hero, speaking out in her own unmistakable voice. It also offers us a view of one of the major sources of contemporary black women's fiction, for today's black women writers revise and recast the same archetypal imagery found in the earliest of black women's autobiographical writings.

Nineteenth-century narratives of isolation and transcendence, and narratives of vision and power, forecast later developments in the tradition. Many of these narratives seem to moderate between the public and the private voice, and between a tone of conciliation and one of confrontation; they are often fraught with gaps in content or chronology and shifting patterns of narrative movement. Almost inevitably, black women autobiographers speak of a perilously intensified adolescence, accompanied by a perception of gender as well as racial difference. The acquisition of the early "womanist"consciousness constitutes an important stage of psychosocial development in the autobiographer's self-awareness and in the formation of her black and female identity, as well as her public voice.[4]

Unlike the "solitary but representative male hero" who rebels with his fists and his feet, the black woman autobiographer uses language—sass, invective, impertinence, and ritual invocation—to defend herself physically and psychologically. As often as not, she celebrates a collective rather than an individual achievement. In *Incidents in the Life of a Slave Girl* Harriet Jacobs celebrates her grandmother's courage and ingenuity and the cooperation of family and friends, both black and white, as she attains her freedom through their collective effort. Not only does *Incidents* represent a cry of outrage against the cruelty and brutality of slavery and the sexual oppression of slave women, it also represents a celebration of community and the bonds of sisterhood that can only be forged in struggle against a common oppressor. This text establishes many of the motifs, images, archetypes, uses of language, and patterns of narrative movement that recur in later autobiography and fiction, for example, in Ida B. Wells's *Crusade for Justice*, Toni Morrison's *Beloved*, and Shirley Anne Williams's *Dessa Rose*.

If the outraged mother emerges in the early narratives and autobiographies by black American women, then so does her counterpart, the visionary. This "Sainted" foremother reappears in mature form in the autobiographies of Zora Neale Hurston and Era Bell Thompson, who react to the outraged mother even as they turn away from the archetypal figure of nurturance and sacrifice to seek self-fulfillment; they return to a childhood perception of unity with nature as one source of inner wholeness. This goal of creative self-integration is realized in the work of Maya Angelou, who closes the circle of tradition when she achieves fulfillment as both a mother and an

artist, even while she celebrates her mother
and her grandmother as carriers of the
maternal archetype and as personal sources
of renewal and revitalization. Angelou's
volumes are testaments to the vitality of
autobiographical writing by black American
women. Another such testament is the
posthumously published autobiography of
the Reverend Dr. Pauli Murray, *Song in a
Weary Throat* (1987), which reflects the
images of both the outraged mother and the
visionary; for although she was never a
mother, Murray's righteous outrage is
representative. Her vision, unlike that of
many of her antecedents, is a vision not of
an individual, but of a collective wholeness
where the words "liberty and justice for all"
are more than mere litany; this is the song
in her weary throat. Although her throat got
weary, she never stopped singing. In the
course of her remarkable life, she kept the
vision and the song in front of her and she
kept on moving. The autobiographies and
memoirs of Lucille Clifton, Gwendolyn
Brooks, Angela Davis, and Marita Golden
continue such testaments. Every individual
work has to end somewhere; had I chosen to
extend this one past *I Know Why the Caged
Bird Sings* (1969), I would have investigated
the subgenres of the political memoir as
represented by *Angela Davis: An Autobiography* (1984) and the back-to-Africa memoir,
as represented by Marita Golden's *Migrations
of the Heart* (1984) and Maya Angelou's *All
God's Children Need Traveling Shoes* (1986).
Nikki Giovanni's *Gemini* (1971) and
Gwendolyn Brooks's *Report from Part One*
(1972) might have represented the autobio-

graphical works of prominent literary
figures published during the height of the
Black Arts movement. But I have chosen to
close this study with *I Know Why the Caged
Bird Sings* because it marks the coming of
age, if not the full flowering, of a long
continuum of black women's autobiography.

The tradition exists because of the
commonality of the black woman's experience, because of what Maya Angelou has
called the "tri-partite crossfire of masculine
prejudice, white illogical hate and Black
lack of power," and because of the uniquely
Afra-American culture and consciousness
that emerge from this experience. After all,
autobiography, perhaps more than any other
literary genre, is a form of symbolic memory,
a confluence of culture and consciousness.
And so there is no single Afra-American
experience, nothing static. This stream of
culture is an expanding one; still, it flows
back on itself, borrowing from the archetypal
imagery, the patterns of narrative and
geographic movements, and the uses of
language from the past. Within the tradition
of black women writing autobiography,
many streams converge, improvising,
dancing and playing, together and with the
rivers from which they emerge.

Notes, References, and Index

Notes

A Tradition Within a Tradition

1. Portions of this introduction appeared in my "Harriet Jacobs' *Incidents in the Life of a Slave Girl:* The Redefinition of the Slave Narrative Genre," *Massachusetts Review* 27 (1986): 379–387, where I argue that the "study of black women's writing helps us to transform definitions of genre, of archetype, of narrative traditions, and of the African-American experience itself." I use the term *Afra-American* (as an adjective) to designate the distinctively feminine aspects of black American literature and culture; the term is, by definition, feminist, or to use the word coined by Alice Walker, "womanist," in that it places the experience of black women at the center and speaks from that perspective. Neither race nor gender is privileged; a united and integrated view is expressed. The speaker is neither a black who happens to be a woman nor a woman who happens to be black, but is an individual whose perspective encompasses the multiple elements of a complex identity. See also James Olney, "Autobiography and the Cultural Moment," *Autobiography: Essays Theoretical and Critical* (Princeton: Princeton University Press, 1980), 26.

2. A woman called "Belinda" dictated "The Cruelty of Men Whose Faces Were Like the Moon: The Petition of an African Slave to the Legislature of Massachusetts." The title of the text suggests an awareness of racial and sexual oppression that is both race and sex specific. Belinda speaks to the cruelty of white men, whose moonlike faces symbolize strangeness, spiritual barrenness, and death. See "Belinda, or the Cruelty of Men Whose Faces Were Like the Moon" in *American Museum and Repository of Ancient and Modern Fugitive Pieces, Prose and Poetical*, vol. 1 (June 1787).

211

3. Ibid.

4. Alice Walker, *In Search of Our Mothers' Gardens* (New York: Harcourt Brace Jovanovich, 1983), 234.

5. Emma Margaret Harrison, quoted in Joanne M. Braxton, "Black Grandmothers: Sources of Artistic Consciousness and Personal Strength," Wellesley College Center for Research on Women Working Papers Series, Working Paper 172, 1985, 9–10.

6. Henry Louis Gates, Jr., Foreword to "In Her Own Write," *Schomburg Library of Nineteenth-Century Black Women Writers* (New York: Oxford University Press, 1988), xviii.

7. Temma Kaplan, Introduction, *Barnard Occasional Papers on Women's Issues* 3, no. 2 (1988): 2–3.

8. Toni Morrison, "Rootedness: The Ancestor as Foundation," in *Black Women Writers*, 1950–1980, ed. Mari Evans (New York: Doubleday, 1983), 342.

9. Stephen Butterfield, *Black Autobiography in America* (Amherst: University of Massachusetts Press, 1974), 49.

10. See Sidonie Smith, *Where I'm Bound: Patterns of Slavery and Freedom in Black American Autobiography* (Westport, Conn.: Greenwood Press, 1974), 121–126.

11. James Olney, ed., *Autobiography: Essays Theoretical and Critical* (Princeton: Princeton University Press, 1980), 15–16.

12. Lillian S. Robinson, *Sex, Class, and Culture* (Bloomington: University of Indiana Press, 1978), 37.

13. Annette Kolodny, "Some Notes on Defining a 'Feminist Literary Criticism,' " *Critical Inquiry* 2 (1975): 75.

14. Estelle C. Jelinek, ed., Introduction, *Women's Autobiography* (Bloomington: University of Indiana Press, 1980), xii.

15. William Andrews, *To Tell a Free Story: The First Century of Afro-American Autobiography, 1760–1865* (Urbana: University of Illinois Press, 1986).

16. Albert E. Stone, *Autobiographical Occasions and Original Acts* (Philadelphia: University of Pennsylvania Press, 1982), 24.

17. Ibid.

18. William Andrews, *Sisters of the Spirit: Three Black Women's Autobiographies of the Nineteenth Century* (Bloomington: Indiana University Press, 1986).

Part I: Making a Way Out of No Way

1. William Andrews, *To Tell a Free Story: The First Century of Afro-American Autobiography, 1760–1865* (Urbana: University of Illinois Press, 1986).

2. For a discussion of black women's spirituality, see Nancy Faires Conklin, Brenda McCallum, and Marcia Wade, *The Culture of Southern Black Women* (University: University of Alabama Archive of American Minority Cultures and Women's Studies Program, 1983), 78–87.

Chapter 1: Outraged Mother and Articulate Heroine

1. An earlier version of this chapter appeared as "Harriet 'Linda Brent' Jacobs' *Incidents in the Life of a Slave Girl*: The Redefinition of the Slave Narrative Genre," *Massachusetts Review* 27 (1986): 379–387.

2. Hazel V. Carby, *Reconstructing Womanhood: The Emergence of the Black Woman Novelist* (New York: Oxford University Press, 1987), 45–46. Carby discusses John Blassingame's idea of "representativeness" in the slave narrative genre, especially with regard to Jacobs's *Incidents in the Life of a Slave Girl*. See also John Blassingame, *The Slave Community: Plantation Life in the Antebellum South*, 2d ed. (New York: Oxford University Press, 1979), 367–382.

3. Frances Foster suggests that "narratives by slave women present a significantly different perception of slave women [from that presented by slave men]. It is this discrepancy," Foster comments, "which has not been duly noted, and it is this neglect of slave women's versions of their lives that is a basic reason for the perpetuation of the current and inadequate images of women slaves." Foster goes on to say that "there is no reason to believe that male narrators deliberately set out to demean or misrepresent slave women. Both social attitudes toward women and literary conventions made the distortion of slave women probable in narratives that featured male protagonists." See Frances Foster, " 'In Respect to Females...': Differences in the Portrayals of Women by Male and Female Narrators," *Black American Literature Forum* 15 (1981): 66. See also Carby, *Reconstructing Womanhood*, 47–51.

4. See Robert Stepto, "Narration, Authentication and Authorial Control in Frederick Douglass' *Narrative* of 1845," in *Afro-American Literature: The Reconstruction of Instruction*, ed. Dexter Fisher and

Robert Stepto (New York: Modern Language Association, 1979). Stepto defines the heroic archetype of the slave narrative primarily in masculine terms. See also Robert Stepto, *From Behind the Veil: A Study of Afro-American Narrative* (Urbana: University of Illinois Press, 1979).

5. See Carby, *Reconstructing Womanhood*, 35–36 for a discussion of the portrayal of black women in slave narratives by men. See also Braxton, "Black Grandmothers," 387.

6. Valerie Smith, Introduction to *Incidents in the Life of a Slave Girl: Written by Herself*, by Harriet A. Jacobs (New York: Oxford University Press, 1988), xxviii.

7. Harriet A. Jacobs, *Incidents in the Life of a Slave Girl: Written by Herself*, edited with an introduction by Jean Fagan Yellin (Cambridge: Harvard University Press, 1987), 49. Hereafter cited in the text as *Incidents*, followed by page number. The original (1861) Thayer and Eldridge edition has been consulted; however, all subsequent citations refer to the Harvard edition, which is more accessible. Contemporary readers will also appreciate the authenticating documents Yellin includes in her edition of this text.

8. Frederick Douglass, *Narrative of Frederick Douglass: An American Slave Written by Himself* (New York: Signet, 1986; originally published 1845), 65. All subsequent references to Douglass's *Narrative* refer to this edition and are cited in the text as *Narrative*, followed by page number.

9. William Wells Brown, *Narrative of William Wells Brown, A Fugitive Slave, Written by Himself* (1847). Reprinted in Gilbert Osofsky, ed., *Puttin' On Ole Massa* (New York: Harper & Row, 1969).

10. See Mary Prince, *The History of Mary Prince, a West Indian Slave, Related by Herself with a Supplement by the Editor, to Which Is Added the Narrative of Asa-Asa, a Captured African* (London: F. Westley and A. H. Davis, 1831).

11. See Marion Starling, "The Slave Narrative: Its Place in American Literary History," doctoral dissertation, New York University, 1946; microfilm, University Microfilms International, Ann Arbor, 1977. Also see Arna Bontemps, "The Slave Narrative: An American Genre," *Great Slave Narratives* (Boston: Beacon Press, 1969), xiii; and Jean Fagan Yellin, "Written by Herself: Harriet Jacobs' Slave Narrative," *American Literature* 53 (1981): 480–486. Yellin's edition of *Incidents* authenticates both Jacobs's authorship and the historical identities of principal characters of the text including Jacobs's first mistress (Margaret Horniblow), her grandmother (Molly Horniblow), "Dr. Flint" (Dr. James Norcom), "Mr.

Sands" (Samuel Tredwell Sawyer), and her two children, Joseph and Louisa Matilda, who are disguised as Benjamin and Ellen in their mother's autobiography. Real identities of the individuals are noted in parentheses. I recommend the Yellin-edited *Incidents* for teaching purposes because of the excellent documentation Yellin has provided.

12. See Yellin, "Written by Herself," 480–486. The autobiographical apprentice piece, "Letter from a Fugitive Slave," published in the *New York Tribune*, June 21, 1853, treats the subject matter that later becomes *Incidents* in Jacobs's distinctive style. The *Tribune* published Jacobs's second letter July 25, 1853. Jacobs composed her apprentice pieces secretly so as not to attract the attention of her employer, the writer and editor Nathaniel Parker Willis, whose sympathies she considered too "pro-slavery." Jacobs's correspondence with Amy Post verifies her claim to authorship of these letters to the *Tribune*.

13. "Linda; Incidents in the Life of a Slave Girl: Written Herself," *Anti-Slavery Advocate* (London) 2, no. 53 (May 1, 1861): 1.

14. Carby, *Reconstructing Womanhood*, 47. See discussion of sexual standards, xiv.

15. For a discussion of its narrative strategies, see *Incidents*, xxxiii. See also Carby, *Reconstructing Womanhood*, 59; and Thomas Doherty, "Harriet Jacobs' Narrative Strategies: *Incidents in the Life of a Slave Girl*," *Southern Literary Journal* 19, no. 1 (1986): 81–91.

16. Patricia Meyers Spacks, "Stages of Self: Notes on Autobiography," in *The American Autobiography*, ed. Albert E. Stone (Englewood Cliffs, N.J.: Prentice-Hall, 1981), 112.

17. See also Laura E. Tanner, "Self-Conscious Representation in the Slave Narrative," *Black American Literature Forum* 21 (1987): 417–419.

18. The Yellin, ed., *Incidents* authenticates Brent's historical identity with a copy of the "deathbed codicil of Margaret Horniblow, Jacobs' first mistress, willing 'my Negro girl Harriet' ...to her three-year-old niece Mary Matilda Norcom, July 3, 1825" (p. 213).

19. Carby, *Reconstructing Womanhood*, 57.

20. For further discussion of Linda in relation to Flint as a "representative slaveholder," see Smith, Introduction to *Incidents*, xxx; and Carby, *Reconstructing Womanhood*, 57.

21. Amanda Smith, *An Autobiography: The Story of the Lord's Dealings with Mrs. Amanda Smith* (Chicago: Meyer and Brothers, 1893), 386–389.

22. See Doherty, "Harriet Jacobs' Narrative Strategies," 88.

23. Tanner argues that while Linda's relationship with Sands is "immoral by conventional standards when viewed within the context of Brent's situation, the relationship principally serves to dramatize one woman's attempt to maintain control over her own body." Tanner, "Self-Conscious Representation," 415.

Chapter 2: Fugitive Slaves and Sanctified Ladies

1. Frances Ellen Watkins Harper, "An Address Delivered at the Centennial Anniversary for Promoting the Abolition of Slavery," in *Masterpieces of Negro Eloquence*, ed. Alice Moore Dunbar (New York: Bookery Publishing, n.d.), 101.

2. Elizabeth Keckley, *Behind the Scenes: or Thirty Years a Slave and Four Years in the White House* (New York: G. W. Carlton, 1868), 43–51. Hereafter cited in the text as *Scenes*, followed by page number.

3. James McPherson, Introduction to *Reminiscences of My Life in Camp with the U.S. 33rd Colored Troops*, by Susie King Taylor (New York: Arno Press, 1968).

4. Susie King Taylor, *Reminiscences of My Life in Camp with the U.S. 33rd Colored Troops* (New York: Arno Press, 1968; originally published 1902), 5. Hereafter cited in the text as *Reminiscences*, followed by page number.

5. Edward L. Pierce, "The Freedmen at Port Royal," *Atlantic Monthly* 12 (1863): 291.

6. William Andrews, *Sisters of the Spirit: Three Black Women's Autobiographies of the Nineteenth Century* (Bloomington: Indiana University Press, 1986), 6.

7. Nancy G. Prince, *A Narrative of the Life and Travels of Mrs. Nancy Prince: Written by Herself* (Boston: The Author, 1853), 1. Hereafter cited in the text as *Narrative*, followed by page number.

8. Amanda Smith, *An Autobiography: The Story of the Lord's Dealings with Mrs. Amanda Smith* (Chicago: Meyer and Brothers, 1893), 505–506. Hereafter cited in text as *Autobiography*, followed by page number.

9. See Robert Stepto, "Narration, Authentication and Authorial Control in Frederick Douglass' *Narrative* of 1845." In *Afro-American Literature: The Reconstruction of Instruction*, ed. Dexter Fisher and Robert Stepto (New York: Modern Language Association, 1979), 178–191. See also Robert Stepto, *From Behind the Veil: A Study of Afro-American Narrative* (Urbana: University of Illinois Press, 1979).

10. *The Life and Religious Experience and Journal of Mrs. Jarena Lee, Giving an Account of Her Call to Preach the Gospel, Revised and*

Corrected from the Original Manuscript Written by Herself
(Philadelphia: The Author, 1849), 20, 23, 54–55. Hereafter cited in the
text as *Life*, followed by page number.

11. Mary G. Mason, "The Other Voice: Autobiographies of Women
Writers," in *Autobiography: Essays Theoretical and Critical*, ed. James
Olney (Princeton: Princeton University Press, 1980), 229.

12. See Jean Humez, "Introduction," *Gifts of Power: The Writings
of Rebecca Cox Jackson, Black Visionary, Shaker Eldress* (Amherst:
University of Massachusetts Press, 1981), 5.

13. Ibid.

14. Ibid., 47.

15. Rebecca Cox Jackson, *Gifts of Power: The Writings of Rebecca
Cox Jackson, Black Visionary, Shaker Eldress* (Amherst: University of
Massachusetts Press, 1981), 47. Hereafter cited in the text as *Gifts*,
followed by page number.

16. Humez, "Introduction," 22.

17. Ibid., 46.

18. Ibid., 37.

19. William Andrews, *To Tell a Free Story: The First Century of Afro-
American Autobiography, 1760–1865* (Urbana: University of Illinois
Press, 1986), 14.

20. Ibid., viii.

21. Sojourner Truth, *Narrative of Sojourner Truth: A Bondswoman
of Olden Time, Emancipated by the New York Legislature in the Early
Part of the Present Century: with a History of Her Labors and
Correspondence as Drawn from Her "Book of Life,"* ed. Olive Gilbert
(Battle Creek, Mich.: For the Author, 1878), 163. Hereafter cited in the
text as *Sojourner*, followed by page number.

22. Sarah H. Bradford, *Harriet Tubman, The Moses of Her People*
(N.p.: For the Author, 1886), 28. Hereafter cited in the text as *Harriet*,
followed by page number.

Part II: Emerging from Obscurity

1. See Estelle C. Jelinek, Introduction, *Women's Autobiography*
(Bloomington: University of Indiana Press, 1980), for her discussion
of the forms assumed by women's autobiographies, especially diaries, 1–20.

2. See James M. Cox, "Recovering Literature's Lost Ground
through Autobiography," in *Essays Theoretical and Critical*, ed.
James Olney (Princeton: Princeton University Press, 1980), 124–125.
Cox discusses the historical memoir as part of literature's lost
ground.

3. Ida B. Wells, *Crusade for Justice: The Autobiography of Ida B. Wells* (Chicago: University of Chicago Press, 1970), 3.

Chapter 3: A Poet's Retreat

1. See Ray Allen Billington, ed., *The Journal of Charlotte L. Forten* (New York: Dryden Press, 1953). Billington omits the fifth and final diary as well as large sections of the first three diaries describing "the weather, family affairs, and other matters of purely local interest." This amounts to about one-third of Forten's five handwritten texts. This edition is hereafter cited in the text as Billington, *Journal*, followed by page number. *The Journals of Charlotte Forten Grimké*, ed. Brenda Stevenson, is a more complete version of Forten's work, which has recently been published in the Schomburg Library of Nineteenth Century Black Women Writers (New York: Oxford University Press, 1988).

2. All five of the original manuscript diaries, along with the typescripts transcribed by Dr. Anna Julia Cooper, can be found in the Grimké Family Papers, Moorland-Spingarn Research Center, Howard University, Washington, D.C. The author gratefully acknowledges permission to quote from this source.

3. Forten's published works include poetry, articles, and autobiography. See also "Interesting Letter from Charlotte L. Forten," "Life on the Sea Islands," "Personal Recollections of Whittier," and *Madame Therese: or the Volunteers of '92*. The most complete bibliographies of Forten's work are in Joan R. Sherman, "Afro-American Poets of the Nineteenth Century: A Guide to Research and Bio-Bibliographies of the Poets," in *But Some of Us Are Brave*, ed. Gloria T. Hull, Patricia Bell Scott, and Barbara Smith (New York: Feminist Press, 1977), 245–260; and Erlene Stetson, *Black Sister: Poetry by Black American Women, 1745–1980* (Bloomington: Indiana University Press, 1981).

4. The Stevenson, ed., *Journals* includes the fifth, until recently unpublished, diary.

5. Dorothy Sterling, *We Are Your Sisters: Black Women in the Nineteenth Century* (New York: Norton, 1984), 119–120.

6. Lydia Maria Child, quoted in Ann Douglas, *The Feminization of American Culture* (New York: Knopf, 1977), 62.

7. Margaret Homans, *Women Writers and Poetic Identity* (Princeton: Princeton University Press, 1977), 17.

8. William Wells Brown, *The Rising Son, or the Antecedents and Advancements of the Colored Race* (Boston, 1874), 475.

9. William Wells Brown, quoted in Joan R. Sherman, *Invisible Poets* (Urbana: University of Illinois Press, 1974), 95.

10. Sherman, "Afro-American Poets," 254.

11. Homans, *Women Writers*, 5.

12. Claudia Tate, *Black Women Writers at Work* (New York: Crossroad Press, 1983), 1.

13. *Diary* 3, September 14, 1862: "I got little satisfaction from the B[oston] Com[mission]," Forten wrote. "They were not sending women at present, etc."

14. Charlotte Forten and John Greenleaf Whittier visited one another frequently during the 1850s and 1860s, and maintained an active correspondence through the 1870s. Forten was one of many women writers Whittier assisted in the mid-nineteenth century; he edited her work, helped her find jobs, and acted as her unofficial literary agent, making contacts with publishers and occasionally receiving funds on her behalf.

15. An undated note written on the stationery of Dr. Anna Julia Cooper and found in the Grimké Family Papers reads, in part: "Nobody wants to take a pig in a poke. Here are two 'samples'—may they help 'sell' the job. The 'At Sea—1862' is not in the notebooks, and it has not been typed." Thus it would appear that "At Sea—1862," an entry written in Forten's hand on white letter paper, was not included in the original notebook manuscript. Dr. Cooper apparently made the decision to add this entry to the typewritten text in an attempt to help sell the manuscript to potential publishers. Dr. Cooper's letter carries no date. See the Grimké Family Papers, Moorland-Spingarn Research Center.

16. For a discussion of the "transcendent present" in slave spirituals, see James A. Cone, *The Spirituals and the Blues* (New York: Seabury Press, 1972), 92–97.

17. See John Greenleaf Whittier, Editor's note to Charlotte L. Forten's "Life on the Sea Islands," *Atlantic Monthly* 13 (1864): 587.

18. See also *The Liberator*, May 13, 1864, for the obituary of Robert Bridges Forten.

19. *Letters of John Greenleaf Whittier*, vol. 8, no. 1198, p. 278. When Forten married Francis Grimké in 1878, Whittier sent a wedding gift of $50.

20. Grimké's sermons, Grimké Family Papers, Moorland-Spingarn Research Center.

21. Douglas, *Feminization*, 92.

22. Charlotte Forten Grimké, "Wordsworth," undated. Anna Julia Cooper Papers, Moorland-Spingarn Research Center.

23. Francis J. Grimké's notebook diaries, Grimké Family Papers, Moorland-Spingarn Research Center.

24. Rayford W. Logan and Michael R. Winston, eds., *Dictionary of American Negro Biography* (New York: Norton, 1982), 233.

25. Undated typescript of Francis J. Grimké's testimonial to the memory of his wife, CFG, on the occasion of her death. Grimké Family Papers, Moorland-Spingarn Research Center.

Chapter 4: Crusader for Justice

1. John W. Blassingame, "Black Autobiographies as Histories and Literature," *Black Scholar* 5, no. 4 (1973–1974): 7.

2. Albert E. Stone, *The American Autobiography* (Englewood Cliffs, N.J.: Prentice-Hall, 1981), 2–3.

3. James Cox, "Recovering Literature's Lost Ground through Autobiography," in *Autobiography: Essays Theoretical and Critical*, ed. James Olney (Princeton: Princeton University Press, 1980), 124–125.

4. See Patricia Meyers Spacks, "Stages of Self: Notes on Autobiography," in Stone, *American Autobiography*, 44–45.

5. Alfreda M. Duster, Introduction, *Crusade for Justice: The Autobiography of Ida B. Wells* (Chicago: University of Chicago Press, 1970), xiii–xiv.

6. Stephen Butterfield, *Black Autobiography* (Amherst: University of Massachusetts Press, 1974), 200.

7. See Estelle C. Jelinek, Introduction, *Women's Autobiography* (Bloomington: Indiana University Press, 1980), 1–20.

8. Erik Erikson, *Life History and the Historical Moment* (New York: Norton, 1975), 135.

9. Ibid., 125.

10. Alfreda M. Duster, letter to Joanne M. Braxton, January 30, 1983.

11. Ibid.

12. John Hope Franklin, Foreword, *Crusade*, x–xii.

13. Duster, *Crusade*, xiii. See also Norman B. Wood, *The White Side of a Black Subject* (Chicago: American Publishing House, 1897), 381–382.

14. Duster, *Crusade*, xiv.

15. Ibid., xxxi.

16. Ida B. Wells, *Crusade*, xiii–xiv. Hereafter cited in the text as *Crusade*, followed by page number.

17. Albert E. Stone, *Autobiographical Occasions and Original Acts* (Philadelphia: University of Pennsylvania Press, 1982), 29.

18. Erikson, *Life History*, 161.
19. See Spacks, "Stages of Self," 48.
20. Erikson, *Life History*, 141.
21. Robert Stepto, *From Behind the Veil: A Study of Afro-American Narrative* (Urbana: University of Illinois Press, 1979), 26.
22. Erikson, *Life History*, 55.
23. Ida B. Wells, *Southern Horrors, Lynch Law in All Its Phases* (New York: Arno Press, 1969; originally published 1892), 2.
24. Ida B. Wells, letter to Frederick Douglass, October 17, 1892. Frederick Douglass Collection, Library of Congress, Washington, D.C.
25. Frederick Douglass, letter to Ida B. Wells, October 25, 1892. Frederick Douglass Collection, Library of Congress.
26. Gerda Lerner, *The Majority Finds Its Past* (New York: Oxford University Press, 1979), 109.
27. Gertrude B. Mossell, *The Work of the Afro-American Woman* (New York: Oxford University Press, 1988; originally published 1894), 38.
28. Paula Giddings, *When and Where I Enter: The Impact of Black Women on Race and Sex in America* (New York: Morrow, 1984), 92.
29. Ibid.
30. Interview conducted by Marcia Greenlee with Alfreda M. Duster on March 8–9, 1978, for the Black Women's Oral History Project at the Schlesinger Library, Radcliffe Collection, Harvard University, 62. Quotes are used with the written permission of Alfreda Duster, August 6, 1981.
31. Ibid., 11.
32. Ibid., 16.
33. Giddings, *When and Where I Enter*, 94.
34. August Meier, Introduction to *On Lynchings*, by Ida B. Wells-Barnett (New York: Arno Press, 1969), i.
35. Duster–Greenlee interview, 4.
36. Ibid.
37. Giddings, *When and Where I Enter*, 126.
38. Ibid., 121.
39. Stone, *Autobiographical Occasions*, 29.

Part III: Claiming the Afra-American Self

1. See Edith Cobb, "The Ecology of Imagination in Childhood," *Daedalus* 88 (1959): 540–541. Cobb claims a "widespread intuitive understanding that certain aspects of childhood experience remain in memory as a psychological force, an elan, which produces the

pressure to perceive creatively and inventively." See also Albert E. Stone, *Autobiographical Occasions and Original Acts* (Philadelphia: University of Pennsylvania Press, 1982), 92. Stone applies Cobb's theory to Richard Wright's *Black Boy* to argue that "most autobiographers... achieve self-consciousness through a kind of *metanoia*. They write as if, and after, some transforming event or inner crises has occurred." Like Wright, both Zora Neale Hurston and Era Bell Thompson meet inner crises and write as if they are transformed by them. In their autobiographies, they return to the middle age of childhood described by Cobb.

2. Pauli Murray, *Proud Shoes: The Story of an American Family* (New York: Harper & Brothers, 1956).

3. Maya Angelou, in interview conducted by Joanne M. Braxton, Los Angeles, California, spring 1975.

4. Alfreda M. Duster, letter to Joanne M. Braxton, January 30, 1983.

5. Barbara Smith, "Notes for Yet Another Paper on Black Feminism, or Will the Real Enemy Stand Up?" *Conditions* 5 (1979): 123. See also "Towards a Black Feminist Criticism," *Conditions* 2 (1977): 25–44.

Chapter 5: Motherless Daughters and the Quest for a Place

1. Edith Cobb, "The Ecology of Imagination in Childhood," *Daedalus* 88 (1959): 540–541.

2. Albert E. Stone, *Autobiographical Occasions and Original Acts* (Philadelphia: University of Pennsylvania Press, 1982), 92.

3. E. Edward Farrison, "Dust Tracks on a Road: An Autobiography," *Journal of Negro History* 28 (1943): 352–355.

4. See Cobb, "Imagination in Childhood," 540–541.

5. Zora Neale Hurston, *Dust Tracks on a Road* (Urbana: University of Illinois Press, 1984), 44. Hereafter cited in the text as *Dust Tracks*, followed by page number.

6. Robert Hemenway, *Zora Neale Hurston: A Literary Biography* (Urbana: University of Illinois Press, 1977), 282.

7. Ibid., 56, 99.

8. Robert Hemenway, Editor's note in *Dust Tracks on a Road*, by Zora Neale Hurston (Urbana: University of Illinois Press, 1984), 288–289.

9. Hemenway, ed., *Dust Tracks*, 300–301.

10. Ibid., 295.

11. Ibid., 324–325.

12. Ibid., 340.

13. Ibid., 340–341.

14. Zora Neale Hurston, *Mules and Men* (New York: Lippincott, 1935), 192.

15. Zora Neale Hurston, *Tell My Horse* (New York: Lippincott, 1938), 30.

16. Zora Neale Hurston, *Jonah's Gourd Vine* (New York: Lippincott, 1934), 204.

17. Ibid., 207.

18. Zora Neale Hurston, *Their Eyes Were Watching God* (New York: Lippincott, 1937), 1.

19. Ibid., 24.

20. Cobb, "Imagination in Childhood," 540–541.

21. Era Bell Thompson, *American Daughter* (Chicago: University of Chicago Press, 1946), 67. Hereafter cited in the text as *Daughter*, followed by page number.

22. Stephen Butterfield, *Black Autobiography* (Amherst: University of Massachusetts Press, 1974), 169.

23. Ibid., 174.

24. Arthur P. Davis, Review of *American Daughter*, by Era Bell Thompson, *Journal of Negro Education* 15 (1946): 647–648.

Chapter 6: A Song of Transcendence

1. Roger Rosenblatt, "Life as the Death Weapon," in *Autobiography: Essays Theoretical and Critical*, ed. James Olney (Princeton: Princeton University Press, 1980), 171.

2. Maya Angelou, *I Know Why the Caged Bird Sings* (New York: Random House, 1969), 71. Hereafter cited in the text as *Caged Bird*, followed by page number.

3. Cedric Clark, "Black Studies or the Study of Black People?" in *Black Psychology*, ed. Reginald L. Jones (New York: Harper & Row, 1972), 6. Clark provides an excellent discussion of the development of black self-esteem in relation to white self-esteem in the American psychology and the culture that surrounds it. As in Reconstruction times, blacks in the twentieth-century American South who did not accept the conception of what was proper for them to do, say, and be were often met with violence. Through a pattern of recognized rules,

the theory went, racial friction could be minimized as long as formal social distance between the races was maintained. The development of a positive black self-image proved difficult under these circumstances.

4. Maya Angelou, "Women Writing Today," address given at Old Dominion University, Norfolk, Virginia, September 24, 1980. During her visit, Angelou read from her own work and spoke on a variety of related topics including "The Creative Writer" and "The Role of the Black Woman in Contemporary Society." Hereafter cited in the text as *ODU*.

5. George E. Kent, "Maya Angelou's *I Know Why the Caged Bird Sings* and Black Autobiographical Tradition," *Kansas Quarterly* 7, no. 3 (1975): 75.

6. James Olney, "Autobiography and the Cultural Moment: A Thematic Historical and Bibliographical Introduction," in *Autobiography: Essays Theoretical and Critical*, ed. James Olney (Princeton: Princeton University Press, 1980).

7. Maya Angelou, *Oh Pray My Wings Are Gonna Fit Me Well* (New York: Random House, 1975), 51.

8. Stephen Butterfield, *Black Autobiography* (Amherst: University of Massachusetts Press, 1974), 203–204.

9. Paul Laurence Dunbar, *The Complete Poems of Paul Laurence Dunbar* (New York: 1913), 105.

10. Sidonie Ann Smith, "The Song of the Caged Bird: Maya Angelou's Quest for Self-Acceptance," *Southern Humanities Review* 7 (1973): 367.

11. See Myra K. McMurry, "Role Playing as an Art in Maya Angelou's 'Caged Bird,' " *South Atlantic Bulletin* 41, no. 2 (1976): 111.

12. Kent, "Angelou's *Caged Bird*," 75.

13. Smith, "Song of the Caged Bird," 369.

14. Erik Erikson, *Life History and the Historical Moment* (New York: Norton, 1975), 43.

15. Maya Angelou, *Gather Together in My Name* (New York: Random House, 1974), 76–77.

16. Carl Jung, *Four Archetypes* (Princeton: Princeton University Press, 1959), 36.

17. Liliane K. Arensberg, "Death as a Metaphor of Self in *I Know Why the Caged Bird Sings*," *CLA Journal* 20 (1976): 291.

18. Kent, "Angelou's *Caged Bird*," 78.

19. Jung, *Archetypes*, 36.

20. Smith, "Song of the Caged Bird," 369.

A Circle Closing and Expanding

1. Alice Walker, *In Search of Our Mothers' Gardens* (New York: Harcourt Brace Jovanovich, 1983), 234.

2. Phillis Cole and Deborah Lambert, "Gender and Race in American Literature: An Exploration of the Discipline and a Proposal for Two New Courses," Wellesley College Center for Research on Women Working Papers Series, Working Paper 115, 1.

3. Cole and Lambert, "Gender and Race," 3. See also Elaine Showalter, "Feminist Criticism in the Wilderness," *Critical Inquiry* 8 (1981): 179–205; and Carolyn G. Heilbrun and Margaret Higgonet, *The Representation of Women in Fiction: Papers from the English Institute, 1981,* New Series, No. 7 (Baltimore: Johns Hopkins University Press, 1983), ix–xxii.

4. Walker, *Search,* xi–xii. Here Walker defines the term "womanist" and its derivation.

References

Andrews, William L. *Sisters of the Spirit: Three Black Women's Autobiographies of the Nineteenth Century.* Bloomington: Indiana University Press, 1986.

_____. *To Tell a Free Story: The First Century of Afro-American Autobiography, 1760–1865.* Urbana: University of Illinois Press, 1986.

Angelou, Maya. *And Still I Rise.* New York: Random House, 1978.

_____. *Gather Together in My Name.* New York: Random House, 1974.

_____. *The Heart of a Woman.* New York: Random House, 1981.

_____. *I Know Why the Caged Bird Sings.* New York: Random House, 1969.

_____. *Just Give Me a Cool Drink of Water 'Fore I Diiie.* New York: Random House, 1971.

_____. *Mrs. Flowers.* Minneapolis: Redpath Press, 1986.

_____. *Oh Pray My Wings Are Gonna Fit Me Well.* New York: Random House, 1975.

_____. *Poems: Maya Angelou.* New York: Bantam, 1986.

_____. *Shaker, Why Don't You Sing?* New York: Random House, 1983.

_____. *Singin' & Swingin' & Gettin' Merry Like Christmas.* New York: Random House, 1981.

_____. "Women Writing Today." Address given at Old Dominion University, Norfolk, Virginia, September 24, 1980.

Arensberg, Liliane K. "Death as a Metaphor of Self in *I Know Why the Caged Bird Sings.*" *CLA Journal* 20 (1976): 273–291.

Belinda. "Belinda: or the Cruelty of Men Whose Faces Were Like the Moon." *American Museum and Repository of Ancient and Modern Fugitive Pieces, Prose and Poetical,* vol. 1. June 1787.

Billington, Ray Allen. Introduction. *The Journal of Charlotte L. Forten.* Edited by Ray Allen Billington. New York: Dryden Press, 1953.

Blassingame, John W. "Black Autobiographies as History and Literature." *Black Scholar* 5, no. 4 (1973–1974): 2–9.

_____. *The Slave Community: Plantation Life in the Antebellum South.* 2d ed. New York: Oxford University Press, 1979.

Bontemps, Arna, ed. *Great Slave Narratives.* Boston: Beacon Press, 1969.

Bradford, Sarah H. *Harriet Tubman, The Moses of Her People.* N.p.: For the Author, 1886.

_____. *Scenes in the Life of Harriet Tubman.* N.p., 1869.

Braxton, Joanne M. "Black Grandmothers: Sources of Artistic Consciousness and Personal Strength." Wellesley College Center for Research on Women Working Papers Series. Working Paper 172, 1985.

_____. "Charlotte Forten Grimké and the Search for a Public Voice." In *The Private Self: Theory and Practice of Women's Autobiographical Writings,* edited by Shari Benstock, 254–271. Chapel Hill: University of North Carolina Press, 1988.

_____. "Harriet Jacobs' *Incidents in the Life of a Slave Girl:* The Redefinition of the Slave Narrative Genre." *Massachusetts Review* 27 (1986): 379–387.

Brent, Linda (Harriet Jacobs). *Incidents in the Life of a Slave Girl: Written by Herself.* Boston: Thayer and Eldridge, 1861.

Brown, William Wells. *Narrative of William Wells Brown, A Fugitive Slave, Written by Himself.* 1847. Reprinted in *Puttin' on Ole Massa,* edited by Gilbert Osofsky. New York: Harper & Row, 1969.

_____. *The Rising Son, or the Antecedents and Advancements of the Colored Race.* Boston, 1874.

Butterfield, Stephen. *Black Autobiography.* Amherst: University of Massachusetts Press, 1974.

Carby, Hazel. *Reconstructing Womanhood: The Emergence of the Afro-American Woman Novelist.* New York: Oxford University Press, 1987.

Clark, Cedric. "Black Studies or the Study of Black People?" In *Black Psychology,* edited by Reginald Jones. New York: Harper & Row, 1972.

Cobb, Edith. "The Ecology of Imagination in Childhood." *Daedalus* 88 (1959): 537–548.

Cole, Phillis, and Deborah Lambert. "Gender and Race in American Literature: An Exploration of the Discipline and a Proposal for Two Courses." Wellesley College Center for Research on Women Working Papers Series. Working Paper 115, 1983.

Cone, James A. *The Spirituals and the Blues.* New York: Seabury Press, 1972.

Conklin, Nancy Faires, Brenda McCallum, and Marcia Wade. *The Culture of Southern Black Women.* Archive of American Minority Culture and Women's Studies Program, University of Alabama, 1983.

Cox, James M. "Recovering Literature's Lost Ground through Autobiography." In *Autobiography: Essays Theoretical and Critical,* edited by James Olney. Princeton: Princeton University Press, 1980.

Davis, Arthur P. Review of *American Daughter,* by Era Bell Thompson. *Journal of Negro Education* 15 (1946): 647–648.

Demetrakopoulos, Stephanie A. "The Metaphysics of Matrilinealism in Women's Autobiography." In *Women's Autobiography: Essays Theoretical and Critical,* edited by Estelle C. Jelinek. Princeton: Princeton University Press, 1972.

Doherty, Thomas. "Harriet Jacobs' Narrative Strategies: *Incidents in the Life of a Slave Girl." Southern Literary Journal* 19, no. 1 (1986): 79–91.

Douglas, Ann. *The Feminization of American Culture.* New York: Knopf, 1977.

Douglass, Frederick. Letter to Ida B. Wells, October 25, 1892. Frederick Douglass Collection, Library of Congress, Washington, D.C.

————. *Narrative of Frederick Douglass: An American Slave, Written by Himself.* 1845. New York: Signet, 1968.

Dunbar, Paul Laurence. *The Complete Poems of Paul Laurence Dunbar.* New York, 1913.

Duster, Alfreda M. Interview conducted by Marcia Greenlee on March 8–9, 1978, for the Black Women's Oral History Project at the Schlesinger Library, Radcliffe Collection, Harvard University, Cambridge.

————. Introduction. *Crusade for Justice: The Autobiography of Ida B. Wells.* Chicago: University of Chicago Press, 1970.

————. Letter to Joanne M. Braxton, January 30, 1983. Private collection, Joanne M. Braxton.

_____. Letter to Joanne M. Braxton, August 6, 1981. Private collection, Joanne M. Braxton.

Erckman, Emilie, and Alexander Chatrian. *Madame Therese: or the Volunteers of '92.* Translated by Charlotte L. Forten. 13th ed. New York: Scribner, 1869.

Erikson, Erik. *Life History and the Historical Moment.* New York: Norton, 1975.

Farrison, E. Edward. "Dust Tracks on a Road: An Autobiography." *Journal of Negro History* 28 (1943): 352–355.

Forten, Charlotte L. "Interesting Letter from Charlotte L. Forten." *Liberator* 19 (December 12, 1862): 7.

_____. *The Journal of Charlotte L. Forten.* Edited by Ray Allen Billington. New York: Dryden Press, 1953.

_____. *The Journals of Charlotte Forten Grimké.* Edited by Brenda Stevenson. New York: Oxford University Press, 1968.

_____. "Life on the Sea Islands." *Atlantic Monthly* 13 (1864): 587–596, 666–676.

_____. "Personal Recollections of Whittier." *New England Magazine* 8 (June 1893): 472.

Foster, Frances. " 'In Respect to Females...': Differences in the Portrayals of Women by Male and Female Narrators." *Black American Literature Forum* 15 (1981): 66–70.

Franklin, John Hope. Foreword. *Crusade for Justice: The Autobiography of Ida B. Wells.* Chicago: University of Chicago Press, 1970.

Giddings, Paula. *When and Where I Enter: The Impact of Black Women on Race and Sex in America.* New York: Morrow, 1984.

Harper, Frances Ellen Watkins. "An Address Delivered at the Centennial Anniversary for Promoting the Abolition of Slavery." In *Masterpieces of Negro Eloquence*, edited by Alice Moore Dunbar. New York: Bookery Publishing, n.d.

Heilbrun, Carolyn G., and Margaret Higonnet. *The Representation of Women in Fiction: Papers from the English Institute, 1981.* New Series, No. 7. Baltimore: Johns Hopkins University Press, 1983.

Hemenway, Robert. Introduction. *Dust Tracks on a Road*, by Zora Neale Hurston. Edited by Robert Hemenway. Urbana: University of Illinois Press, 1984.

_____. *Zora Neale Hurston: A Literary Biography.* Urbana: University of Illinois Press, 1977.

Higginson, Thomas Wentworth. *Life in a Black Army Regiment.* Boston: Fields, Osgood, 1870.

Homans, Margaret. *Women Writers and Poetic Identity.* Princeton: Princeton University Press, 1977.

Hull, Gloria T., Patricia Bell Scott, and Barbara Smith, eds. *But Some of Us Are Brave.* New York: Feminist Press, 1977.

Hurston, Zora Neale. *Dust Tracks on a Road.* New York: Lippincott, 1942.

———. *Dust Tracks on a Road.* Edited by Robert Hemenway. Urbana: University of Illinois Press, 1984.

———. *Jonah's Gourd Vine.* New York: Lippincott, 1934.

———. *Tell My Horse.* New York: Lippincott, 1938.

———. *Their Eyes Were Watching God.* New York: Lippincott, 1937.

Jackson, Rebecca Cox. *Gifts of Power: The Writings of Rebecca Cox Jackson, Black Visionary, Shaker Eldress.* Edited and with an Introduction by Jean McMahon Humez. Amherst: University of Massachusetts Press, 1971.

Jelinek, Estelle C., ed. *Women's Autobiography.* Bloomington: Indiana University Press, 1980.

Jung, Carl. *Four Archetypes.* Princeton: Princeton University Press, 1959.

Keckley, Elizabeth. *Behind the Scenes: or Thirty Years a Slave and Four Years in the White House.* New York: G. W. Carlton and Company, 1868.

Kent, George E. "Maya Angelou's *I Know Why the Caged Bird Sings* and Black Autobiographical Tradition." *Kansas Quarterly* 7, no. 3 (1975): 72–78.

Kolodny, Annette. "Some Notions on Defining a 'Feminist Literary Criticism.' " *Critical Inquiry* 2 (1975): 75–92.

Lee, Jarena. *The Life and Religious Experience and Journal of Mrs. Jarena Lee, Giving an Account of Her Call to Preach the Gospel, Revised and Corrected from the Original Manuscript Written by Herself.* Philadelphia: The Author, 1849.

Lerner, Gerda. *The Majority Finds Its Past.* New York: Oxford University Press, 1979.

Logan, Rayford W., and Michael R. Winston, eds. *Dictionary of American Negro Biography.* New York: Norton, 1982.

McMurry, Myra K. "Role-Playing as Art in Maya Angelou's 'Caged Bird.' " *South Atlantic Bulletin* 41, no. 2 (1976): 106–111.

McPherson, James. Introduction. *Reminiscences of My Life in Camp with the U.S. 33rd Colored Troops.* 1902. New York: Arno Press, 1968.

Mason, Mary G. "The Other Voice: Autobiographies of Women Writers." In *Autobiography: Essays Theoretical and Critical*, edited by James Olney. Princeton: Princeton University Press, 1980.

Meier, August. Introduction. *On Lynchings*, by Ida B. Wells-Barnett. New York: Arno Press, 1969.

Mossell, Gertrude B. (Mrs. N. F.). *The Work of the Afro American Woman.* 1894. Introduction by Joanne M. Braxton. New York: Oxford University Press, 1988.

Murray, Pauli. *Proud Shoes: The Story of an American Family.* New York: Harper & Brothers, 1956.

———. *Song in a Weary Throat.* New York: Harper & Row, 1987.

Olney, James. "Autobiography and the Cultural Movement: A Thematic, Historical Bibliographical Introduction." In *Autobiography: Essays Theoretical and Critical,* edited by James Olney. Princeton: Princeton University Press, 1980.

———. *Metaphors of Self.* Princeton: Princeton University Press, 1972.

Pierce, Edward L. "The Freedmen at Port Royal." *Atlantic Monthly* 12 (1863): 291–315.

Prince, Mary. *The History of Mary Prince, a West Indian Slave, Related by Herself with a Supplement by the Editor, to Which Is Added the Narrative of Asa-Asa, a Captured African.* London: F. Westley and A. H. Davis, 1831.

Prince, Nancy G. *A Narrative of the Life and Travels of Mrs. Nancy Prince: Written by Herself.* Boston: The Author, 1853.

Robinson, Lillian S. *Sex, Class, and Culture.* Bloomington: University of Indiana Press, 1978.

Rosenblatt, Roger. "Life as the Death Weapon." In *Autobiography: Essays Theoretical and Critical,* edited by James Olney. Princeton: Princeton University Press, 1980.

Sherman, Joan R. "Afro-American Poets of the Nineteenth Century: A Guide to Research and Bio-Bibliographies of the Poets." In *But Some of Us Are Brave,* edited by Gloria T. Hull, Patricia Bell Scott, and Barbara Smith, 245–260. New York: Feminist Press, 1977.

———. *Invisible Poets.* Urbana: University of Illinois Press, 1974.

Showalter, Elaine. "Feminist Criticism in the Wilderness." *Critical Inquiry* 8 (1981): 179–205.

Simmons, William. *Men of Mark.* 1887. New York: Arno Press, 1968.

Smith, Amanda. *An Autobiography: The Story of the Lord's Dealings with Mrs. Amanda Smith.* Chicago: Meyer and Brother, 1893.

Smith, Sidonie Ann. "The Song of a Caged Bird: Maya Angelou's Quest After Self-Acceptance." *Southern Humanities Review* 7 (1973): 365–375.

———. *Where I'm Bound: Patterns of Slavery and Freedom in Black American Autobiography.* Westport, Conn.: Greenwood Press, 1974.

Smith, Valerie. Introduction. *Incidents in the Life of a Slave Girl: Written by Herself,* by Harriet A. Jacobs. New York: Oxford University Press, 1988.

Spacks, Patricia M. "Selves in Hiding." In *Women's Autobiography,* edited by Estelle C. Jelinek. Bloomington: University of Indiana Press, 1980.

———. "Stages of Self: Notes on Autobiography." In *The American Autobiography*, edited by Albert E. Stone. Englewood Cliffs, N.J.: Prentice-Hall, 1981.

Starling, Marion. "The Slave Narrative: Its Place in American Literary History." Doctoral dissertation, New York University, 1946. Available on Ann Arbor University Microfilms, Ann Arbor, 1977.

Stepto, Robert B. *From Behind the Veil: A Study of Afro-American Narrative.* Urbana: University of Illinois Press, 1979.

———. "Narration, Authentication, and Authorial Control in Frederick Douglass' *Narrative* of 1845." In *Afro-American Literature: The Reconstruction of Instruction*, edited by Dexter Fisher and Robert Stepto, 178–191. New York: Modern Language Association, 1979.

Sterling, Dorothy. *We Are Your Sisters: Black Women in the Nineteenth Century.* New York: Norton, 1984.

Stetson, Erlene. *Black Sister: Poetry by Black American Women, 1746–1980.* Bloomington: Indiana University Press, 1981.

Stone, Albert E. *The American Autobiography.* Englewood Cliffs, N.J.: Prentice-Hall, 1981.

———. *Autobiographical Occasions and Original Acts.* Philadelphia: University of Pennsylvania Press, 1982.

Tanner, Laura E. "Self-Conscious Representation in the Slave Narrative." *Black American Literature Forum* 21 (1987): 415–424.

Tate, Claudia. *Black Women Writers at Work.* New York: Crossroad Press, 1983.

Taylor, Susie King. *Reminiscences of My Life in Camp with the U.S. 33rd Colored Troops.* 1902. New York: Arno Press, 1968.

Thompson, Era Bell. *American Daughter.* Chicago: University of Chicago Press, 1946.

Truth, Sojourner. *Narrative of Sojourner Truth: A Bondswoman of Olden Time, Emancipated by the New York Legislature in the Early Part of the Present Century: with a History of Her Labors and Correspondence as Drawn from Her "Book of Life."* Edited by Olive Gilbert. Battle Creek, Mich.: For the Author, 1878.

Walker, Alice. *In Search of Our Mothers' Gardens.* New York: Harcourt Brace Jovanovich, 1983.

Wells, Ida B. *Crusade for Justice: The Autobiography of Ida B. Wells.* Chicago: University of Chicago Press, 1970.

———. Letter to Frederick Douglass, October 17, 1892. Frederick Douglass Collection, Library of Congress, Washington, D.C.

_____. *Southern Horrors, Lynch Law in All Its Phases.* New York: Arno Press, 1969.

Whittier, John Greenleaf. Editor's Note. "Life on the Sea Islands," by Charlotte L. Forten. *Atlantic Monthly* 13 (1864): 587.

_____. *The Letters of John Greenleaf Whittier,* edited by John B. Picard. 8 vols. Cambridge: Harvard/Belknap Press, 1975.

Wood, Norman B. *The White Side of a Black Subject.* Chicago: American Publishing, 1897.

Yellin, Jean F. "Written by Herself: Harriet Jacobs' Slave Narrative." *American Literature* 53 (1981): 479–486.

Index